"Don Bain is the only jazz musician I know who's also written 80 books. There's 'good vibes' on every page."
—Jazz Great Lionel Hampton

"Don Bain is the consummate professional, having written more than 80 books over a long and impressive career. He's an inspiration for anyone seeking success as a writer."
—Bill Adler,
Bill Adler Books

"Don is the hardest working writer in the business. He isn't married to any one genre or voice. He can write mysteries, westerns, anything. Few writers have that amazing ability."
—Lee Goldberg, Author of the
Diagnosis Murder and *Monk* novels

"As a devotee of Long John Nebel, Bain's biography of the legendary talk king was must reading for me. So is this wonderful memoir by a man who has had a brilliant career making others look good. Thank you, Donald for finally giving up the ghost."
—Alan Colmes, Fox News Channel

"When there's a Writer Hall of Fame, Donald Bain will have a golden plaque in his honor. With affection and a great sense of humor, his book has much to teach aspiring writers about the real world of commercial publishing."
—Paul Fargis, President & Publisher,
The Stonesong Press

"I've known Don Bain for two decades, but it wasn't until I read this book that I realized I've spent my life trying to be him. Should be required reading for any life-hungry, wandering soul who thinks he or she wants to make a living as a writer."
—Mike Levine, Legendary DEA Agent &
Best-selling Author of *Deep Cover*

Murder, HE Wrote

Murder, HE Wrote

A Successful Writer's Life

Donald Bain

NotaBell Books
An imprint of
Purdue University Press
West Lafayette, Indiana

Copyright © 2002 by Donald Bain. All rights reserved.

Printed in the United States of America.

First NotaBell paperback printing by Purdue University Press 2006.

ISBN 978-1-55753-421-7
    1-55753-421-7

Library of Congress Cataloging-in-Publication Data

Bain, Donald, 1935-
  [Every midget has an Uncle Sam costume]
  Murder, HE wrote : a successful writer's life / Donald Bain.
    p. cm.
  Originally published: Fort Lee, NJ : Barricade Books, c2002.
  "Books written by Donald Bain" : p.
  Includes index.
    1. Bain, Donald, 1935- 2. Novelists, American—20th century—Biography.
  3. Authorship. I. Title.
  PS3552.A376Z464 2006
    813'54—dc22
                                                      2006003853

DEDICATION

My two families:

The one that was there for me in the beginning—My mother and father, George and Constance; my sister, Connie; and cousins Jack and June, Marge and Emlyn, Cliff and Loraine, Diane and Bob, Greg and Donna, Janet, Frank and Jill, and all their children.

And my family today—My wife, Renée; daughters Laurie (a fine writer and editor) and Pamela (the professor in the family); grandchildren Zachary, Alexander, Jacob and Lucas; my son-in-law Stuart; stepdaughter Marisa, husband Ron, and daughters Abigail and Eleanor; and stepson Billy, his wife Jessica, and their son, Sylvan.

Sometimes you get lucky.

TABLE OF CONTENTS

ACKNOWLEDGMENTS

My agent, *Ted Chichak*, a famous opera singer in a previous life, who has guided my career for more than 25 years. He kept me from throwing in the towel during lean times, and encouraged me to send my angry letters to him instead to those editors and publishers who used to be on the receiving end . . . *Sam Vaughan*, an extraordinary editor and fine gentleman, the Strunk-and-White of my professional life, whose editing not only improves manuscripts, it serves as a primer on what good writing really is . . . *Ellen Edwards*, who's everything an editor should be, and nice, too . . . *Paul Fargis*, as decent a man as he is a wellspring of ideas . . . *R.H. "Red" Sutherland*, boss, friend and mentor who taught me many things, including integrity, courage, and to appreciate the art practiced by a good short order cook . . . *Jack Pearl*, a cousin and best friend who wrote nearly 100 books, and who got me into the writing business. Most of the time I've appreciated it . . .

Tony Tedeschi and *Joe Scott*, with whom I had the pleasure of collaborating. They taught me a lot about writing—and friendship. That they married wonderful women like *Candy* and

Priscilla doesn't surprise me ... *Long John Nebel,* king of late night talk radio in New York, a complex friend who included me in his radio family, allowing me to chat all night with hundreds of fascinating people over the years ... Comedy writer and friend, *Jack Douglas,* the funniest man I've ever known; and his wonderful wife, *Reiko,* who continues to keep me laughing ... *Dan O'Shea,* my first agent and good friend. Although we eventually parted ways, he helped launch my career as a writer, and I thank him for that ... *Sam Post,* who saw gold in airline stewardesses ... *Sandy Teller,* my quick and bright friend with whom I've shared so many interesting moments, and his talented wife, *Roberta Dougherty* ... *Lyle* and *Carole Stuart* and *Allan Wilson,* who've always liked what I've written ... My attorney, *Frank Curtis,* of Rembar & Curtis ... *Robert Half,* whose friendship I treasured, and his wonderful wife, *Maxine* ... Agents *Russell Galen* and *Jack Scovil* ... And friends *Bob* and *Georgia Baumann, Ralph* and *Kay Bergl, George* and *Rosalie Brown, Cindy Chang, Charles Flowers, Tom Detienne, Ed* and *Elaine Filler, George Gibbs, Rosemary Goad, Arthur Goldberg, Hap* and *Regina Gormley, Jim* and *Elizabeth Grau, Phyllis (P.D.), James, John* and *Peg Johnson, Roy* and *Billie Kramer, Ruth* and *Frank Lazzara, Phil* and *Joan Leshin, Mike Levine* and *Laura Kavanau Levine, Bob London, Joyce Clemow London, Dick* and *Anne Mann, Bill* and *Kathy Miller, Peter* and *Wally Peckham, Lisa Rock, Jim* and *Susan Shevlin, Joe Stockdale, Craig* and *Jill Thomas, Nick* and *Bea Vasile, Karen Welch, Rob Wilson, Bill Wooby,* everyone at the *Jolly Fisherman* where I spent half my adult life, all my friends from the *North Salem Chamber of Commerce,* and so many others whose friendship I've enjoyed over the years. And special thanks to Purdue University Press's managing editor, *Margaret Hunt.*

READ THIS FIRST

There's this elderly man who's hit by a New York City taxi. The impact tosses him into the air, and he lands with a painful thud on the sidewalk. A woman rushes to him, slips her coat beneath his head, looks down and asks, "Are you comfortable, old man?"

He opens his eyes and rasps, "I make a living."

I repeat this old joke whenever someone asks me to sum up my 45-plus years as a professional writer. It doesn't represent false modesty. That I've been able to make a living—a pretty good one at that—for all these years in a profession not known for providing much of anything except frustration and hard times, sometimes impresses me. It also might amuse those who haven't liked what I've written, or in a few cases have envied my relative success. But for the most part, I've been able to satisfy publishers, editors, and the reading public by treating writing as a business, *my* business. I've written more than 90 books. Most of them have been ghostwritten for people more famous than I. Which leads to a question I'm often asked when talking to groups about my career: "How can you stand to see someone else's name on a book that you've written?"

Easy. Ghostwriting is primarily responsible for my having been able to make a living doing what Kurt Vonnegut once described as stringing little black marks together on paper. Vonnegut also said that while he loves being a writer, he hates writing. I share that sentiment at times, although I've found that the more I write, the more I enjoy it. Shaping a scene that works, or coming up with the perfect line for a character, brings pleasure.

I especially enjoy the rewriting process. Initial drafts tend to be longer than necessary, with a half dozen words saying what one or two more judiciously chosen ones would accomplish. One of my favorite sayings is "If I had more time, I would have written less." Getting that initial draft down on paper is the tough, fatiguing part of the process. Reworking it is a joy; you can take all the good work you did and make it better by cutting, finding a word that more accurately says what you'd originally intended, picking up the pace where it flags because you were tired and ended up pushing words around, injecting background into a character where the reader needs it to understand that person's motivation, and myriad other "fixes" destined to elevate your manuscript from good to very good.

Even after you've rewritten and polished to the point that the manuscript has gone to your editor, you'll eventually get it back with lots of suggestions on how to make it better. A good editor is invaluable. If you have faith in your editor's skill and experience, as well as in his or her motivation—in other words, believing in you as a writer, wanting your book to be the best it can be, and not suffering from the "I always wanted to be a writer" syndrome—the editor's comments and suggested changes should be heeded. Sometimes editors are wrong, and will suggest a change that violates everything you intended. But don't write off a good editor's comments and reactions. As for working with a bad editor, the best you can hope for is that there'll be another merger and your bad editor will end up at a different publishing house.

A problem with editor—writer relationships sometimes has to do with age. If the writer is of another generation, perceptions based upon life experiences can get in the way. I once created a husband-and-wife team of characters for a book in a series I was ghosting. My characters were in their 50s, erudite, physically fit, and madly in love. My editor on the series went to another publisher, and I was assigned an attractive young woman with an ego not supported by her abilities. She said the characters had to go: "They're too old," she told me. "People in their fifties don't have any passion left!"

I balked, and prevailed. The characters stayed, and went on to become particular favorites of critics and readers of the series. Last I heard, this editor had become a successful literary agent, which doesn't mean she no longer edits manuscripts. Top agents today function as editors as well as negotiators for their clients. I trust she's matured, and has found passion later in her life.

Good editors don't allow personal preferences and prejudices to influence their work. I once described a major league baseball stadium as being "a beautiful sight" at night, all lit up, the grass vividly green, the base paths meticulously manicured. I didn't say this as the author; my character said it. The editor didn't like baseball, and thought it was a ridiculous comment for the character to make. "Baseball stadiums aren't beautiful," she said. But my character felt they were, and said so in the published book.

A homosexual editor insisted a villain in a book I'd written be made a heterosexual in order to not give homosexuals a bad name. It wasn't my intention to give anyone a bad name. It just so happened that the character's homosexuality was crucial to the story. It turned out to be a moot point because the book was never published, a situation that spawned one of the few legal actions I've ever taken in my career. More about that later.

I suppose it's impossible for editors, agents, and publishers to completely put aside their own particular little quirks when working on a manuscript. I did a series of books years ago for Fawcett, one of the preeminent paperback publishing houses in the business. It was headed by a lovely gentleman, Ralph Daigh, the only non-Fawcett on the board of directors. Ralph had his own peculiar idiosyncrasy. He refused to allow Native Americans—Indians— to appear on the cover of any book he published, including numerous western novels. It wasn't that he disliked Native Americans. He just didn't want them on his covers. Go figure.

The difference between a good and a bad editor, aside from professional skill, can be the attitude toward the writer. Some editors display anger or frustration each time they make an editorial change or offer a suggestion, as though you, the writer, have caused a terrible, sour-tasting burden to be inflicted upon them. This is counterproductive for the writer. Writing a 400-page book is hard enough. Having to deal with an editor's hostility only increases the pain.

*   *   *   *   *

I've spent some time thinking about why I've been successful as a ghostwriter for all these years. It boils down to attitude. My ego is intact; I don't need public recognition, although I admit to moments of frustration when a book I've written receives a wonderful review, or spends weeks on the *New York Times* bestseller list. I would have enjoyed having people outside my circle of friends and family know I'd written that particular book. I don't feel that way, however, when a book I've written receives a negative review, or fails in the marketplace. You can't have it both ways.

I'm not without an ego. When I wrote *Coffee, Tea or Me?* in the mid-60s, it carried the by-line of two former Eastern Airline stews (they were called stewardesses back then). I dedicated it to myself: *"So many thanks to Don Bain, writer and friend, who's flown enough to know how funny it really can be. Without him, Coffee, Tea or Me? would still be nothing more than the punch line of an old airline joke."* I went on to write three sequels to that remarkably successful book, as well as a half dozen others in the same frothy vein, and dedicated them all to me. (Shameless.) I've whimsically wondered whether some person would read those books and question who this guy Bain is who has all these attractive young women dedicating their books to him. It hasn't happened. There are two reasons for a writer to ghostwrite for others. One, of course, is money. There are ghosts, I'm sure, who apply their skill solely for that reason, hoping to save enough to be free to eventually write their own works. The second reason is *craft*. Writing is a craft, involving tools, as carpentry is a craft utilizing tools. Once a carpenter has mastered his hammer, level and miter box, he's free to be creative with them. The same is true of writing. When my daughters were little, and I was spending my days in the basement of our home working at a manual typewriter, neighborhood kids would ask them what their father did. "He types," they replied. They were right, I suspect. Early in my career I was doing more typing than writing. I turned out books without having honed the writer's craft. Years later, my agent, Ted Chichak, called me after I'd submitted a manuscript and said, "You've finally learned how to write."

It takes time and practice to develop useful writing muscles.

I take pride in my craft, whether it's applied to a book bearing my name, or someone else's. I've never considered a ghostwriting assignment to be less important than something I've written of my own. I operate on two basic premises: The first is that whatever I'm writing at the moment—even a letter—is the most important writing I'll ever do. The second is that what I'm working on at any given time might be the last thing I'll ever write, and I treat it that way. These "attitudes" have, I believe, been at the root of whatever success I've achieved as a writer. More than anything, I've strived to be a professional, and to be viewed in that light.

I've known writers who've taken on a ghostwriting job who would never consider using something from their own life in the book. They'd rather save such things for when they write under their own name. I realized I'd reached a level of professionalism when I'd dropped such views. I was writing a book for a well-known person, one of a number of books I'd written for this individual in a best-selling series. I'd reached a point in the manuscript where an episode from my own life would fit perfectly. I paused. Should I waste it on someone else's behalf? My two "rules" came into play: This is the most important thing I'll ever write, and it may be the last. I used my personal experience in the book, and have continued to do so throughout my ghostwriting career.

While my professional life has focused on the writing of books, both for the byline of others and for my own, it's taken me into a variety of other activities. I've written for magazines, radio, and television, and spent many years working in public relations, particularly in the aviation and travel industries.

What I've found interesting about my career is that it's plunked me in the center of fascinating, sometimes bizarre circumstances, and allowed me to get to know a wide range of interesting people, some wonderful, bright and kind, others strange and, in a few instances, downright mean. I've been a jazz musician my entire adult life, and continue to perform as a vibraphonist, although less frequently these days. I find creating music more immediately satisfying than writing, but writing has opened up greater opportunities to make a decent living. I've been an on-air personality on radio and television, once owned a piece of a nightclub, and have given yearly lectures about writing while crossing the Atlantic on the magnificent QE2, and on the equally splendid Seabourn Sun.

Although this is a book by me and about my career, the people I've come to know and work with are infinitely more interesting. *Murder, HE Wrote* is really about them.

Duke Ellington once told me that the reason he refused to do his autobiography was that once you did, it meant your life was over.

I hope the Duke was wrong.

Most names in the book are real, although I've changed an occasional one to stay out of court.

CHAPTER ONE

"HE WANTED TO BE
ED SULLIVAN"

I never wanted to be a writer.

My four years at Purdue University in West Lafayette, Indiana were spent planning a career in radio and television. My heroes were Steve Allen and Jack Paar, not Faulkner, Hemingway or Mailer.

I went off to Purdue after four uneventful high school years during the pleasant Eisenhower era of the 50s. Sewanhaka High School in Floral Park, Long Island, New York, was a big, happy, positive place at which to spend your teens. Everybody's white bucks were quickly and deliberately made dirty, acne proliferated, hair goop to create a wave was in style, and the popular music of the day was actually based on melodies. Like most high school students, I tried to figure out who I was and what I might become. I had my jock side—basketball, soccer, and track-and-field. I was six feet four, the big guy on the basketball team. They called me "Moose." Today, I'd be considered short on a basketball court. The truth was, I was not a very competitive athlete; winning never seemed especially important. My only claim to playing field fame was having "taught" the great four-time Olympic champion, Al Oerter, how to throw the discus.

I was a discus thrower on Sewanhaka's track-and-field team. Our coach, Jim Fraley, brought Oerter to the practice field one afternoon, introduced us, and asked me to give him some preliminary pointers until the coach had time to get back to us. Oerter, who was a year behind me, made the initial mistake everyone does; he spun the discus off his pinky rather than his index finger. I corrected him.

There was a fence at the far end of the practice field that was historically unreachable by any discus thrower. Within weeks, Al was scaling that fence, to the chagrin of passing motorists. He was a natural at the sport, and his incredible career testifies to that fact. You owe it all to me, Al.

Sewanhaka had its own student radio station. I spent considerable time there dreaming of one day becoming a broadcasting star, and looking on with envy at the station's most talented student, Dave Potts, who went on to a successful career in radio and TV (under the name Dave Michaels). I also formed a comedy team with a funny, one-eyed guy named Mike Venezia. We appeared in a number of student shows and left 'em rolling in the aisles. Fortunately, our appearances were never recorded or filmed. Students laughed at anything in those days. I suspect we were pretty lousy.

It was in high school that I developed my lifelong love of music, particularly jazz. My sister had a close friend, Carolyn Kelsch, who owned a small portable record player. She occasionally loaned it to me so I could listen to the two jazz albums I owned, both 10-inch LPs. One was the first recording by the great Canadian pianist Oscar Peterson, a solo effort. The second was a Dixieland band led by Muggsy Spanier. There were days when I left for school, waited around the corner until everyone had gone off to work, then returned to the house and played those records over and over until they were worn out.

I also used to travel into Manhattan from Long Island to sit in the non-alcoholic bleachers at the famed jazz club, Birdland, where I sipped Cokes and was carried away by the remarkable music of Basie and Miles Davis, Dizzy Gillespie and Sarah Vaughan. And there was a jazz club in Hempstead, a half hour from home, where the vibraphonist Terry Gibbs, and multi-instrumentalist Don Elliot, often performed. Watching Gibbs's vividly colored mallets fly over the vibes's keyboard, and hearing the rich, complex improvisations flowing from it, was mesmerizing. I decided I wanted more than anything to become a vibes player. I gently broached the subject to my parents of possibly buying a set, and was informed they couldn't afford it. I knew they were right and didn't question it. But the dream endured.

I mention my love of music, and the tangential career I eventually forged in it, because I think it has a direct bearing on my writing. Good writing has a rhythm. Each character speaks at a different tempo, some using carefully arranged phrases, others improvising in the best tradition of Charlie Parker and Bill Evans. An audience knows when a band isn't together, when the "time" laid down by the drummer or bass player isn't quite in-sync with the other musicians. Readers have the same negative reaction when a character's inherent voice falls behind or gets ahead of the beat. Even narrative passages must have the right musical quality. And, of course, like any properly constructed song, stories on paper must have a beginning, middle, and end, properly structured, logical, and consistent.

When it came time for me to go to college, I wanted three things: A large university away from home; one with a good radio and television station; and a scholarship. Purdue, primarily an engineering and agricultural school, offered me a special merit scholarship, which paid my out-of-state tuition. It had what sounded like an impressive educational radio and television station (now called "public" radio and TV). It was big. And it was in Indiana, miles away from New York.

The scholarship was crucially important. My mother and father did not have the money to send me away to college, although we weren't poor. My father managed to keep his job during the Depression as manager of the Keiner-Williams Stamping Company, which made those old-fashioned milk cans, painted versions of which are now seen on the porches of faux country homes. The owners of the company were shrewd, and benevolent. They kept their employees on the payroll during those bleak years by cutting everyone's salary in half. A half a loaf was decidedly better than none.

My father defined the word "dour." His family had originally emigrated from Wick, Scotland, the former herring capital of the world, and settled in Nova Scotia. I visited Wick as an adult and understood why they'd left. The northern coast of Scotland is a stunning visual feast. It's also a sadly depressed area. The Scandinavians introduced technologically superior herring boats and ate the Scots's lunch, so to speak.

My father, his brother, Robert, and sister, Ada, left Halifax in the early 1900s and settled in New York, where my father pursued a career in baseball. (A younger brother had fallen through the ice in Newfoundland and drowned.) My father signed with the Brooklyn Dodgers in 1916 but never got to pitch professionally because he fell off a roof shortly after signing and broke his pitching arm.

Boxing was a popular sport in our house. A close family friend, Jimmy Quigley—known to me as "Uncle Jimmy"—was a frequent weekend visitor to our home on Madison Avenue, in Franklin Square. Jimmy was a small man who always dressed impeccably, and drove the biggest car I'd ever seen. He was a dandy, a lifelong bachelor whose full-time job was selling paint for the Sherwin-Williams Company. In his spare time he managed a few tank fighters. Jimmy and my father thought I'd make a good boxer and set out to train me. I was in junior high at the time, and was as fascinated by the sport as they were. A regulation size ring was erected in our basement, which was moved outdoors in the summer. An unofficial tournament was launched in the neighborhood in which many kids my age participated. It was fun, although I didn't enjoy getting hit in the face by a particularly tough friend, Jimmy Ziegler, who lived a few blocks away.

Listening to professional fights on radio, and later watching them on TV, was also a part of our routine. Prior to television, I would plan all week to hear the Friday night fights on radio, fortifying myself with special sweets from a local bakery and secluding myself in a small room at the rear of the house. Those were magical nights; I "saw" the action through the excited words of the commentators, and projected myself into the ring, fighting for a world title, taking the blows but always coming back, a warrior, driving the ringside fans wild with my skill and courage. Later, a local appliance store got the first TV set in the neighborhood, and my father and I would join friends of his in the store on Friday nights to enjoy the marvel of actually being able to see the bouts. The classic featherweight battles between Willie Pep and Sandy Sadler remain etched in my memory. Joe Louis, Rocky Graziano, Jake La Motta, Tammy Mauriello, Marcel Cerdan, Gus Lesnievich, Billy Conn, Kid Gavilan, Charlie Fusari, and dozens of other names have stayed with me all these years. Those were wonderful moments spent with my father and Uncle Jimmy.

George Sutherland Bain (Sutherland is my middle name, too) was a man who seemed to carry the world on his shoulders. He seldom laughed. We had one of the first TV sets on the block, and my mother, sister and I would occasionally see him break a smile when the comedian, Arnold Stang, was on the small, round, black-and-white tube. This grave approach to life undoubtedly played a role in the succession of heart attacks he suffered, and his death at the age of 56. He wasn't helped by that era's "smart" cardiac care. His physician suggested my father eat plenty of eggs, which he did at three meals a day, and to not exert himself. He went up the stairs on his backside, one step at a time. I was in my third year at Purdue when he had his final coronary. I took the train to New York from Chicago, and arrived in time to say goodbye. He died a few days after I got there. I was on the couch with my mother and sister when the call came from the hospital. I remember being both sad and relieved at the news. He'd been sick for a long time, and those years caring for him had taken a toll on my mother. That there was a sense of relief in my bag of emotions created a feeling of guilt in me that lasted for many years.

My mother, Connie, was born in Brooklyn, and served in the Navy during WWI. Her father, my grandfather, Cornelius "Con" Dailey, had played major league baseball, a catcher with a variety of teams from 1884–1896. His brother, Ed, was also a major league player from 1885–1891. Their records are included in the *Baseball Encyclopedia*. I never met Con Dailey, but evidently he was quite a man about town in Manhattan, a pal and drinking buddy of Diamond Jim Brady. For years, he took a baseball team from a Long Island Episcopal boys' school to Cuba to compete against Cuban high school players. I wish I'd gotten to pal around with him.

My mother was very different from my father. She was tall, slender, and pretty—and flighty, a nervous woman with a wonderful sense of humor. That helped when dealing with her somber husband. She reminded me of Edith Bunker, the Jean Stapleton character on the TV sitcom "All in the Family." My fondest memories of her occurred in the kitchen after dinner. My father would retire from the dinner table to his recliner where he would enjoy his favorite dessert—white bread and butter, and chocolate ice cream—while the three of us—my mother, sister and I—did the dishes. I was a collector of joke books, and regaled my mother and sister with my delivery of material from them. They laughed so easily, like the students at high school shows. It was a warm kitchen, full of love.

My father's frequent illnesses put a strain on the household budget, and my mother was forced to pawn her engagement and wedding rings more than once to pay the bills. But they always managed, and the financial strains they felt were seldom made known to me. I had two cars while in high school (not at the same time), a 1935 Ford coupe with a rumble seat, which I hand-painted a brilliant green (I paid $50 for it with money I earned working parttime and during summer vacations); and an Aero-Willys, a strange vehicle that cost me $95. And there was always enough money for a pitcher of beer at local hangouts with high school buddies Bob Baumann, Bill "Boopsie" Miller, and George Gibbs.

The scholarship from Purdue meant I would be able to go away to college. My parents drove me to Indiana that first year. I knew that it was crucial for me to keep the scholarship, which meant maintaining a 3-point average each semester. My parents paid my room-and-board bill, but that was it. Any pocket money would have to come from my working.

I became involved that first semester with WBAA, the student radio station. To Indiana it was more than that. It broadcast to every corner of the state, and was as popular as many of the area's commercial stations. It was managed by a lovely man, Jim Miles, but the day-to-day operations fell to John DeCamp, who did the play-by-play for Purdue football games when he wasn't overseeing the dozens of students working at WBAA. I say working because there were a limited number of paid announcer slots; I was fortunate to land one. It didn't pay much, but I didn't need much those days. As I progressed through my four years at Purdue, I ended up spending what seemed like half my life at the station. For my final two years I opened the station six days a week, showing up at six and doing the morning show until nine when I headed for class. I returned at noon to do a one-hour classical music show. At four, I went on the air at WASK, a commercial station in town, where I broadcast until seven.

Each year, a senior was chosen to receive The Durwood Kirby Award for work at the university's stations. Kirby, who'd once attended Purdue, and who spent years as second banana to TV star

Garry Moore, was the guest speaker at the dinner when I accepted the honor. He told me to look him up when I returned to New York. I did. He brushed me off.

My dream of becoming a professional musician came true during my last three years at Purdue. I'd become close friends with George Brown, who played jazz trumpet and piano. He put together a sextet that worked many student parties, as well as clubs and other college campuses around the state. George had run across a used two-and-a-half octave set of Jenco vibes for sale during my second year at Purdue. The owner wanted $150, which I scraped up, and spent every spare free minute teaching myself to play. My first professional job occurred two weeks after buying the vibes. I was sworn into the musicians union on the dance floor before the party started, and struggled through the evening with George's verbal help from the piano bench. I have pictures of that engagement. I looked good. How I sounded is another matter.

We bought uniforms for the band, dark gray suits with irregular gray stripes that gave us the look of zebras. We rehearsed whenever we could find the time, and found ourselves much in demand, not only in the West Lafayette area, but throughout Indiana. One winter, George got us a two-week, six-night a week gig in a nightclub in Kokomo. It meant staying at school during the Christmas break to rehearse, but the booking represented the big time for us, and we took it seriously. The club owner demanded that we include a female singer, and we found one, Julie, divorced and living with her two children. Julie couldn't sing, but she was blonde and had a nice figure, which we correctly analyzed as being all that mattered to the club owner. It was torture rehearsing with her. We once worked for the better part of a day trying to get her to sing the Gershwin song, 'S Wonderful. She could barely carry a tune, and had absolutely no sense of time, rhythm or phrasing. Eventually we taught her four songs, and decided to play a lot of Latin tunes. She looked great shaking a pair of maracas.

The club, a classic "cheater's joint," was an hour's drive from

West Lafayette. The routine was for George Brown to pick up Julie at her home in the block-long yellow Lincoln convertible he'd bought from Teddy, the Chinese owner of the Black & Gold, a student hangout on the Purdue campus, and pick me up at WASK where I was on the air five days a week from four until seven in the evening. The three of us then drove to Kokomo where we played from nine until two in the morning.

Things went relatively well the first two nights. The club owner wasn't happy with the latin tunes. They were too up-tempo: "Keep it slow," he told us, "so the guys can get the broads to dance with them." Other than that, he really liked having Julie on the bandstand with her low-cut sequined dress and big smile. She provided the band a value-added talent, too. She'd studied theatrical makeup at some point in her life, and insisted upon making us up before we started playing.

Disaster struck on the third night.

George arrived at WASK as scheduled. Julie wasn't with him.

"Where's Julie?" I asked.

"Bad news, man."

"What happened?"

"She's been arrested."

"Arrested? For what?"

"Armed robbery."

"Oh."

Earlier that year, two men wielding guns had stuck up a large bakery in Lafayette and walked away with the cash payroll. According to witnesses, the gunmen were heavily made up to disguise their identity, and obviously knew when the payroll would be there, ready to be distributed to workers. Julie, our maracas-shaking blonde bombshell, had been in charge of the bakery's payroll up until a month before the robbery. She was charged with having masterminded the holdup.

"Where's Julie?" the club owner asked while we were setting up.

George explained what had happened.

"Jesus," the owner muttered, and walked away.

The atmosphere in the club was heavy that night. Men who'd sat at the bar ogling Julie complained about her absence. At the end of the night, the owner fired us. "Don't come back tomorrow," he said. "I already got another act." Our replacement turned out to be a stripper who did her act on stage in a huge plastic wine glass.

Julie pleaded guilty to her complicity in the holdup. She told the judge at sentencing that she did it because she didn't have money to buy her kids new bikes at Christmas. It was the last I heard of her.

Those four years at Purdue were heady ones. Between my studies and making money doing things I enjoyed, there wasn't much time for sleep. My ambition to do something in what could roughly be called show business seemed well on its way.

Each year, Purdue University mounts *Varsity Varieties*, a huge student show held in the main theater, as large and lavish as Radio City Music Hall, and professionally managed at the time by a former manager of Radio City. A friendly rivalry existed between the two venues, with one adding a few extra seats to enable it to proclaim itself the larger of the two. And then the other would slip in extra seating and reclaim the title.

I auditioned for MC of the show my freshman year and won. It was the first time a freshman had ever been chosen. I won the audition the next two years, too. When I stepped onto the stage in my senior year, it was the only time in the university's history that the same student had been selected in all four years. Talent scouts from Chicago were there, and they invited me to talk to them about representing me after I graduated. I did, but nothing came of it because as an Air Force ROTC student, I owed Uncle Sam my first three post-college years.

My favorite professor was theater professor Dr. Joseph Stockdale, who wasn't much older than his students. He cast me as Mitch in *A Streetcar Named Desire*, the role played on Broadway and on the screen by Karl Malden. I didn't especially aspire to become an actor, although I enjoyed being with theater people and taking my bow in front of an appreciative audience.

What did I want to be? *Who* did I want to be? The answer was all too vague at that juncture in my life. My goal seemed to become anything that would bring me fame and adoration. I wanted to live in a Manhattan penthouse and sign autographs. Beautiful women would find me irresistible. With all this, however, I would remain humble and never forget my roots. That was the future I envisioned for myself. How to get there was the big question.

Forty years later, I attended a reunion of the Purdue Theater Department at the West Lafayette campus. Joe Stockdale was there. He'd gone on from Purdue to head the drama department at SUNY-Purchase, in New York, from which he retired as dean emeritus after 16 years. As teacher and director, he's launched the careers of a number of well-known actors and actresses, and continues to direct and to write plays; he's considered one of the leading experts on the works of Tennessee Williams. He introduced me to someone: "This is Don Bain. He wanted to be Ed Sullivan."

Which wasn't true, although his comment accurately served as shorthand to describe who I was and what I wanted to become after graduation. Joe and I are now friends, and communicate regularly. He was one of those people in my life who made the sort of impression that sticks to your ribs; when I was his student, I wanted to look like him, talk like him, and be him.

Ed Sullivan indeed! Steve Allen maybe.

Indulge me a few final comments about my first 22 years of life.

My sister, Connie, wasn't my biological sister. Her name was Constance Dailey. Her mother and my mother were sisters. Connie's mother died giving birth to her, and the father, a politically connected man on Long Island, simply walked away. He wasn't about to raise a daughter without a mother. Hell of a guy. My mother and father assumed Connie's upbringing. At that time, the prevailing wisdom was to not tell a child that he or she was adopted, or being brought up by someone other than natural parents. We know today that that's the wrong approach, more potentially destructive to a child than when they're told the truth.

Connie didn't learn that she wasn't George and Constance Bain's real daughter until she was 16 and applied for working papers. I remember as a little kid crouching outside our kitchen window while she loudly, and tearfully, confronted my mother after returning from the labor department offices. I don't think Connie, affectionately nicknamed "Mutzi," ever really got over it, although it was never raised as an issue after that initial confrontation, at least not within my earshot. She never married, and died too soon. My mother and father, who eventually legally adopted Mutzi, loved her as much as they loved me, and did what they could to provide a happy life for her. They were only partially successful, I'm afraid. But they tried. They did their best. They always did.

When I MC'd *Varsity Varieties* my sophomore year at Purdue, my mother and father made their only visit aside from having driven me there my freshman year. It was the year I worked with a partner, a guy named John Peterson. One bit had me singing a few lines from a popular song.

Mom and Dad came backstage after the show. My mother was bubbling with pride and happiness. My father came up to me, shook my hand, and said, "You shouldn't sing."

When I tell this story, the usual response is negative. People consider it a cruel comment, an insensitive father failing to support his son. I disagree. With the exception of people who abuse their children, I believe that most parents do their very best within the parameters of who they are, their personalities, life experiences, and the problems they face each day in their own lives. I have little patience with adults who blame their failings on their parents. I was loved. My mother and father believed in me, and wanted only the best for their son. I smile when I think back to my father's backstage comment that night. I knew he was as proud of me as my mother. It just wasn't in him to express it.

I thank my mother and father for many things, including creating a home in which I never once heard a word of prejudice or bigotry, and for instilling in me a love of four-legged animals. My father was fond of sayings, including this from Abraham Lincoln.

"I am in favor of animal rights as well as human rights. That is the way of a whole human being."

I've enjoyed the friendship and companionship of a variety of four-legged animals over my lifetime, and a number of two-legged animals, too. All of the four-legged ones were smart and loving, loyal and forgiving. Most of my two-legged friends have been, too.

CHAPTER TWO

"One of Our Sand Dunes is Missing"

Everything gets used.

Life experiences create a bank of images and recollections from which a writer draws every day. That certainly has been true with me. Everyone I've met, every situation in which I found myself, has been "used" in one way or another in my books. Someone's facial tic, unusual speech pattern, physical description, or response to a difficult situation becomes grist for characters in a novel, never to the extent of identifying the real people, of course, but modified and shaped to suit the needs of the creative process of the moment. Entire episodes from one's life can become the basis for a story, screenplay, or novel. That was true of a portion of my time in the United States Air Force.

After successfully completing the Air Force ROTC program at Purdue, I was commissioned a second lieutenant upon graduation. I'd intended to go to flight school, and was in the first group of AFROTC college seniors to receive government sponsored private flying lessons, the Air Force having decided it was cheaper to wash out potential pilots in college than waiting until they'd actually entered the military. The private flying program involved 35 hours of training, eight hours of dual instruction, 27 hours of solo. My instructor pilot was an old-timer named "Pop" who had to hold his trembling right hand with his left to sign my logbook. That impairment aside, he was a hell of a good flight instructor.

On the morning of my eighth hour of dual instruction, Pop had me shoot takeoffs and landings for the first half hour before telling me to taxi to the small building that served as West Lafayette's terminal. "You're on your own for the next half hour," he said. "It'll feel different with my weight out of the right seat, so be aware of it." With that he was gone. Terror gripped me. Could I do it alone after so few hours of training? But once the wheels of the Cessna 172 left the ground, my fears were replaced by exhilaration. I'd never before felt so free and in control of my life.

I had 32 hours under my belt when the Air Force changed the commitment military pilots were required to serve from three years to five. I didn't want to put in that much time and chose to drop out of the pre-flight program. They allowed me to complete my private training, however, and I received my pilot's license.

I loved being up in a plane, and do to this day, although I no longer am an active pilot. Airplanes, and the experience of flight, fascinate and thrill me; I can happily spend hours at the end of an active runway watching planes take off and land. I would go on to spend a portion of my adult life working in the airline industry, three years on the public relations staff of American Airlines, and more than a dozen years as a consultant to Pan Am. These were among the happiest years of my life; I still have trouble coming to grips with there no longer being a Pan Am, the big blue ball on its planes' tails a once proud symbol of America around the world. (Investors eventually bought the Pan Am name and today operate it as a small charter airline.) Pan Am was mismanaged into the ground, although the Lockerbie tragedy didn't help, nor did introducing the first jumbo jet, the 747, with all those seats to fill just as a recession was starting. I wrote the speech Pan Am's chairman gave at a somber gathering at Lockerbie, Scotland, after the plane had been brought down by a terrorist's bomb. It was the most difficult thing I've ever written.

A few days after graduation—and while awaiting orders where to report for my first military assignment—I traveled to Europe with a Purdue variety show, playing vibes with the university's big band, and emceeing the show. We toured military bases in France and Germany under the auspices of the USO. When I returned home a month later, my orders were waiting: Report within two weeks to Bordeaux Air Force Base, France. Not bad.

The joy of returning to France was short-lived, however. After a few months there, I received papers transferring me to Dhahran, Saudi Arabia, as officer-in-charge of that desert air base's Armed Forces Radio and Television Station (AFRTS). Not so good.

In September of 1957, I flew to Dhahran on an overnight TWA Constellation flight from Paris. People in Bordeaux had told me that while it would be hot in Arabia, it would be bearable because it was the desert—dry heat. They lied. Dhahran sits directly on the Persian Gulf. I stepped off the plane early in the morning and was hit with the hottest, wettest air I'd ever experienced. The only place that comes close is Washington D.C. in August.

Our military presence in Dhahran was confusing, to be kind. The primary mission was to train Saudi jet pilots, some who were making the transition from camel to T-33, which made for interesting training flights. Aside from fulfilling that mission, however, America's presence in Saudi Arabia was considered extremely important, a strategic location in support of our overall Middle East foreign policy. The Saudis imposed a number of stringent restrictions on our being there. There was to be no alcohol, of course, to conform to strict Muslim laws, nor were there to be any weapons in the hands of anyone except Saudi military. The Saudi government allowed us to fly a single American flag, but only on the condition that it be embedded in a huge block of concrete to prevent the staff from touching sovereign Saudi soil.

Prohibition was as much a failure in Saudi Arabia as it had been in this country. Dhahran was home to thousands of bright engineers working for ARAMCO, the huge oil company that had entered into an agreement with the Saudi government to bring up its rich energy reserves. Many of these engineers built elaborate stills within their homes to produce a wide variety of alcoholic beverages. For years after I'd left, I received a photo Christmas card from a friend, posed with his smiling family in front of their still, cleverly hidden behind their living room wall. The wall had been opened for the photo; with all the metal tubing and wiring exposed, it looked like a Dupont plant.

Another condition of our being allowed to be in Saudi Arabia was that no religious services were to be observed. That wasn't a problem with the Jewish religion because every serviceman assigned to Dhahran had to provide a baptismal certificate along with a passport to prove that he or she wasn't Jewish. There was a certain hypocrisy involved in this restriction. RCA had built the country's communications system, and many of its engineers were Jewish. Pragmatism evidently prevailed because the Saudis turned their back on those skilled folks they needed at the time.

Despite the prohibition on conducting religious services, they were held nonetheless, in the base theater. Catholic and Protestant chaplains were brought into the country as "recreation officers." Services were announced in the weekly base newsletter: "Recreation Group Number One will meet in the theater Sunday morning at nine." (Read Catholic). "Recreation Group Number Two meets at ten." (Read Protestant.) Guards were stationed at the theater entrance to dissuade locals from wandering inside. Wine was served at Catholic communion, smuggled in on flights from Bahrain. The Christian God was alive and well, no matter what the Saudi government decreed.

But breaking the rules in Saudi Arabia was a risky business. The government's approach to law-and-order was not based upon so-called compassionate conservatism. Steal something and you lost your hand in the public square. Commit a more serious crime and your head rolled. A woman who'd committed adultery was often buried in the sand up to her neck, and townspeople threw rocks at her head until she was dead. My timing in arriving in Dhahran was fortunate. Only a year earlier, groups of foreigners were required to attend hand and head choppings as a reminder of how harshly the government treated lawbreakers, foreign and domestic. I missed that, but the practice of hanging the severed heads and hands on ARAMCO's main gate was still very much alive during my year there.

After settling into my room at the bachelor officer's quarters, and locating the officer's mess where the bar served a variety of milk shake flavors made with powered milk, I strolled over to the radio and TV stations, housed in a one-story concrete building across a sand-covered road from a Saudi military compound. The building also contained the offices of the base information officer, who was scheduled to arrive in a month. When he eventually showed up, he brought with him something that would play a major role in how I spent the ensuing 11 months in Dhahran.

I introduced myself to the 18 enlisted men working at the stations, and made my first of many mistakes. I gave a little speech in which I said something like, "Look, this isn't a great place to be stationed for a year, but we'll all get through it if we just do our jobs and keep our senses of humor. Let's do away with all the military formality and just get along as friends. I'm Don, not Lieutenant Bain. Okay?"

They seemed pleased with my laid back approach, and I ended the meeting confident that things would go smoothly. My immaturity was showing.

Our two stations were the only sources of broadcast entertainment, not only for the Air Force base, but for ARAMCO employees as well. The radio station was on the air 24 hours a day, playing a variety of recorded music that came from the States on large discs, and announcing upcoming events that might be of interest to listeners. The enlisted men manning the microphones had not been announcers in civilian life. They were rough at the edges, comically at times, but did their best.

On the TV side, programming consisted primarily of recorded shows from the States, including movies, sporting events, and a variety of dramas and sitcoms. In addition to military and oil company personnel, the audience also included the Saudis. That created problems. Their taste in programming, and the myriad moral restrictions required by their faith, often bumped heads with the content of the shows. In order to attempt to censor out material that would prove offensive, I had two airmen do nothing but screen shows in search of such material. Each worked an eight-hour shift, peering at a small TV screen and consulting a long list of things to be looking for—sexual content, Christian religious scenes, programs dealing with Israel and all things Jewish, scenes in which alcohol was consumed, and a range of other situations that might offend our hosts.

Big problems.

I found myself being summoned to the base commander's office on an almost daily basis to answer for something that had been on TV the night before. A menacing looking Saudi, replete with headdress and chains and flowing robes, whose job was to monitor our broadcasts in search of offensive material, always attended those meetings. He could find offensive material in the most innocuous of shows, Disney cartoons, period musicals, even *Lassie*, the base commander's wife's favorite program. A six-second camera pan of a cemetery with white crosses in a movie had me on the general's carpet. An inappropriate word that had escaped my two censors would also have me explaining things to the general and the big, scowling Saudi. Each time I returned to the station from those command performances, I would try to inspire the two airmen screening shows to be more diligent. I was sympathetic to their plight. Sitting for eight hours a day squinting at a small TV screen in search of seemingly innocent comments or scenes wasn't easy. But they weren't the ones suffering the accusatory gaze of the Saudi censor. I was. What was the punishment for allowing such things on the air? I wondered. Would I lose a hand? An eye? Be tied to a stake in the middle of the desert and left to shrivel and die?

One night, while at dinner at a friend's home at ARAMCO, we watched my TV station while sipping homemade hooch. Wrestling was on. No fear that something offensive could happen on a wrestling show. That comforting thought was dashed when the participants in the next match entered the ring. One was a wrestler of obvious Arabic origins wearing traditional Arabic garb and with a distinctly Arabic name. Across the ring was a muscular guy wearing a yarmulke and prayer shawl. He was the Jewish wrestling champion, the ring announcer intoned. This was to be a fight to the death, for the honor of their respective peoples.

I grabbed the phone and tried to call the station. Busy. I kept one eye on the TV as I continued to call. Still busy. The Jew was beating up the Arab pretty good, body slamming him and pretending to gouge out his eyes.

"I need your car," I told my host.

His car was a Messerschmitt, a three-wheel vehicle built by the German military aircraft manufacturer of the same name. It was a little bubble of a vehicle that accommodated the driver and one very short person behind. The plastic canopy lifted up, like a fighter plane. The wheel was a half-moon, like the type used in aircraft. I wedged myself into the car, started it up, and headed for the base, a half hour drive from the ARAMCO compound. Driving in Saudi Arabia involved *assuming* you were on the road; daily sandstorms invariably covered it.

I ran into the station and went directly to the TV control room where the engineer on duty was reading a magazine. The match between the Jewish champion and the Arab was over. I didn't even have to ask; I knew it in my bones. The Jew had won.

"Didn't you see the match between the Jewish guy and the Arab?" I growled.

"Wasn't watchin', Don."

I found the airman screening programs. "How come you let that wrestling match between the Jew and the Arab go on?" I asked, forcing calm into my voice.

"I didn't figure there could be nothing bad in wrestling, Don. I cut out all the beer commercials."

Maybe the Saudi censor wasn't watching, I thought, hoping. Maybe nobody was watching. I considered pursuing the matter with the engineer and airman doing the screening, but decided there was nothing to be gained. I drove the Messerschmitt back to ARAMCO and further fortified myself with a drink from my friend's living room wall.

The call came first thing in the morning. I entered the general's office, threw him a snappy salute, and said, "Lieutenant Bain reporting as ordered, Sir." I tried to avoid the ominous glare of the Saudi censor, convinced he was envisioning my head hanging from the ARAMCO gate. The general, whose last name I remember was Clark, gave me what had become a standard dressing down for my negligence in allowing such offensive material to hit the airwaves. Usually, that meant I was free to leave. But this morning he told me to stay after the censor left the office, robes flowing behind him. The general smiled and asked me to sit. When I had, he gave me what passed for a heartfelt, fatherly talk about the sensitivity of the situation, and how important it was to the base and its mission that nothing like this occur in the future.

I explained how I had two airmen working sixteen hours a day screening shows, but promised we'd try even harder.

His fatherly demeanor suddenly evaporated. He leaned across the desk, fixed me in a hard stare, and said, "You'd damn well better, Lieutenant."

Things improved at the station after that, at least regarding the censoring of programs. But my informal approach to military leadership began to kick back on me. While most of the 18 enlisted men responded favorably to my easygoing leadership style (maybe naïve is a better way to describe it), one grizzly veteran sergeant, whose name was Zeke, did not. I suspect he was scornful of all young officers who'd achieved their commissioned rank through college ROTC programs, and I was no exception. He was the only one of the 18 who insisted upon calling me Lieutenant.

Looking back, I must admit that my elitist view of music—as far as I was concerned, jazz was man's highest calling and the only music worthy of being broadcast on *my* radio station, along with some classical—didn't help the situation. I changed music programming to reflect my personal taste, substituting jazz for what had been primarily country-and-western music and vapid pop tunes. This didn't sit well with my sergeant. He grumbled constantly about the "stupid" music being played, and since most of the enlisted men were from the South, he found many receptive ears.

One day, Zeke came to me and asked if he could do a two-hour country-and-western music show every Saturday. I told him I'd think about it, although I'd already made up my mind. This was on a Saturday. I informed him the next day that I didn't think changing programming was a good idea, but thanked him for the suggestion. He left my office cursing under his breath.

That night, the television station broadcast its weekly episode of *Lassie*, the general's wife's favorite program. The show had just started when TV screens all over the area went blank. We were off the air.

The phone rang. It was Mrs. General, who was positively distraught. I assured her we'd do everything in our power to get back on the air and resume the program. I rushed to the control room. Zeke, who was the station's chief engineer, was browsing a magazine and seemingly unconcerned about what was occurring.

""What happened?" I asked.

"Damned if I know, Lieutenant."

"We've got to get back on the air," I said. "The general will be furious with us. It's his wife's favorite show."

"Hard to tell what the problem is, Lieutenant. All this fucking sand blowing around screws everything up. The equipment is sensitive."

I retreated to my office and analyzed the situation. It didn't take long for reality to dawn. I returned to the control room and told Zeke I'd reconsidered, and that he could do his program starting the following week. Minutes later, *Lassie* was back on the air. He'd gotten his way. He had me over a barrel because I knew nothing about the technical side of radio and TV. He did. It was my turn to grumble.

Although Zeke was now an on-air personality ("Good morning, Dhahran!"), he became increasingly surly and uncooperative. I eventually filed a formal complaint against him with my superiors at the Armed Forces Radio and Television command center in Frankfurt, Germany, and Zeke was transferred to some remote outpost in Turkey. I'd grown to despise Zeke and was glad to see him go, although I suppose for someone who'd spent as many years as he had in the military, it was in his blood to dislike dumb young lieutenants who hadn't paid their dues.

It didn't take long for the monotony of Saudi Arabia to set in. The routine never varied—three meals a day at the Officer's Club, the food flown in from Europe on C-54s, and a couple of milkshakes after dinner while watching a movie. I spent most of my time at the station making sure the airmen censoring the programs stayed on their toes.

One morning, about a month after I'd arrived, I was walking down the hall of the Bachelor Officers' Quarters when the sound of musical notes behind one of the doors stopped me. I cocked my head in an attempt to determine where the sound was coming from. More followed, nothing melodic, just random notes. I knew one thing. The instrument on which the notes were being played was familiar.

I found the right room and knocked. The door opened and I was faced with a tall, movie star handsome major with a moustache and a wide smile. I introduced myself, and asked whether he was a musician. He shook his head and invited me in. His name was Henry Tracy, the new base public information officer whose office would be in the radio and TV station building. I looked past him. Standing in the middle of his quarters was a three-octave set of Musser vibes.

"You play them?" I asked.

He laughed. "No," he said, "but I always wanted to. I figured a year in Saudi Arabia was a good place to learn. Nothing much else to do, is there?"

I went to the vibes and started a tune.

"You play," he said.

I explained that I'd sold my vibes before leaving the States for Arabia because I didn't think I'd have an opportunity to use them.

"How about giving me lessons?" he said. "I'll pay you."

I suggested a different arrangement. I'd give him lessons if he allowed me to borrow the instrument in case I had a chance to play with a band. It wasn't wishful thinking. I'd become friendly with some ARAMCO employees, including a jazz drummer named Paul Burt. There was a pickup band at the Dhahran oil facility, and Paul occasionally performed with it. When I told him I was a vibes player, he'd expressed his disappointment that I hadn't brought my set with me.

"It's a deal," Tracy said.

That was the beginning of an unusual and lucrative musical experience for me. I joined Paul's band and we started getting bookings at ARAMCO facilities up and down the Persian Gulf. The oil company's employees were starved for entertainment, and were willing to pay top dollar for live music. The band was pretty good. Paul was an excellent drummer, and the piano player, George, from Pittsburgh, played nicely, too, provided he had sheet music in front of him. I never did understand how he could play a song like *Stardust* a thousand times and still need to read the music. A roly-poly friend of Paul's, Charlie Simmons, was the bass player, and we had a trumpet player named Parker Hendricks. A few months after we'd started working together, a team of engineers from the Netherlands arrived, including a Benny Goodman-inspired clarinet player named Harry Kyper. When he joined the band, things really started cooking.

For the band, all transportation was in cabs driven by Saudis. It took three vehicles to haul the instruments and us to the gigs, and these trips were not without incident. Once, while returning to Dhahran from a job up the coast, we were stopped at a Saudi military checkpoint at two in the morning. The Saudi soldiers wanted to know what the instruments were, but since none of us spoke Arabic, we couldn't explain. They made us drag the instruments from the cabs, set them up, and play. I've performed in strange settings, but never anything like that. I think we played *Night and Day*. Playing *The Sheik of Araby* would have been politically incorrect.

I started some live programming on the TV station that included a weekly jazz show featuring the band. My secretary, a vivacious Italian gal from Brooklyn whose husband was a major on the base, put together a weekly Charades show that was a big hit until the Saudi censor decided the women on it showed too much neck and ankle.

The band made up for the day-to-day drudgery of military life. I found myself spending every spare minute with Paul and his friends at their house, and slept there many nights after too much homemade whiskey.

The rest of my one-year tour of duty in Dhahran would have been uneventful were it not for the unsettled political and military situation in the Middle East. Crisis after crisis seemed to erupt, and tension ran high on the base. We were told to look for signs of unrest among the Saudi military that might foreshadow some sort of action against us. This vague apprehension suddenly turned into real fears when the U.S. Marines landed on the beaches of Lebanon in the summer of 1958.

A top secret base defense meeting was called. I was ordered to be there, although I couldn't imagine what role I would play in defending the base against a Saudi uprising. I found out soon enough.

The general and two ranking colonels conducted the meeting. Because I never intended to become a writer, I didn't take notes. But this is what I remember.

One of the colonels explained why it was necessary to prepare to defend the base against a Saudi attack. He then got specific about how a defense would be mounted. Pardon my paraphrasing.

"Three plans have been formulated, each different depending upon the situation. They are known as Plan A, Plan B, and Plan C. The written details of each plan will be distributed to every unit commander." He turned to me. "Lieutenant Bain, the radio station will provide the first alert that one of these plans is about to be put into action."

He explained. I was to have someone make a box with a glass front, and hang it in the radio studio. There was to be a small hammer tethered to the box. Three slips of paper were to be placed in the box. One said Plan A, another Plan B, and the third Plan C, and each contained a brief set of instructions. Should it be necessary to activate one of the plans, the announcer on duty would receive a call from the general, or one of the two colonels. The announcer was to call back to confirm that one of them had, indeed, made the call, and would be informed which of the three plans was to be put into action. He was then to break the glass and read over the air what was written on the appropriate piece of paper. Every dayroom on the base was to have a radio tuned to the station twenty-four hours a day, with someone assigned to monitor it around the clock.

He asked me if I understood.

"Yes, Sir," I replied.

The second colonel took over. "Because your radio station will issue the initial alert, Lieutenant Bain, it will be necessary for you to defend the station."

I waited. We all waited. There wasn't a weapon in American hands anywhere on the base. The Saudis were heavily armed, with bandoleers of bullets strung across their chests, and plenty of lethal looking firearms.

"You are to send some of the men under your command to the base recreation office," he told me.

Base recreation office? To do what, pray? Take Communion?

"Have them check out baseball bats and strategically place them within the station."

Baseball bats? Louisville Sluggers to defend the radio station?

He continued: "Don't send them all at once. Stagger them so we don't arouse suspicion on the part of the Saudis."

"Yes, Sir," I managed.

"In addition, send others to the woodworking shop to make clubs."

"Clubs?"

"Correct."

With handles?

I looked across the table at another lieutenant, a friend, who was the real base recreation officer. "*Please, don't let me laugh,*" his expression said.

The weaponry decided, attention was turned to the evacuation of women and children. Depending upon the plan put into effect, they would gather at designated sand dunes close to the runway from which C-54s would fly them to safety. The dunes were numbered clockwise starting with true north—or counterclockwise. I forget.

Another officer broke in with, "Sir, the dunes are constantly shifting. Besides, I think it will be difficult for the women and children to differentiate between sand dunes."

This brought forth a suggestion from my friend, the real base recreation officer. "We can use numbered golf staffs, Sir. I have a set of eighteen at the office. We can place them on the dunes."

After some discussion, his suggestion was accepted.

"They're serious," I said to my friend as we left the meeting.

"Looks like it."

"Jesus. Baseball bats? Clubs? Numbered sand dunes?"

"Start sending your guys over," he said grimly, starting to walk away. "I'll save a bat for you."

I stayed close to the station for the next few weeks, sitting in my office, my baseball bat leaning against the desk. Was it a Willie Mays model, or a Mickey Mantle? It didn't matter. At night, I would stare out the window at the Saudi military compound across the road where bonfires burned until the early morning hours. Heavily armed Saudi soldiers sat around the fires chanting, or singing, or arguing among themselves. What they were doing was irrelevant. All I knew was that if they came bursting through the door in search of the announcer on duty, and the small glass-fronted box on the wall behind him, they could take everything, including the announcer. If Zeke had been there, I would gladly have offered him up as a human sacrifice.

Hank Tracy, whose office was directly across from mine, didn't seem especially concerned about the situation. He was a man who found humor in almost everything; it was comforting to have him on the scene. The only time I ever saw him angry was when, just prior to the end of the fiscal year, every rated pilot on the base was ordered to take planes up and, in effect, fly around the flag pole until all the fuel on the base had been depleted. Military thinking: if you don't get rid of it, they won't give you more next year. Tracy thought that was pretty dumb. So did I.

I never got to use my bat. Tensions eventually calmed down on the base. I returned the Louisville Slugger to the base recreation office and started spending more time with friends at ARAMCO again, and working with the band.

Toward the end of my tour in Dhahran, I put in for a week's leave to go to Beirut. I'd been there earlier in the year, and found it a wonderful city, visually lovely and culturally vibrant. My room-mate was Pat Patterson, a C-54 pilot who was scheduled to fly a mission there, and I hitched a ride with him. Because I'd applied to be a passenger on the flight, I was asked to act as a courier for classified material contained in a locked briefcase. Upon landing at Beirut, I would be met by a designated officer who, once he'd presented me with the proper credentials, would take possession of the briefcase. This seemed simple enough—until just prior to leaving when the briefcase was handcuffed to my wrist. The officer at the other end would have the key, I was told.

I didn't give it much thought until we were over-flying Syrian airspace. Patterson was informed by ground control that the aircraft serial number he'd filed with the Syrian authorities when requesting permission to enter their airspace was not the same one he'd radioed in once we'd reached that segment of the flight. He tried to talk his way through it, but the Syrians were adamant. They ordered us to land. Pat protested. Minutes later, I looked out a window and saw a Russian MIG sitting just off the wing. Same thing on the other side of the plane.

We landed. Pat was escorted into a building, and armed Syrian soldiers quickly surrounded the aircraft. I kept eying the briefcase handcuffed to my wrist. Would I put up a fight to keep it from falling into enemy hands? Enemy *hands*? I envisioned hands hanging at the main entrance to ARAMCO. Maybe they could call in a local locksmith.

Immediately outside my window was a young soldier, a machine gun cradled in his arms. He looked angry, combative. I smiled at him a few times, but all I received in return were hateful looks. Minutes passed. A half hour later, Patterson returned, grinning. We'd been cleared to take off and continue through Syrian airspace to Beirut. The engines were started, and I cast a final glance at the soldier outside the window. He smiled at me, and shrugged. Yeah, I thought, I agree with you. This was pretty stupid, a waste of time and men. Like all war.

The briefcase was removed from my wrist at the airport in Beirut, and I spent the next week soaking up everything that wonderful city had to offer.

My musician friends at ARAMCO threw me a party the night before I was scheduled to leave Dhahran, and I remember getting pretty drunk on homemade scotch. We pledged to stay in touch, and Paul Burt and I have. He stayed at my home in New York when he left ARAMCO prior to heading to Las Vegas where he worked as a drummer with Vegas lounge bands before becoming a real estate mogul. Thanks, Paul, for helping make a year in Saudi Arabia tolerable, even pleasant.

The average Saudi citizens I met were decent, loving, peaceful people forced to live by virtue of their birth in a harsh, unforgiving place, and victims of their leaders. Like everywhere else in the world, I suppose. One day the sky turned black with locusts, and everyone was out with sticks and paper bags knocking down the insects in anticipation of a special feast. And I was complaining about powdered milk shakes in the air-conditioned officer's club.

I had a week at home in New York before reporting to my next assignment, Amarillo Air Force Base, Texas. There were four things I longed for during my year in Saudi Arabia—a cold glass of *real* milk; a properly mixed Martini with *real* gin; a ride in the fall through New England in a convertible with the top down; and listening to jazz at what had become my favorite New York jazz joint, the Café Bohemia, in Greenwich Village, where I'd spent many nights listening to such jazz giants as Miles Davis, Cannonball Adderly, Art Blakey, and dozens of other idols. I achieved two out of the four. I never got to New England. I did get to the Café Bohemia, but could only stand in front and read the sign announcing that it was now a strip club.

For this I risked my life to defend my country with a baseball bat?

* * * * *

Years later, after I'd become entrenched in my writing career, I wrote a treatment for a screenplay, *One of Our Sand Dunes is Missing*. I never sold it, although the comedian and actor Jerry Lewis expressed interest. I remember dropping off a copy for him when he was staying at the Plaza in New York City. I still have it, and read it before starting this chapter. It had, as they say, potential.

CHAPTER THREE

"Did You Really Say That?"

You can't edit your words on live TV.

I wasn't happy about being assigned to Amarillo AFB. As far as I was concerned, it represented an intra-desert transfer from Saudi Arabia. My position was assistant base information officer, which represented my first real writing experience. I put out a weekly newspaper, and wrote press releases that went to the local papers. The base's information officer was Dennis L. O'Brien, a no-nonsense captain who took an instant dislike to me. The feeling was mutual. I did my job and counted the days until my discharge, a little more than a year away.

As anyone who's ever been in uniform knows, the military does things in strange ways. Helping me put out the base paper was a young airman who'd worked in his father's bakery before enlisting. I learned that the base bakery had an airman who'd graduated from the University of Missouri's respected school of journalism. I suggested they swap jobs. Couldn't be done. So I had a baker writing stories, and the bakery had a journalist making donuts. Brilliant.

My off-duty life was considerably more interesting than days spent on the base. Before leaving Dhahran, I'd purchased Hank Tracy's vibes from him, and had them shipped to Texas. The base supported a large Air Force band and orchestra, and I quickly got to know the airmen who played jazz when not providing march music. They, in turn, introduced me to jazz musicians in town, and I was soon busy working with various groups in clubs around Amarillo. Officers were prohibited from fraternizing with enlisted men, but I successfully managed to ignore that rule.

I also started working as a disc jockey at KRAY, a small radio station owned by a fine gentleman named Ray Hollingsworth, who pretty much gave me free rein on weekends to play the sort of music I liked. Amarillo is C&W territory, and I received my share of angry calls about the music I chose: "You stop playin' that fuckin' nigger jazz music or I'll come by and shoot your balls off." Ornette Coleman and Charlie Mingus evidently weren't to his liking.

I played with a wonderful young black bass player from the base, Tommy Cope, whose mother and father were highly respected educators in Washington, DC. Tommy was a terrific guy and a good musician. One night, when returning from a job, we stopped at a pizza place owned by a friend, Carmine, and his wife. Originally from Brooklyn, Carmine had been discharged from the service in Amarillo and stayed to open its first pizza parlor. Tommy came in with me and we took a booth. Angry looks from other customers. Carmine motioned for me to come behind the counter. Tommy had to leave, he said. He was dismayed at having to tell me that; I don't think he was a prejudiced man. I understood his dilemma, but was disgusted with the situation that spawned it. Tommy went to the car, and I brought our food out to it. Another night, we were pulled over simply because I was a white man driving with a black man as a passenger. Racial profiling is nothing new.

Ray Hollingsworth didn't seem to care that the station's ratings fell off dramatically on weekends with me at the mike. He was a big band buff, and often told me my shows were his favorites.

Working as a musician and DJ on off-hours had to be negotiated with care. There was a policy that no member of the military was allowed to take jobs that otherwise could have gone to civilians. This was an agreement worked out with local unions, whose members had the most to lose. I did my weekend shifts at KRAY using my grandfather's name, Cornelius Dailey. Working as a paid musician was trickier. Most of my musical work was with a quintet led by a wealthy local real estate broker, Hugo Lowenstern, a wonderful jazz clarinet player and good guy who, I think, found real estate boring, and played jazz on weekends as therapy. He wasn't especially impressed with local civilian jazz musicians, and built his quintet around four players from the base, a pianist, Chuck Gardner; bassist Morty Rosenberg; a drummer whose name I forget; and me on vibes. He got around the musicians union by calling its rep at 8:45, fifteen minutes before a job was to start, and saying, "This is Hugo. I need a pianist, bass player, drummer, and vibraphonist by nine." The rep told Hugo that was impossible. "Well, then," Hugo said, "I'll just have to use some boys from the base tonight." We, of course, were all set up and ready to play. The union rep was used to the calls. I suspect he didn't take some sort of action because Hugo and his family were well connected in town.

Toward the end of my tour in Amarillo, and while still working at KRAY and playing with jazz groups, I landed a part-time job as a booth announcer at the ABC TV station in town. I couldn't go on camera as long as I was still in the Air Force, but knew that prohibition would soon end. I was now married, had an infant daughter, Laurie, and had decided to stay in Amarillo for at least a while after my discharge. I had a lot of things going, including plans to open a nightclub with Carmine, the pizza parlor owner. I was doing everything I wanted to do—playing music I loved on the radio, working in TV, performing live music, and was now poised to become part owner of a nightclub. Show business! Maybe it was only Amarillo, Texas, and I was the proverbial big fish in a small pond, but I was enjoying every minute of it.

I received my honorable discharge, although it was a close call. Capt. O'Brien brought me up on charges of insubordination four months shy of the end of my three-year hitch. The secretary we shared had volunteered to type letters for me to go with the resumes I'd started sending to radio stations in anticipation of becoming a civilian. One day, after returning from the firing range, I asked her how the letters were coming. Her response was to point to a wastebasket next to her desk, and then to nod toward O'Brien's office. In the basket were a half-dozen letters she'd typed. O'Brien had walked in on her during her lunch hour, seen the letters, decided a government employee was being misused by me, and tore them up. I blew my stack and said things I shouldn't have. He filed the charge against me.

I was determined to fight it and went to see a friend in the judge advocate's office. After he allowed me to rant and rave about O'Brien, his advice was, "Go back into his office—on your knees—and plead that he drop the charge. He's got you, Don. You're dead meat." I took his advice and it worked. O'Brien transferred me to another unit where I spent my final months counseling airmen with bad debts.

My wife, Jackie, whom I'd met in Bordeaux and married in Amarillo, wasn't happy in Texas, but went along with my decision to stay. I was elevated to full-time announcer and on-air talent at the ABC TV station, and went to work with my "partners"— another young lieutenant who'd recently been discharged, and the pizza parlor owner who financed the deal—to get our nightclub opened. It was my brainchild. Amarillo was not a large city but had a surprising number of radio and television stations, as well as advertising and public relations agencies. Although I wasn't the partner putting up any money, the concept of the club and how to promote it was my responsibility.

Bars and restaurants in Amarillo were hardly what you would call sophisticated, and I was convinced there was room for a private club that made customers feel special, even elite. I came up with the name Backstage Club, and positioned it as a members-only club, with membership open to those in the communications fields. The definition I used of "communications" was broad enough to allow as many people as possible to join. After all, everybody communicates in one way or another, don't they? It didn't cost anything to become a privileged member of the Backstage Club, but you had to have received a letter of invitation.

We found a rundown former roadhouse on the outskirts of town and leased it from the owner. A husband and wife lived in a trailer on the property, and we made a deal with them to help fix up the place, provide ongoing maintenance, and work the kitchen. We kept the menu simple—shrimp cocktails, steaks, chops and chicken, and a couple of seafood items. Because Amarillo was dry, liquor served in private clubs had to belong to the members for their own use, and be kept in secured small compartments behind the bar with the members' names on them. As in Saudi Arabia, liquor laws in Texas were meant to be broken. Dozens of phony compartments were established with members' names attached to them, each containing a different type of whiskey. All a customer had to do was ask for a drink from "Mr. Smith's locker" and the drink was poured.

I found a white grand piano, had it installed in the club, and hired pianists from the air base to play during the cocktail hour. I put together a quartet and provided live jazz four nights a week.

The invitations went out and the response was overwhelming. The Backstage Club was an instant success. Everyone in Amarillo was talking about it, and we were inundated with requests to join.

I was ecstatic. I had my own place in which to play live music, the radio station gave me an outlet for my taste in recorded music, and because I no longer had to remain anonymous, I was becoming a well-known face and voice on the ABC TV affiliate. I was insanely busy, and happy. I put to good use what I'd learned about public relations from my military job as assistant base information officer, pumping out press releases and feature stories about the club on a regular basis. The wife of a local dentist, an aspiring jazz singer who went by the stage name Jeannie Jennay, started working with the band. Because Dallas was a radio jingles production center, and I was the only vibes player in Texas at the time (at least that I knew of), I made a few trips there to record. Everything was good. Ed Sullivan, move over. Steve Allen, watch your back.

While I accept the truth that all good things come to an end, I didn't expect them to blow up quite so fast.

The agreement I had with the partners of the Backstage Club was that once profits started rolling in, we would share in them, fifty percent to Carmine, who'd put up the money, and twenty-five percent each to me and to my Air Force buddy. We sat down after two months and went over the books. Judging from the fact that the club was packed on most nights, and people were spending freely, I was certain I'd be in for a healthy check. But according to Carmine's books, there weren't any profits. Names I'd never heard of were receiving checks.

"Who's he?" I asked Carmine.

"My wife's brother. He's a consultant. He really knows the night-club business."

"Where is he?"

"In Brooklyn. We consult on the phone."

"Who's she?"

"My sister-in-law. She's moving out here. We need her."

"How come she's getting paid before she comes?"

"Expenses. It'll cost a lot to get her out here. It's an advance."

I believe I've recently seen Carmine in some episodes of "The Sopranos," although I can't be sure.

The following weekend, on a Friday night, the club was filled to capacity. I devoted the band's first set to ballads to get everyone up dancing. Toward the end of the set, and in the middle of a tune, I stopped playing and told the band to do the same. People on the dance floor looked at us quizzically as the musicians followed my instructions and started packing up. Carmine came to me.

"What the hell are you doing?" he demanded.

"Packing up."

"You can't do that."

"Watch me, Carmine. Just watch me."

When I arrived home that night earlier than expected, I announced to my wife that I'd had it with Amarillo and wanted to return to New York. She was delighted with that decision.

I stayed at KRAY and ABC for a few more months until we were ready to head east. My star had faded in Amarillo, Texas, although I inadvertently created one final and memorable moment before leaving.

Each Sunday afternoon, I hosted a movie on the ABC TV station. I wore a suit, and sat in a living room set, legs casually crossed, dry ice in a coffee cup giving off what looked like steam. I would introduce that day's film, do commercials during intermissions, and then re-introduce the movie and its stars. I don't recall the name of the film on this particular Sunday, but I do remember it starred Adele Mara and Forrest Tucker.

I did my bit during one of the intermissions, looked into the camera, and said, "And now we return to our featured film starring Adele Mara and Torrest Fucker." I couldn't believe it had come out of my mouth. I heard raucous laughter through the heavy glass window separating the studio from the control room. Phones started ringing. The lines were jammed. One of the calls was from the station manager, who shouted at me, "Did you really say that?"

"It was a mistake. It just came out."

He yelled some more but eventually hung up, and I got through the rest of the movie, never again daring to name the actors.

I turned in my resignation a week later and drove to New York with my wife and child. Amarillo had been small time. New York was where the action was, and I was certain it was waiting to welcome me with open arms. My confidence knew no bounds.

I was young.

CHAPTER FOUR

"All He Wanted to Talk About Was Roses"

He got me!

I had two immediate goals when I got to New York. The first was to support my family. The second was to continue to pursue the sort of career I'd always envisioned for myself. I wasn't sure what it was, but I knew it didn't involve some of the jobs I took in the interim.

I sold children's shoes at the department store, A&S. If anything is destined to turn a person into a W.C. Fields and his famous dislike of children, it's fitting shoes on little kids while their mothers tell you you're doing it wrong. My salvation was the jazz jobs I began to pick up, including a year of Friday nights at the Sombrero Club in Queens. A drummer I'd met, Mike Fahn, had the job but wanted out, and asked if I was interested in replacing him. I bought a used set of drums and joined a trio led by a pianist, Joe Ziehl, with whom I'd one day end up in a business partnership.

Joe left the trio after several months and was replaced by piano player named Tommy Raymond, who stayed a short time. When he left, Val Anthony took the piano chair and suggested we turn the group into a quartet, with a different drummer and me on vibes. That was toward the end of my run there, and it was a musical nightmare.

Anthony, who went on to open his own nightclubs, and who was a favorite of Sinatra whenever the crooner was in town, played everything in sharp keys—D, E, B and A. Well-trained musicians wouldn't have had a problem playing in those keys, but I did. Having to transpose tunes every Friday night took the fun out of working with Anthony, and I left, devoting more time to playing weddings and bar mitzvahs. I occasionally performed in some of Val Anthony's clubs during the ensuing years, including one that was closed down because Long Island "housewife hookers" were allegedly selling their bodies out of it. Sol Yaged, a clarinet player who'd taught Steve Allen how to finger the instrument when Allen portrayed Benny Goodman in the biographical film of the "King of Swing," worked that club from time to time, and I ended up playing vibes or drums with him on a few occasions. I didn't especially enjoy those jobs because Sol's personality and mine didn't mesh. Years later, a dear friend and wonderful musician, Hap Gormley, became Sol's regular drummer. That he stayed with him so long is a testament to Hap's good nature. Of course, the tenuous living jazz provides also played a role, I'm sure. Work is work, regardless of the leader's personality.

Maybe the fact that Yaged played like Goodman contributed to Sol's prickly personality. Benny Goodman, as wonderful a jazz musician as he was, engendered more resentment among those who played with him than perhaps any other musician in the business. Goodman was a musical giant. That the musician's union newspaper devoted only a small space to his obituary says volumes about how his passing was viewed.

My first encounter with Sol Yaged was at the Metropole, on Broadway, in New York City, now a topless joint. Back then, it was a swinging jazz club, the musicians strung out along a narrow stage behind the long bar. Drummer Cozy Cole and trumpeter Henry "Red" Allen were stalwarts there, pouring out classic jazz for the admiring crowd. During one Christmas break from Purdue, I came home with two musician friends, George Brown, who'd found for me my first set of vibes, and a brilliant jazz pianist and accordionist, Bob Sardo. We stayed at my home on Long Island, but spent lots of time in the city haunting jazz clubs. One Saturday afternoon, we stopped in a musical instrument store where I bought a new set of vibe mallets, and then went to the Metropole where Sol Yaged was leading a group. There was an unused set of vibes on the stage belonging to Harry Shepherd. Harry and his brother, Harvey were both vibraphonists, and I got to sub for Harry on jobs years later. George and Bob encouraged me to ask if I could sit in. Yaged didn't sound too happy about it but invited me up. He asked what I wanted to play, and in what key. I suggested *After You've Gone*, a jazz evergreen, in the key of F. He counted it off at an unusually fast tempo. That was okay; I knew the tune and could move through the changes at any tempo. But then, after one chorus, Yaged signaled the pianist to go up a full step, to G. Then to A flat. And B flat. And B natural. I became hopelessly lost and left the stage in disgrace, and anger. Yaged had done it to embarrass and get rid of me. He succeeded. I suppose it could be considered a rite of musical passage. But at the time, I just considered it a nasty act.

I told him that story years later when I played with his band. He said he didn't remember, of course. But I did, and still do.

I love being around musicians, particularly jazz musicians. They're bright, funny, and never at a loss for stories about their profession and the characters in it. But there are those who are petty, insecure, and in some cases, downright nasty. Fortunately, my exposure to such people has been minimal and tangential because music has never been my full-time occupation. But I've made lifelong friends because of music: John Johnson, an extremely talented pianist with an intellect to match, and one of my favorite people in the world; impish bassist and trumpeter Willie Wayman, who lives and breathes music (I've introduced him from the bandstand by saying that if he ever has to have surgery, hundreds of quarter and eighth notes will float up out of the incision); drummer Hap Gormley whose humor and decency rivals his strong playing; reedman and jokester Artie Miller; pianist, vibist and bon vivant Bob Smith; the late clarinetist Charles Nostrand with whom I've played hundreds of jobs ("We've never played a bad job" he was fond of saying, and he was right); and baritone saxophone virtuoso Gerry Manecke, who decided he'd learn to play piano, too, in order to get more work and soon was playing it professionally.

I'd brought audition tapes with me from Amarillo and sent them to radio stations in New York City and environs. I was offered jobs by stations on Long Island (Freeport and Huntington), and in Mt. Kisco in Westchester County. I turned them all down because they didn't pay enough for me to quit selling children's shoes. I was interviewed at night by the program director at one of the stations, and knew immediately that I wouldn't work there no matter what the salary. Everyone wore sunglasses even though it was dark. I don't trust people who wear sunglasses at night, any more than I eat in restaurants that have colored pictures of its food in the window. A man has to have some standards.

One day, I received a call from the program director at WNEW in the city. WNEW at the time was a wonderful radio station that featured such famous DJs as William B. Williams and Jim Loew, and that played my kind of music—Sinatra, Ellington, Ella, Basie and Goodman. The station wanted me to come in for an interview because they liked my audition tape. I was thrilled. My big break had arrived.

The program director was very gracious as I sat across the desk from her. We chatted about many things before she asked how much money I was looking for. I gave her a figure, explaining that I had a wife and infant daughter to support. Her response was, "There are hundreds of announcers in this city as good or better than you, who'll come work here for nothing just for the exposure. Give me a reason to pay you to work here."

I didn't have a good answer. The interview was over. I still don't have a good answer.

On my days off from A&S, I pursued more lucrative and fulfilling full-time employment. I was interviewed by the vice president of public relations for AMF Industries, and offered a job in his PR department. I remember this particular gentleman from a brief scene in the men's room at corporate headquarters. I'd had my final interview with him, and we were leaving to have lunch. When we entered the restroom, he immediately went to the sink and scrubbed his hands. He noticed my interest in his doing that prior to using the urinal, turned and said, "Yale. We always wash before and after."

That Ivy League idiosyncrasy aside, I wanted the job and readily accepted the offer. It was cause for celebration in our apartment. It represented the start of a career with a major corporation, and the salary was considerably more than I was making at the department store.

The celebration didn't last long. I called to confirm my start date and was informed by someone in the personnel department (now called human resources) that they'd received a negative reference about me.

"Negative reference?" I said, flabbergasted. "I didn't give any references. I just got out of the Air Force."

"Yes, Mr. Bain, I know, but we checked back with the Air Force and spoke with one of your former commanders, Captain Dennis L. O'Brien. I'm sorry, but we have to withdraw the job offer."

It had never occurred to me that they'd go to that extent. I'd received an honorable discharge. Aside from the personality conflict with O'Brien toward the end of my year at Amarillo AFB, I'd had a perfectly respectable military record. But my rationalization didn't matter. He got me! He hadn't court-martialed me, but he cost me a good job. I've thought of him often over the years, and not kindly.

I was taking a break at A&S one day when I bumped into a childhood friend, Jim Potamos. Jim and Chris Potamos lived a few houses from where I grew up in Franklin Square, and we were best of buddies. Their father, Frank, owned a Greek diner in Franklin Square that served the best greasiest hamburgers on earth. Jim told me he'd just started working for Underwood-Olivetti, the business machine manufacturer. The Italian firm, Olivetti, had bought Underwood, a name synonymous with the typewriter. For years, the Russian word for typewriter was "Underwood." According to Jim, the company was hiring hundreds of salesmen. He encouraged me to apply, and gave me the name of someone to call. By this time I was ready to take any job that didn't involve kids' feet and snarling mothers.

I was hired, and was sent to Hartford, CT for a month of training. I drove home one weekend with two of my fellow salesmen-trainees. It was mid-winter, and the roads were icy. We were on Hillside Avenue on Long Island, a few blocks from where one of my passengers lived, when I braked for a red light. A small panel truck was stopped at the light in front of me. I skidded and bumped into its rear, gently, just a tap. The truck's driver, a short, wiry, older man leaped out and started yelling at me in Italian. I pointed out to him that it was an accident due to the slippery road, and that no damage had been done. We got back into our vehicles as the light turned green and continued down the road. We came to the next light. He stopped. I tried to, but slid into him for the second time. Again, no damage, but I'm sure that if he'd carried a weapon, he'd have shot me.

I was one of many new salesmen that had been hired. The Olivetti management decided that the best way to sell its products in the United States was to send a couple of thousand salespeople out into the business community to put the typewriters, adding machines and calculators on trial. Once the potential buyers used them, they reasoned, they'd gobble them up. I worked out of the Garden City, Long Island office where each salesperson was expected to place two machines on trial each day, with the business owner signing a card verifying that he or she had, indeed, taken in one of the machines. I was paid $6-thousand a year. I used my own car; no expenses were reimbursed.

Sound easy getting two people each day to accept a free, no-obligation trial? It wasn't. Part of the problem was that I was a lousy salesman. Once I recognized that, my estimation of good salesmen was elevated. Selling is a creative art, an art I simply don't possess. Like some of the others in the office, I began fulfilling my two-a-day quota by either falsifying the cards and storing the machines in the trunk of my car—"trunk trials" they were called—or finding enough small businesses willing to take multiple trials off my hands. At one time, a deli in which I often bought lunch had as many as a dozen of my machines lined up on a shelf in the kitchen. The fear was, of course, that the supervisor would decide to spend a day with you in the field. That happened a few times, and it took some fast-talking to get off the hook.

Two significant events occurred during that year peddling business machines.

The first, and most important, was the birth of my second daughter, Pamela, eleven months after Laurie had been born in Texas. It was a difficult delivery, and my wife was hospitalized for weeks. I hired a woman, aptly named Mrs. Warden, to come in each day to care for my two infant daughters. I paid her more each week than I was making. It was a traumatic, stressful, financially devastating time, and I was desperate for money

Which led to the second significant event. I started my writing career.

CHAPTER FIVE

FLYIN' HIGH

My cousin's name was Jacques Pearl, although no one ever called him Jacques. He felt that name sounded pretentious and instead introduced himself as Jack. He was my best friend, a very good novelist and storyteller, and the reason I became a writer.

Jack spent a portion of WW II liberating Europe from the Nazis. I vividly remember the night before he shipped out from Long Island. My parents threw a party for him that lasted into the wee hours. Mutzi and Carolyn Kelsch were there, along with Jack's sister Marge and her husband, Emlyn, and a dozen of Jack's friends. I was a little kid who idolized his big cousin and was bitterly angry when my father sent me to bed before the party ended. I sat at the top of the stairs and cried. I wanted to spend every possible minute with Jack, and would have happily gotten on the train with him the next day and gone off to war.

When Jack was discharged from the Army, he enrolled at Columbia University in its highly respected writing program. He married a lovely gal, June, and set his sights on a career as a novelist, with Hemingway his role model, perhaps not in a personal sense but certainly as a stylist. Jack and June had a rough go early in their marriage. He came down with TB, arguably the result of his wartime experiences, and was bedridden for more than a year at the home of June's parents. This was before the advent of drugs that cure TB a lot faster. And June suffered a life-threatening disease that she beat, and has beaten, for more than 50 years. Not a smooth launch to a marriage and a career, but they persevered and went on to forge a happy life together, and to have two daughters, Jill and Janet.

Jack began writing articles for men's adventure magazines, not of the *Playboy* or *Penthouse* ilk, but publications such as *Man's World, MALE, MEN,* and *SAGA.* He was eventually hired as editor of *SAGA,* the most high-toned of such magazines.

He came to me one day to say that he'd taken on too many freelance magazine assignments. Would I like to ghost a few for him? I jumped at the opportunity. The pieces were of the type found in today's tabloids and scandal sheets—exposés, shocking truths from history, and the sexy escapades of movie stars.

I kept a portable typewriter with me in the car while trying to place business machines on trial for Underwood-Olivetti, and worked on the stories during lunch breaks, as well as at home. The money was welcome—as I recall, $150 per article—and I felt good doing something creative. I would learn later that Jack had not been overburdened with work as he'd claimed. Aware of my money problems, he'd thrown me those assignments to help me financially. What I most appreciated was that he provided an opportunity for me to earn my pay, rather than being on the receiving end of a handout. He couldn't have known at the time that he'd set into motion a writing career that would encompass more than 90 books.

I continued to write occasional magazine pieces under Jack's byline while looking for a better full-time job than selling typewriters and calculators. I found it a year after joining Underwood-Olivetti at the large advertising agency, McCann-Erickson, where

I was hired to work in its public relations division, Interpublic, headed by Chet Burger, a leading light in the PR business. I was assigned to the Luxtrol account, a Connecticut company that manufactured an early type of light dimmer. My immediate boss was a gentleman named Frank LaClave, who seemed to take a fatherly interest in me. One of his early pieces of advice was to leave very early for meetings so that you weren't racing around town and raising your blood pressure. "Life is too short," was his mantra. The new job meant a raise of $1,200. I was now making $7,200 a year, although the train fare from Long Island to the city consumed some of that.

I enjoyed the job. Ghosting the articles for Jack had whetted my appetite for writing, and I turned out dozens of pieces for trade magazines on behalf of Luxtrol. One of my assignments was to seek celebrities who would allow us to install Luxtrol dimmers without charge, in return for our being able to photograph their apartments and homes. My greatest success with this involved the film director, Otto Preminger. We had dimmers placed in every room of his opulent Manhattan apartment, and I generated plenty of space for the client in myriad magazines.

After six months, I was reassigned to a new unit that had been established within the agency. The three of us in this division were responsible for writing and placing stories for the agency's many clients. My two colleagues, a stunningly beautiful woman named Pat Morrison, and a suave Greek-American, Michael Crissan, were PR veterans, and I had much to learn from them. Most of the writing fell to me because Morrison and Crissan spent most of their days wining and dining editors of major publications, and reporting back to our immediate supervisor, Lida Livingston, that major stories about our clients were on the horizon in these leading national publications, a very distant horizon it usually turned out. I worked the nuts-and-bolts side of the street, grinding out story after story for lesser magazines. I began to resent the division of labor, especially since I was being paid less than half the salary either of them was receiving. I'd gotten a few raises, which brought me up to $9,000 a year, but it was far below their pay. After having been at the agency for almost a year, I sat down with Chet Burger and voiced my complaint. He told me I was lucky to be making less than Morrison and Crissan because my lesser salary meant lower hourly charges against clients for my services, which meant, in return, being assigned to more interesting projects. Smooth.

I started looking for another job.

Before I left McCann-Erickson, Jack Pearl approached me with a new proposition. He'd been asked to ghostwrite a book on the history of stock car racing, which would carry the byline of Bill France, president of NASCAR, the sport's sanctioning body. The book was under contract to Pocketbooks, a division of Simon & Schuster. The pay was a flat fee of $1,000, no royalties. Was I interested? I said I was, and Jack took me to meet the editor, Ed Brown. I was certain Brown would turn me down. I'd never written a book before, and my other writing experiences upon which he could judge my qualifications consisted of only PR articles for agency clients; Jack was reluctant to admit that he'd had me ghost magazine pieces for him.

I was wrong. Based upon Jack's recommendation, Brown signed me to ghost the stock car book.

We were renting a small house on a farm in Old Westbury, Long Island at the time, at which race horses from nearby Roosevelt Raceway were stabled and otherwise cared for, and I set up a corner of the kitchen as my writing area. I was spared having to research the subject of stock car racing because, in reality, I was the second ghost on the project. The first go-around had been by Bloys Britt, a journalist who covered car racing for the Associated Press. Like many newspaper reporters, he'd had trouble pulling together an entire book. Writing a book is like running a marathon, as opposed to newspaper writing, which more resembles a sprint. Britt had all the material, but it was disjointed, and written like a series of short articles. Nothing fit together.

I worked on the book at night after commuting home from the city, and on weekends. I attacked the project with enthusiasm. This was my first book. It may not carry my name, and was not a subject in which I had much interest (although I found the history of stock cars to be fascinating and the lives of the top drivers colorful; I made use of what I learned in another book years later). But it would demonstrate to at least one editor and publishing house that I was, in fact, capable of writing a book. It had to be good because it was my initial credential in the publishing world, my best foot forward.

I turned in the manuscript on time and awaited Brown's reaction. There is nothing more frustrating in this world than writing something and having to wait for a reaction. Because writing is of necessity a lonely profession, a lack of feedback from editors can be excruciatingly painful. Depending upon your level of paranoia, not hearing creates all sorts of negative visions. Sam Vaughan, formerly president of Doubleday and currently editor-at-large for Random House, once told me that the cruelest thing you can do to a writer is not call. He's right. I've often thought that every major publishing house should have one person on staff whose only duty is to call the writers under contract to ask how they're doing, and to let them know someone at their publisher is, at least, thinking of them.

After six weeks had passed, I summoned the courage to call Brown.

"How did you like the manuscript?" I asked.

I was met with his long, pained sigh. "I had to do a hell of a lot of work on it," he said. "A-lot-of-work."

I was devastated. I'd failed. What I'd written was obviously sub-par, amateurish, not worthy of publication unless saved by an astute, experienced editor. Writing for a living was not in my future.

The Racing Flag, by Bloys Britt and Bill France (I didn't know that the original ghost would have a byline), was published in an oversized paperback format in early 1965. I eagerly opened the copy sent to me by Brown and read it against the manuscript I'd submitted. Aside from some minor editorial alterations, little had been changed. The book had been published virtually as I'd written it. What was going on here?

Dan O'Shea, my first literary agent, gave me his take on Brown's negative reaction. "He's probably one of those editors who's a frustrated writer, and has to put down those who actually write," Dan said. "Besides, by making it sound as though he had to save your manuscript, he can lowball the advance when you come to negotiate your next book with him."

I don't know whether O'Shea's analysis was accurate. If it was, it made me feel better. At the same time, it's sad that any writer who's devoted months, or even years, to writing a book has to be subjected to such self-serving editorial reactions. I've come to learn over the course of my career that writing for a living isn't for the faint of heart, or for those lacking a reasonable amount of self-esteem. There are always editors who'll put you down as a writer, just as there are jazz musicians who'll keep changing keys on you in the middle of a tune to make you feel inadequate. They should all suffer a terminal case of prickly heat.

Once I'd decided to leave McCann-Erickson, I contacted a head-hunter who specialized in placing people in PR jobs, and he set up a number of interviews with companies, including IBM. I'd also learned of a job opening at American Airlines, and applied for it. IBM hired me. The job I really wanted was with American, but they'd offered it to someone with airline experience. I accepted the IBM offer, resigned from McCann-Erickson, and planned to take a week's vacation with my family on Cape Cod between jobs. Just before leaving McCann-Erickson, IBM sent me a huge package filled with everything I should know about the company and its products before reporting for my first day at corporate headquarters in Westchester. I took a fast look at it and realized I'd made a mistake. The extremely formal IBM corporate culture, and my

"Just call me Don" style, was not a match made in heaven.

Almost simultaneously with receiving IBM's package, I received a call from John Squire at American Airlines, who'd interviewed me for the job there. The person they'd hired had decided to go with another airline. Was I still interested? You bet I was. Squire suggested we have lunch at Costello's, a watering hole on the East Side popular with media and PR people, only a few blocks down Third Avenue from McCann's offices. With Squire was his boss, Bob Crimley, balding, built like a fire hydrant, and with a raspy, tough guy way of talking straight out of a Mickey Spillane novel. In contrast, the Canadian born Squire was tall and had a mane of silver hair. What they had in common was an appreciation of the drinks served by Costello's head barman, Freddie, who arrived at work each day on his bicycle, which he rode through the front door to the rear of the establishment, scattering customers in his wake.

We talked and drank, martinis, lots of them, and parted on the sidewalk at three. They'd get back to me, Squire said. As I made my uncertain way back to McCann-Erickson, I knew I really wanted the job with American. I wasn't in my office fifteen minutes when Squire called. Could I come back to Costello's at five to meet one of the airline's VPs?

"Sure," I said.

The vice president was a very nice, professorial gentleman named Karl Dahlem. We drank martinis and talked. I don't remember how the subject came up, but Dahlem started telling about his prize rose garden at home. I knew nothing about roses, but wasn't about to admit it. I wanted that job so I could bail out of IBM before heading for the Cape. I waxed poetic about my love of roses, their scent, brilliant colors, symbolism—I don't remember what I said except I know it had to do with roses.

They hired me on the spot. I would be American's PR man for the three area airports, JFK, LaGuardia and Newark. The headhunter wasn't happy when I called to tell him I'd changed my mind. I offered to pay the fee he was losing but he said that wasn't necessary. He did question my decision, however. IBM, he said, was a powerhouse, a highly respected corporation with a wonderful future. Airline PR departments had a bad reputation, he claimed. Airline PR people all drank too much and caroused and were always traveling.

I'd made the right decision.

A few months after I'd started work, Squire told me what Dahlem had said after we parted in front of Costello's.

"I like the guy, but is he gay?"

"I don't think so. He's got a wife and a couple of kids. Why?"

"All he wanted to talk about was roses."

I spent three of the happiest years of my life with American Airlines. These were the high flying days of airline PR. Air travel was still glamorous. Celebrities seemed always to be on our flights between New York and Los Angeles, and we made hay with them. This was a time when New York had seven daily newspapers. The tabloids—the *Daily News* and *Daily Mirror* in particular—were always looking for photos of film stars getting on planes, and we accommodated them. My office, which I shared with Vinnie Modugno, one of two photographers on American's staff, had a full dark room. Squire or Crimley would alert me when a celeb was flying, and Vinnie and I would knock off some shots, preferably of male stars posing with one of our stewardesses (now called flight attendants). While Vinnie processed the film, I wrote the caption. An hour later a messenger service was on its way with a print to every paper in town.

There seemed to be an unlimited budget for American's PR department, which probably helped sustain its reputation as the most aggressive and effective PR department in the airline business. I'd not experienced lavish corporate spending before, and it took me a while to get into the swing of it. Nancy, Crimley's secretary, told me on my first day on the job at the airport that she would open a checking account for me in the bank on the ground floor of corporate headquarters, on Third Avenue.

"How much do you want me to deposit in it every week?" she asked.

"I don't know," I said. "Fifty dollars maybe."

At the end of the first week, I sent my expense report to Nancy. I'd legitimately spent twenty-six dollars, and I attached a personal check made out to American Airlines for the difference between that and the fifty that had been deposited, twenty-four dollars. The next day, the person I'd replaced, Ed Brett, who'd been transferred to Detroit, called me.

"We haven't met," he said, "but I just got a call from Nancy."

"And?"

"She says you sent back some of the expense money she deposited for you."

"That's right."

"That's not the way it works, Don. It doesn't matter if you have to throw the money at passengers, *never send it back!*"

I never did again.

The seemingly unlimited expense accounts we enjoyed were treated by virtually everyone in a strangely honorable way. You never kept any of it for your personal use, for things like helping make your car or mortgage payment, or to buy gifts for your wife or kids. But you did use it to live high as an extension of your job. If you worked later than seven, or were out drinking and dining with press after office hours, you ordered a car service to drive you home. You ate lunch at the best places, with or without a media contact, and charged it to the airline.

Not everyone, however, honored the "rules" of how to use the expense account. There was one man in the department, who I'll call Henry, who viewed his expenses as a supplement to his salary. His lunch each day was a Sabrett hot dog from a sidewalk vendor, but he put in for expensive lunches at the city's best restaurants, listing members of the press he'd entertained, their names lifted from a media guide listing the city's working journalists. One day, his boss, Dave Frailey, who would go on to become VP of the department, called Henry into his office. He laid Henry's most recent expense report in front of him and said, "I don't mind you lying on your report, Henry, but at least pick somebody who's alive. I attended this guy's funeral a year ago." What was remarkable to me was that Henry wasn't fired. Because there seemed to be an endless budget, our excesses were overlooked.

I received a call one day from Jack Sterling, who'd taken over WCBS's morning show after Arthur Godfrey had retired from it. I'd become friends with Jack, and he gave the airline constant plugs on the show. His call to me was to request a trip to San Francisco for him and his wife. He confided in me that they had been having some problems between them, and needed to get away for a week. I immediately arranged for two first-class tickets, a suite at the Mark Hopkins, and sent a limo to drive them to the airport. The limo driver called later to report that only Mrs. Sterling had taken the flight. I called Jack, who said they'd had a fight. He wanted to take another flight and meet her in San Francisco. I accommodated, of course.

The bill from the Mark Hopkins came in a few weeks later. Jack had purchased a couple of thousand dollars worth of jewelry at the hotel gift shop, evidently as a peace offering to his wife. I took the bill into Dave Frailey and asked what to do.

"Pay it," he said without blinking.

That's the way things were done in those flush days at American Airlines. Sterling couldn't say enough good things about the airline for months after that.

Press trips were extravagant orgies of eating and drinking, the best hotels, limos for all. Milestones in the airline's life were celebrated with inventive and expensive promotions. When we introduced the first commercial jet aircraft, the 707, we rigged the interior of one with a complete bowling alley, and held a professional bowling tournament at 30-thousand feet from New York to Los Angeles to demonstrate the stability and size of the plane. Later, the tri-engine 727 was brought into service, the first three engine aircraft since the Ford Tri-Motor of the 30s. One of these corrugated metal, tri-motor planes, flown by American in its early days, had crashed in a southwest desert many years ago. A family of Native Americans had moved into it, inserted a metal chimney, and lived there for years. The airline eventually discovered it, bought it back from the Indians—shades of the purchase of Manhattan—whipped it into flying shape, and used it as a barnstorming promotional vehicle. I commandeered it to promote the introduction of the 727, whose initial flight was between Chicago and New York. I staged a mock air race between the two planes, giving the Ford Tri-Motor a head start, of course. They arrived at JFK simultaneously; seeing these two generations of three engine aircraft taxing side-by-side to the gate provided a superb photo opportunity.

I got to log flying time in the old Tri-Motor. I'd been put in charge of an American Airlines hospitality trailer at the Atlantic City Airport for the 1964 Democratic convention, and hitched a ride in the plane back to New York for a weekend. I knew both veteran American pilots assigned to the Tri-Motor, and one of them was aware I held a private pilot's license. He put me in the left seat, and once we were off the ground allowed me to take over the controls, advising, "All the control cables are strung on the outside of the plane. You have to turn the yoke once to take up the slack before it responds."

I flew it as far as the Verrazano Bridge. It was a crystal clear night, and I felt like king of the skies. I brought my flight logbook with me on the return flight to Atlantic City and the captain signed it, verifying my time at the controls.

On another occasion, I spent the morning in the Tri-Motor flying around the New York area with Johnny Carson's sidekick, Ed McMahon, who'd been a Marine pilot before his TV career. While we were having lunch at JFK, John Squire called. Arthur Godfrey, also a professional caliber pilot, wanted some time in the Tri-Motor. We ferried the plane to LaGuardia where Godfrey arrived in his Bentley. He was driving; his chauffeur dozed in the back seat. It was a memorable afternoon, with McMahon and Godfrey at the controls shooting landings and takeoffs at Teterboro Airport. I have a photo of the two of them that I treasure to this day.

Promoting the 727 wasn't all pleasure, however. The plane had three serious accidents during its early days in service, including an American 727 that went down one early evening in Cincinnati, crashing into a hill during its landing approach. I was dispatched to the scene to handle the press, and I spent the night on that hill while they brought down the bodies. You don't forget experiences like that, nor will I ever forget the work of the Red Cross, who'd established a station at the bottom of the hill from which they served up hot coffee and plenty of comfort. As I recall, the official finding in the three crashes was that the pilots of the aircraft hadn't been properly trained to compensate for the 727's sink rate, which was faster than other commercial aircraft in service. Modified cockpit procedures were introduced in which the rate of descent was verbally called out during the landing process. That seemed to solve it; the plane continues to this day to be a workhorse of commercial aviation.

After a year and a half as the PR representative at the airports, I was brought into the city to work directly for R.H. "Red" Sutherland, a bigger-than-life character who headed up the airline's film, radio and television department. I've met outspoken people during my career, but none to rival Red. He was a huge man who wore red suspenders, and always had a red-and-white railroad handkerchief hanging out of his rear pants pocket. His feet were broken down from the weight they had to carry and he walked with a waddle. Red was a chain smoker; a large ashtray overflowing with butts, dominated the center of his desk. He kept his office dark except for a single gooseneck desk lamp that cast a pool of light over the ashtray, as though it was starring in some theatrical production.

Red's motto was, "Drive it like you owned it." He had that philosophy translated into Latin by a friend, Dan Solon, and it appeared on all his stationery and business cards.

Working for Red Sutherland meant an increase in travel. I'd done a fair amount of it during my first 18 months with the airline, but now I found myself on the road a good part of the time. I flew around the country with film crews making travel movies of American's prime destinations. Cleveland was one, but an enticing travel film about a city whose river had once caught fire because of pollution, wasn't easy. The city sits on Lake Erie, but the water and shorefront looked so grimy and unattractive that I decided to not shoot the lakefront. After putting together a rough cut, I sat with Red in our screening room and showed him the result. When it was over, he asked why Lake Erie wasn't in the footage. I explained. Red picked up an empty metal film can and threw it at me from across the room. It missed my head by a few feet and clanged off the wall. "You can't do a fucking film about Cleveland without including Lake Erie in it." A few days later I was back in Cleveland shooting the lake from a helicopter.

Aside from an occasional film can heading my way, working for Red was a joy. American's PR department was headed up by a remarkable man named Willis Player, who defined what an enlightened leader should be. Player believed that his primary role was to support the people working for him, and to tout their achievements to higher management. Red was his man, and in turn echoed that philosophy. I once proposed a project that came under discussion during a department meeting. Karl Dahlem, the VP who'd made the decision to hire me, said, "I can't relate to Bain's project."

Sutherland shot back, "The only thing you can relate to is your fucking mortgage in Scarsdale."

He would have been fired, I'm sure, if he'd worked at IBM. But no one challenged Red at American. He knew more about airline operations, flight procedures, and promoting an airline through films, radio and TV than anyone else in PR, not only at American but in the entire aviation industry. His approach to making travel films was enlightening. He believed in hiring the best filmmakers around, giving them a broad idea of what he wanted to accomplish, and sending them on their way to apply their expertise. A particular favorite was John Peckham, the founder of Peckham Productions, one of New York's top industrial filmmakers. Working with Peckham, and others, was a wonderful opportunity for me. I got to write many of the film narrations, and did scratch track voice-overs for them. I struck a solid friendship with Peckham and others at his company, including his brother, Peter, who heads the company to this day (John died of lung cancer years ago). Among the others were his excellent film editor Hoyt Griffth; one of his freelance writers, Bill Littlefield; and members of Peckham's production staff. There were times when Peckham was working on films for clients other than American that he called Red and asked if he would spring me to write those films, or to do a narration. Red would dispatch me to wherever Peckham was shooting, and cover for my absence at American.

He was utterly fearless. Red was a recovered alcoholic; years before he joined American Airlines, he'd once woken up on a street in Philadelphia without any idea how he'd gotten there. He quit drinking that day.

When he worked for American, Red commuted daily to Manhattan from a home he'd built in Westhampton Beach, a two-and-a-half-hour trip each way. He used the time to learn everything he could about selected subjects by reading dozens of books on a topic. His train stopped at Carle Place, Long Island, where I was living at the time, and we'd ride into the city together. Occasionally, when we got off at Hunter's Point to catch a subway for the rest of the trip into Manhattan, he'd say, "Let's go catch some art, kid." We'd walk to a local diner, order a big breakfast, and admire the way the short order cooks handled the dozens of simultaneous requests flung at them by the waitresses. "It's like a ballet," he would say. "Just watch." We'd waltz into work late those days, but I didn't have to worry about that. I was with Red Sutherland.

When I wasn't shooting travel films, I was crisscrossing the country making promotional deals with radio and TV stations. The stations would run contests, and we'd provide trips to favored American destinations for the winners. I also spent a lot of time in Los Angeles setting up mentions of American Airlines in motion pictures. American's PR rep there was a corpulent bachelor named Joe Hardy. Joe was independently wealthy. He drove a big Cadillac and seemed to know everyone in the Hollywood movie community. Every once in awhile he'd pull into the parking lot of a strip club and we'd go inside. The girls squealed the moment they saw Joe, and ran to him. He'd pull out a wad of bills and hand them out to the strippers' delight. He didn't seem to be looking for any favors in return because we never stayed. Once the money had been dispensed, we left and got back to business. I think Joe just liked being liked.

At Los Angeles International Airport, Joe introduced me to a man who had some connection to Zsa Zsa Gabor, a sometime actress and full-time celebrity. Zsa Zsa was flying to New York that night on American to appear on the Johnny Carson Show. For three hundred dollars, she would say nice things on the show about the flight. The guy wanted the money in cash. I gave it to him. Later that night, I watched the broadcast. Zsa Zsa waxed poetic about American's superb service, and said it was her favorite airline. She also plugged a half-dozen other products and services, all of which had evidently paid three hundred bucks for the privilege.

Life was good, very good. My two daughters were healthy and happy, I liked my work, and living on the horse farm was idyllic, although an incident occurred that proved how stupid I could be about mechanical things, and that got me space in the papers.

When I took the job with American, we needed a second car to get to the airport each day, and I bought a used Volkswagen Beetle convertible from a United Airlines pilot. It was nifty looking little car, but it had electrical problems. You turned the key and the horn blew. You blew the horn and the lights went out. The worst part was that it seldom started, which meant getting a push from my wife each morning, and finding someone at the end of the day to jump-start, or give me a push.

One cold winter morning, my wife was suffering with the flu and I didn't want to have her come outside. I got in the Volks, put it in first gear, turned on the ignition, got out, climbed in our second car, came around behind the Volks and pushed it. It started. Of course it started. But there was nobody in it. The Volks headed down a narrow road that paralleled a paddock in which many of the expensive trotters were grazing, with me in pursuit on foot. It turned left on its own, leveled the fence, and was headed directly at one of the horses, who seeing it coming, reared up on its hind legs and neighed. Fortunately, the car stalled before hitting the horse. I probably shouldn't have told this story to people at American because one of them called reporters he knew and the story hit the papers, in Norton Mockeridge's column in the *World Telegram*, complete with a cartoon of me chasing the car.

As busy as I was with my job at American Airlines, I continued to seek other careers. I worked occasional weekends as a jazz musician, and continued writing pieces for the men's adventure magazines. What changed was that I started writing them under my own name, or to be more accurate, under pseudonyms I created. This came about when I was introduced to The Count.

CHAPTER SIX

THE COUNT AND ME

No, not Count Basie.

As I go back through diaries covering the first half of the 1960s, I realize how insanely busy I was. I'd adopted the philosophy that to be successful at this stage of my career, it was necessary to *turn down nothing and to say yes to everything*. I still believe in that approach for young people launching careers. Now, of course, I'm more selective in the projects I choose to take on. But back then, there wasn't a person with a proposal that wasn't worth, at least, listening to.

There seemed to be nothing but opportunity. Everyone I met represented a potential for a new project, a book, screenplay, or business prospect. My main focus, of course, was my full-time PR job with American Airlines. But there were always nights and weekends to develop these extracurricular ventures.

Jack Pearl introduced me to Dan O'Shea, who would become my first literary agent (I've only had two, Dan, and Ted Chichak). Dan was an attorney whose father had been a Hollywood executive during the filming of *Gone With the Wind*; original costume sketches from that movie decorated the walls of an apartment he kept in Hollywood. The elder O'Shea was a gruff old guy. The first time I spoke with him was on the phone.

"This is Don Bain."

"Yes. How are you?"

"Couldn't be better."

"I doubt that."

The senior O'Shea's frequent trips to Los Angeles were marked by the seating arrangements he made on the plane. He always flew first class; Mrs. O'Shea was relegated to coach.

Dan, the son, a lawyer who'd decided to become a literary agent, and my cousin Jack Pearl, decided I should be writing material for the men's adventure magazines under my own name, and took me to the offices of Magazine Management to meet Hans Ashbourne, who oversaw the myriad magazines published by that company. Hans was a glib, intelligent, impeccably dressed gentleman who claimed to be descended from European royalty. He was Count Ashbourne, he insisted, and I wasn't about to challenge him. I didn't care if he was King Ashbourne as long as he gave me assignments.

We went to lunch that first day, and the Count held court, weaving a long, often hilarious explanation of the philosophy behind the magazines, much of it tongue-in-cheek. But it was obvious to me that although he was in a position to mock many of the magazines' formulas, his writers had damn well better take them seriously. I was eager to do that, and by the end of the meal he invited me to submit article ideas directly to him.

There was a routine for writers to follow when submitting proposals to The Count. One day each week, the writers would gather in a waiting room for their fifteen minutes with Hans to pitch new ideas. As journalistically suspect the stories might have been, the pay attracted a heavy-duty roster of writers. I shared the waiting room week after week with people like Mario Puzo, Bruce J. Friedman, and Mickey Spillane. Friedman, who went on to great literary success with such novels as *Stern* and *A Mother's Kisses*, actually worked at Magazine Management as an editor at one point, and I have correspondence with him concerning a story I'd pitched. Puzo, of course, reached publishing and motion pictures heights with his *Godfather* series, and Spillane cashed in big with *I, The Jury*, and dozens of other best-selling hard-boiled detective novels.

The weekly proposals submitted to The Count, and to other editors working under him, consisted of a single paragraph, augmented by the fifteen minutes the writer was allotted to verbally enhance the ideas. I started selling regularly to Magazine Management; at one point I had an article in its various magazines every month for a year, writing under such pseudonyms as Christopher Blaine, Stanley Jacob, Hugh Lambert, Cornelius Dailey, and John Southwick. The titles say it all: *I Am a POW in Vietnam; Stewart Raffill: He Tames the Killers* (profile of a Hollywood animal trainer); *The Soccer Game that Killed 400 People; Weekend Sailors: Joyriding Killers; Taiwan: Pleasure Island for Weary Viet Heroes; Labor's Prettiest Negotiator; Mr. Frederick of Hollywood; The Lady Eichmanns: Why Have They Gone Unpunished?* ; and *Massage Parlor Prostitutes.* There were dozens of others. Some of the articles demanded quotes from a psychologist, but I didn't have the time or the inclination to seek out a real one, so I created a fictitious psychologist whom I often quoted.

The highlight of my relationship with Count Ashbourne and Magazine Management occurred one day while I was pitching story ideas to him. He took me to lunch and made a proposal. I paraphrase the conversation.

Ashbourne: "We're about to launch an exciting new project."

Me: "Oh? What's that?"

Ashbourne: "We're going to start running excerpts in the magazines from soon-to-be-published best-selling novels. We'll splash banners across the covers announcing it each month."

Me: "That's great, Hans. You're going to be buying rights to novels."

Ashbourne: "Buy rights? Of course not. I was wondering

whether you'd like to write the excerpts."

Me: "Me? Write the excerpts? I don't understand."

Ashbourne: "All you have to do is write exciting stories that *could* have come from a novel. Twice as long as the articles you've been writing. It pays double."

Me: "Ah, I see. Okay."

I wrote three or four "excerpts" from novels for The Count's magazines. The first was from the "soon-to-be-published" novel, *Flight to Erotica*. The excerpt was titled "I Fly the Charter Passion Route." The money was great, the writing easy.

The Count and his magazines paid a lot of bills for me, and for dozens of other writers making a living until the big break came along. The standards might not have been high, or the approach to subject matter kosher, but aside from the money, the experience was invaluable. I took the articles seriously and approached them with my two basic rules: Each article was the most important thing I'd ever write, and may be the last thing I'd write. As with any craft, you learn by doing. I was proud of the work I turned in during that period, and still am, although rereading them while writing *Murder, HE Wrote* has provided plenty of laughs.

Whether Hans Ashbourne was, in fact, a Count is irrelevant. He was a charming, witty gentleman with whom I shared many lunches over the years as part of an entourage in which I was pleased to be included.

CHAPTER SEVEN

"HUMAH! HUMAH! HUMAH!"

While still with American Airlines I picked up the strangest ghostwriting job of my career. It involved a retired physician named Louis Sunshine, who was introduced to me by Jack Pearl. How Jack ever got involved with Dr. Sunshine is beyond me but he did, and so did I by extension.

Louis Sunshine had been a physician during the days of vaudeville, and many of his patients had been the leggy chorus girls who did their high kicking in that era's glossy revues. The rumor about the good doctor, according to Jack, was that he was the prime undercover abortionist for many of these young women. Whether he was or not remains conjecture. He never admitted it to me.

He'd written three or four novels based upon his years administering to the stars of vaudeville, and had submitted them to publishers, all of whom had sent back rejections. Sunshine decided he needed a professional writer to rewrite the books, and had approached Jack, who turned him down. But he had this talented cousin. . . .

I arrived for my initial meeting with Dr. Sunshine on a freezing cold night, made more so because John Lindsay had just been inaugurated as Mayor of New York, and the transit workers promptly went on strike. I had to walk from American's offices at Third Avenue and 44th Street to the good doctor's large apartment on the Upper West Side. I was greeted at the door by his wife, a voluptuous blonde wearing a bathrobe, who I judged to be in her midforties. She told me the doctor would be with me shortly and led me to a small room dominated by a dentist's chair. She had me sit in it, turned off the overhead light, turned on a gooseneck floor lamp behind my right shoulder, and handed me a manuscript. "Read this while you wait," she said.

Ten minutes later Louis Sunshine arrived. He was a wizened little old man who needed a shave, and whose gray hair headed in many directions. He wore a flannel bathrobe over pajamas, and slippers. In a Jewish accent, he asked me what I thought of the manuscript.

"I've only had a chance to read a few pages," I replied, "but from what I've read, it's . . . well, it's good."

He told me of his disappointment with the publishing industry for having turned down his novels, but knew that with a little professional help, they could be made into bestsellers. Was I interested in helping him?

When I said I was, he outlined how we would work together. He would give me 40 pages that night, which I would take home and rewrite. I was to return the following week with what I'd done, and he would give me the next 40 pages. I would be paid each week for my previous week's efforts. I don't recall the amount we agreed upon but it was in the neighborhood of a hundred dollars a week.

I took the pages home, rewrote them, and delivered them as scheduled the following week. He paid me, gave me the next forty pages, and sent me on my way.

The job lasted six weeks. Nothing ever varied in the routine. His blonde wife would greet me at the door and take me to the dentist's chair where she would hand me that week's 40 pages. Her husband would eventually arrive and critique the work I'd done. I never saw either of them in anything but pajamas and bathrobes.

Our relationship ended in the sixth week. He stood over me as I reclined in the dentist's chair and started yelling about the work I'd done on the previous week's pages. "You don't have any sense of humah," he said. "No sense of humah. Say it after me. Humah! Humah! Humah!"

He'd become agitated and was bouncing up and down as he continued to shout, "Humah! Humah! Humah! Say it! Say it!"

I got out of the chair, grabbed my coat and hat from where I'd left them in the foyer, thanked him and his wife for their hospitality, and ran.

I later learned that Louis Sunshine had died. I suspect his novels were never rewritten and published, although I don't know that for certain. What I do know is that those six weeks of getting to his apartment in the winter after a long day at American, and receiving his lecture on developing a sense of humor, justified to me every cent I'd been paid.

CHAPTER EIGHT

COFFEE, TEA AND ME

Toward the end of 1965, I picked up a call in my office at American.

"Don, this is Ed Brown at Pocketbooks."

I wasn't expecting a call from my editor on the stock car racing book; it had been a long time since we'd spoken.

"Jack Pearl told me you were with American Airlines. I have a book you might be interested in."

He went on to tell me that the NBC news anchor, Chet Huntley of the popular Huntley-Brinkley Report, who'd written books for Pocketbooks, had brought in a couple of young Eastern Airlines stewardesses who wanted to write about their flying experiences. Wally Westfeld, producer of the New York portion of the Huntley-Brinkley Report, had met them on a flight, found their tales amusing, and introduced them to Huntley.

"They've got some pretty funny stories," Brown said. "You might be perfect with your airline experience. Would you like to meet them?"

"Sure," I said. *Say no to nothing.*

A few nights later, I met Melva Hicks and Jo Ann Blaisdell at the bar at Toots Shor's, a fabled watering hole in midtown Manhattan where I had a house charge. Melva was a big, breezy blonde, Jo Ann a demure young brunette with porcelain features. Over drinks, they spent the first half hour telling me funny stories about their escapades as airline stewardesses. Over more drinks, they spent the second half hour repeating the first half hour. One thing was clear: If there was a book in this, most of it would have to come out of my own head and experiences.

We made a handshake deal. I'd write a proposal for Ed Brown. If it resulted in a publishing contract, we'd split all money 50-50, half to me, fifty percent for them to share.

I submitted a proposal and sample chapter to Ed Brown in January 1966. As I was writing, and developing a chapter-by-chapter outline, a working title came to me, the punch line of an old airline joke. A stewardess goes to the cockpit and asks the captain, "Coffee, tea or me?" He replies, "Whatever is easier to make." Boffo!

Brown sat on the proposal until March when he asked for two additional sample chapters, which I promptly provided. Each time I called to see where the project stood, Brown told me it was "under consideration," which was hardly news. If they weren't considering it, they would have sent it back.

While waiting for a decision from Pocketbooks, I continued making promotional deals around the country for American. One such project brought me into contact with a young fledgling filmmaker, Mark Carliner, who was seeking funding for a short subject film. Short subjects were popular with moviegoers in those days; theaters played them prior to screening the feature. The premise of Carliner's short was interesting; a couple from the rural Midwest vacation in New York City, and film their adventures—badly. The film would cut off heads, be shaky, and suffer all the mistakes made by amateur picture takers. In return for our financial help, the couple would fly American on their vacation, with plenty of footage in the film of our planes in action. I agreed to the deal.

One of the scenes Carliner wanted to shoot was of a homeless man on the Bowery. I was with him when he made contact with such a person, a scruffy, disheveled guy who was surprisingly well-spoken, and who said he would be happy to appear in the film. Carliner handed him twenty dollars and told him to be at the same place the following day. When we arrived twenty-four hours later with the camera crew, we were faced with a different man. He'd used the twenty to get a haircut and shave, and to buy a used suit. He looked absolutely spiffy. The scene was scrapped.

I liked Mark Carliner, and we remained in touch after he'd completed the film and it had been shown in theaters throughout the country. Years later, we'd cross paths again professionally. That time, my view of him wasn't quite as sanguine.

I had frequent lunches with Dan O'Shea during this period. He'd officially become my first agent, and I was his first client. I told him about the proposal for *Coffee, Tea or Me?* and how it was just sitting at Pocketbooks. He called me the following day: "Don, I'm having drinks tonight at the Bull & Bear, in the Waldorf, with an editor named Sam Post. Come join us and tell me about the stewardess book as though you hadn't told me before."

I showed up and did as Dan had suggested. Two days later Post called O'Shea to say he wanted to publish *Coffee, Tea or Me?* Dan withdrew the proposal from Pocketbooks and gave it to Post, editor-in-chief at Bartholomew House, the newly created hardcover division of Macfadden-Bartell Publications. Macfadden-Bartell had been established in 1940 as a magazine and softcover book publishing company, and had published hundreds of paperback books. Post had been brought in only that year to launch its hardcover operation.

Post's interest in *Coffee, Tea or Me?* didn't translate into a quick contract. I refined the outline for him, and played the now familiar waiting game. The holdup was Post's boss, Fred Klein, Bartholomew House's publisher, a gentleman with perfectly coiffed silver hair, a pinky ring, and a fondness for shiny suits. He insisted on personally meeting Melva and Jo Ann, which proved logistically difficult. Both women had left Eastern Airlines. Jo Ann married a Mexican physician, became Sra. Jo Ann de Cancino, and moved to Mexico City; Melva packed up her Atlanta apartment and headed west to San Francisco. Eventually, Melva and Klein met up at the Beverly Hills Hotel in Hollywood where, as I recall it, she amused the publisher with her half hour of funny airline stories.

While this was going on, I left American Airlines after almost three wonderful years. I say "almost" because the final months had turned unpleasant. A new vice president, Holmes Brown, was brought in to run the PR department, and it became evident that his primary mission was to put an end to the department's free spending habits. His immediate solution was to get rid of people. Red Sutherland had already resigned.

Holmes Brown (I seem to have been involved with many Browns during my life) was a short man with a gray crew cut who wore large glasses. He'd held top executive positions with other major corporations, including the Ford Motor Company; tales of his abrasiveness and temper followed him from previous jobs, and his behavior at American did nothing to dispel that reputation.

American's public relations offices comprised a large open area, a bullpen of sorts, surrounded by private offices. Brown began a ritual of appearing at the edge of the bullpen at four o'clock every Friday afternoon. He would scrutinize the staff like a commander surveying his troops, then point to someone and indicate with his finger that the individual was to follow to his office—to be fired. Losing your job was bad enough. Being publicly humiliated was worse. Brown wasn't the only executive at the airline who seemed to enjoy the executioner's role. There was another, not in the PR department, whose primary function seemed to be firing people around the airline's system. He, too, enjoyed his work. His *modus operendi* was to travel to a city and take the victim to dinner at a fancy restaurant. After much drinking and backslapping, he would pull out an organization chart, place it in front of the employee, and say it was the new management structure. It took the employee a few minutes to realize that he or she wasn't on it.

"I don't see my name."

"That's because you aren't on it. You're fired."

After weeks of watching Holmes Brown indulge himself, I decided to take the offensive. I met with him and asked about my future at the airline. I was pleasantly surprised. He told me he intended to increase my budget and give me greater responsibility. I left his office that morning feeling pretty good.

That same day, I stopped in the offices of Peckham Productions on East 48th Street after lunch just to chat with John Peckham, who was there with his new wife, Sarah, his brother, Peter, sales director Tom Detienne, and others with whom I'd become friendly through our work together for American. John and Peter had spoken with me before about coming to work for them, but this day they made a firm offer. I was making $12,000 a year at American after three years. They offered me $14,000, and a chance to write and direct films for clients including IBM, Union Carbide, Avon, Pan Am, American Airlines, and others. Although my meeting with Holmes Brown had been positive, I wasn't excited about continuing to work for him. I shook hands with the Peckhams, returned to my office at American, drafted a letter of resignation, and sent it in to Brown.

He was furious. As far as he was concerned, I'd set him up by gaining a commitment, knowing all the while I intended to leave. Which wasn't true. The lunchtime meeting with the Peckhams, and the job offer, hadn't been planned.

I gave the airline a 30-day notice. Brown wouldn't even look at me during my remaining month, turning his head when he passed me in the hall. I knew I'd made the right decision to leave.

Although Brown had put on the money squeeze, going away parties for PR department employees continued to be lavish affairs, and mine was no exception. It was a festive, yet sad evening. I loved most of the people I worked with and had mixed emotions about no longer spending my days with them.

I put *Coffee, Tea or Me?* on the back burner and got busy writing industrial films for Peckham Productions. It was a great place to work, informal yet with plenty of deadline pressure and lots of travel. It wasn't until September 9, 1966, that I signed a contract with Bartholomew House for the stewardess book, which by this time I'd almost finished writing despite the lack of a contract. The advance was $5000, ten percent of which went to Dan O'Shea as the agent (agents today routinely receive 15 percent), fifty percent of what was left to Melva and Jo Ann, and half to me. The royalty on the hardcover was a flat 13 percent of the book's cover price, which was $5.95.

I delivered the first draft of the manuscript to Sam Post in mid-October of that year and soon found myself involved in publication and promotion plans. The publisher hired a marvelous publicist, Anita Helen Brooks, with whom I met frequently in late 1966. She went on to choreograph an incredibly effective publicity blitz for *Coffee, Tea or Me?*

Sam Post and Dan O'Shea decided that the book needed illustrations, and Bill Wenzell, a successful cartoonist best known for sexy girls he'd provided to such magazines as *Esquire*, was hired to create sketches to begin each chapter. He was a big, taciturn, tough looking guy with a burr cut who came off more like a Marine drill sergeant than an artist. When we were first introduced, I called him Bill. He said he preferred William. Okay. His drawings were noteworthy in that the shapely young women in them didn't have any knees. There wasn't a female knee in any of his illustrations that ended up in the finished book.

"William," I once said at one of our lunches, "How come your girls never have any knees?"

"I don't like knees," he said, his lips barely moving.

I never brought it up again.

Wenzell provided illustrations for other books I would go on to write in the *Coffee, Tea or Me?* style, and I grew fond of "William" and our lunches together.

What *was* the *Coffee, Tea or Me?* style?

I wrote it when air travel was considered glamorous, and many viewed stewardesses as sex objects. I knew the book had to be sexy, but didn't want to lose a broad segment of the market by being graphic. I made a little sign which I hung over my typewriter: **Boys chasing girls but no heavy breathing**, and constantly heeded that "rule" as I wrote. I kept it frothy, downright silly at times, and was conscious of the need to write in the first person voice of two females. (Most of my ghosting has been in the female voice and I have been fairly successful in being true to that voice, although I know there have been times when my masculine side showed.)

While waiting for the hardcover edition of *Coffee, Tea or Me?* to be published (it was scheduled for November 1967), I kept busy writing industrial films for Peckham Productions. I'd helped John Peckham open a Washington D.C. office, and wrote treatments and proposals for clients based there. In New York, I wrote scripts for the New York Coffee and Sugar Exchange, Union Carbide, Avon, and the Italian Line. It was during this period that Tom Detienne, Peckham's sales manager, introduced me to Duke Ellington and the Duke Ellington Society, a wonderful organization that held monthly dinner meetings at which virtually every top jazz musician who'd ever had professional contact with The Duke spoke. Their comments were taped, providing a treasure trove of jazz history. I obtained an option through Tom to develop a book based upon those tapes. It was a chance to combine two loves in my life, jazz and writing. Dan O'Shea's efforts to sell it were unsuccessful. My option eventually ran out and I dropped the project.

I took a stab at writing a spec script for a popular TV show, *Mr. Terrific*, but received a rejection from the show's producer. I also failed to sell an article on talk radio and its renaissance to *Esquire*, my favorite magazine at the time, and continued to pitch book ideas to O'Shea. He delivered good news to me about *Coffee, Tea or Me?*. Alan Barnard, the top editor at the paperback house Bantam, put in a preemptive bid for the softcover rights to the book. The advance was $75,000, $10,000 paid on the signing of the contract, $32,500 when Bartholomew House published the hardcover edition, and $32,500 upon publication of the Bantam edition a year later. If a motion picture was released within three years of Bantam's edition, an additional $10,000 would be paid, and an extra $20,000 if the book showed up on the *New York Times* bestseller list for five consecutive weeks. The deal's structure pretty much followed industry standards. As the hardcover publisher, Bartholomew House would receive half of all monies advanced by Bantam, as well as fifty percent of what the book earned in softcover. The authors would receive the other half, after the agent's commission had been deducted. The softcover edition would be priced at $2.95; the author's royalty was a flat 10 percent, somewhat higher than customary. We're talking big money in 1967.

This was cause for celebration, although it was tempered by a medical problem my daughter, Pamela, had been suffering for a couple of years. She'd been having recurring urinary tract infections and was being treated by the chief of urology at a leading Long Island hospital. Eventually, my wife and I decided it was time to get a second opinion, and a series of calls led us to Dr. Victor Marshall at New York Hospital. Marshall, a big, handsome Texan who looked and talked like Lyndon Johnson, had developed a surgical procedure that would fix Pam's medical problem. After a series of appointments with him, Pam's surgery was scheduled for April 3, 1967. She was almost six at the time.

When they took her up to the OR the morning of the operation, my wife and I went to the hospital coffee shop. To our amazement, Dr. Marshall was at the other end of the counter eating a slice of pie and drinking coffee. What did *that* mean? we wondered. Had he handed over the scalpel to an associate, an intern or resident? I got up the nerve to approach.

"Dr. Marshall, my wife and I were wondering why you aren't upstairs operating on Pamela."

He looked up at us, smiled, and drawled, "I'll be getting' around to that just as soon as I finish mah pie."

The operation was a success, but an infection of a different kind set in during her post-surgery days in the hospital that extended her stay there. It was a trying time for everyone, although the Peckhams made it as easy as possible for me. After getting Pam's sister, Laurie, who was eleven months older, to school, my wife and I would drive from Long Island to the hospital each morning. I would then go to work, late, of course, and leave early to spend as much time at the hospital as possible. In those days, parents weren't allowed to stay overnight with their child, and we'd leave a very unhappy and frightened Pamela at eight o'clock and drive home. Laurie was cared for after school by neighbors, which was tough on her, too.

If I ever have to recall the date of Pamela's surgery, I need only to open my wallet and check my American Express card. During her extended hospital stay, I learned that the bill there would be about $2,000, and that it would have to be paid before we could take her home. While sitting in my office at Peckham Productions one morning, a full-page ad in the *Times* caught my eye. The Franklin National Bank was introducing a gold American Express card with a $2,000 credit line. The bank had a branch a half block from the office, and I ran there and applied. I got the card and used the credit line to bail Pam out of the hospital. I haven't left home without it since.

Coffee, Tea or Me? was published on November 21, 1967, with considerable fanfare. Anita Helen Brooks booked Melva and Jo Ann on dozens of radio and TV shows, although not under those names. They used pseudonyms on the book; Melva became Rachel Jones, and Jo Ann was Trudy Baker. Eventually, because of the book's phenomenal success, Melva legally changed her name to Rachel Jones to capitalize on her sudden fame.

They made appearances on "The Today Show"; "Monitor"; "The Barry Gray Show"; "Mike Wallace Show"; Barry Farber's radio program; "Girl Talk"; "To Tell the Truth"; and many others. Lengthy interviews with them appeared in *Newsday, King Features Syndicate, Look,* the *Daily News, Travel,* and the *Park Avenue Social Review.* The Coffee Tea or Me Girls were a hot commodity, and hardcover sales reflected the wave of publicity they generated.

Surprisingly, reviews were good. *Look* Magazine said ". . . a nuisance to own. Everyone wants to borrow it. Reads like a footnote to *Human Sexual Response.*"

Publishers Weekly: "Parents will move heaven and earth to prevent their daughters from becoming stewardesses."

"Hilarious experiences," wrote the Chicago *Sun-Times.*

"This is a funny, funny book," someone wrote in the Palm Springs *Desert Sun.* And Jack O'Brien wrote in his *Voice of Broadway* column, "A very funny saga."

I was especially pleased with what Barry Farber said on his show about the book: "The chapter on public relations and press flights is outstanding. It is the most brilliant exposé of the public relations business. I couldn't read it in one sitting; I had to put it down and rest."

Holmes Brown, VP of public relations at American Airlines who'd thought I'd suckered him by quitting, now made some noise about recognizing himself in the chapter on PR, and said he was considering suing me. It would have been a frivolous suit; would I ever consider making fun of someone I admired as much as Mr. Brown?

We made the bestseller lists, including the *Times,* and received our bonus. While most reviews were good, a *Times* writer who put together a list of the best-selling paperback books of 1969 (it was on their list for most of that year), and who summed up each book with a pithy comment, wrote of *Coffee, Tea or Me?* "Phooey!"

Phooey on you, man!

Hollywood took notice, too. Frank McCarthy at 20th Century

Fox optioned the book for a movie but allowed the option to lapse. It was picked up three days later by Robert Aldrich at MGM, but he, too, dropped the project after the option period had expired. I loved the experience of optioning a book to Hollywood. You get paid to allow someone to decide not to make the movie, and then get paid again by the next person optioning the property. Pretty neat deal.

During this period of film options, Julie Stein and Anita Loos approached O'Shea about turning *Coffee, Tea or Me?* into a Broadway musical. The subject matter and timing were perfect. It would have made a wonderful youthful, happy, wacky, romantic musical. But I turned it down because everything was back-ended. The up-front option money these two immensely talented people were offering was far less than the Hollywood studios were coughing up, and I went with cash-in-hand. It's one of those situations I've second-guessed ever since.

Two film versions of *Coffee, Tea or Me?* were eventually made.

CBS produced a made-for-TV version in 1973 starring John Davidson and Karen Valentine. As often happens, they used the title but wrote their own story, stealing from the film *Captain's Paradise* in which Alec Guinness plays a sea captain with a wife in two different ports. In this case, the bigamist was, of course, an airline captain. It was a dreadful movie, which didn't stop CBS from using it to launch their 1973 season, and it ranked as one of the most watched TV movies in history. The experience with CBS was dismal, and eventually led to Dan O'Shea and me parting company as agent and author.

Here's what happened.

Sam Post at Bartholomew House received a call from a producer, Mark Carliner (remember him as having made the short subject film with my help at American Airlines?), asking whether the performing rights to the book were available. He wanted to produce a film version for CBS. Post referred him to O'Shea. When Carliner learned I'd written the book, he became enthusiastic, and he,

O'Shea and I met for lunch in January 1972 at the Lamb's Club, where I was a member. I made the point during that lunch that because the book had earned me so much money, I wasn't interested in simply optioning or selling it again. I wanted screenwriter experience and credentials. Carliner agreed. Ironically, I received a call in the middle of lunch from a good friend, Jim Grau, who wanted to know whether performing rights for *Coffee, Tea or Me?* were still up for grabs.

*   *   *   *   *

I'd met Grau during my American PR days when he was director of promotion for WNBC in New York, and we developed a number of promotional tie-ins involving some of that station's on-air talent, including "Big" Wilson and Brad Crandall. "Biggie," who did the morning show, was also a talented pianist and bass player; we went on to become friends, performing together in jam sessions around New York. I became friendly with Crandall, too, one of the brightest men I've ever known.

Grau went on to open his own TV and film production company, Charisma Productions, a successful venture that he continues to head today. He's also Donald Trump's brother-in-law by virtue of having married Elizabeth Trump, and is intimately involved in booking entertainment provided at Trump's casinos and clubs.

A few years ago, Jim invited me to put on a murder mystery weekend at Mar-a-Lago, Donald Trump's magnificent club in Palm Beach where membership fees run into the hundreds of thousands of dollars. I contacted Ron and Joni Pacie, who perform interactive murder mysteries around the globe through their production company, Murder Mysteries, Inc., and invited them to join me in the project. I'd met the Pacies aboard the QE2 while giving one of my yearly lecture series on mystery writing, and was impressed with their professionalism and that of their acting troupe. They joined me one weekend, along with Grau and assorted other people in

Trump's entourage, for a trip to Palm Beach on Trump's private 727. We planned the mystery weekend, and returned in that opulent aircraft a few months later to put on the show. It went over big, although it was hard to read Trump's reaction. One minute he was extremely friendly, the next minute aloof to the point of arrogance. But he was pleasant and courteous to my wife and me on the way back from Palm Beach that second weekend. We shared the popcorn he'd made in the galley, and watched some of his favorite Kung Fu movies; there must be fifty titles onboard.

I don't envy people like Donald Trump. His wife at the time, Marla Maples, and some of their children, were with us on the second trip. Their beautiful daughter, Tiffany, was never allowed to go anywhere without a nanny and armed security guard at her heels, and the entrance to the Trumps' private quarters was under twenty-four hour armed guard. Such precautions are necessary, of course, for someone of his wealth, and maybe you get used to it. I'm not sure I ever would.

*   *   *   *   *

I told Grau I was meeting at that moment with Carliner regarding a CBS film version of the book, but assured him he'd get first crack at it if the CBS deal fell through. Carliner, O'Shea and I left the Lambs Club with a handshake deal. Carliner would pursue a deal at CBS to buy the rights to make a film of *Coffee, Tea or Me?*, and I would be hired to write a screen treatment for the Writer's Guild minimum fee.

I met frequently with Carliner over the ensuing months as I worked on the screen treatment. CBS tendered a letter-of-intent to O'Shea, which I never saw. But he assured me it covered everything that had been agreed upon with Carliner. A formal contract for the purchase of the property, as well as an agreement for me to write the treatment, came from CBS in March 1972. I didn't pay any attention to the business end of the deal, which was a mistake. Writing a book or screenplay is only the first step in the process of maximizing the potentials of a property. Writers who fail to pay attention to every aspect of "the deal," including promotion plans and contractual matters, are asking for trouble, no matter how much faith they have in an agent and publisher. All I knew was that CBS was paying $12,500 for the right to make a movie from the book. Because made-for-TV movies don't include participation, there are no royalties to hope for, no percentage of profits; it was a flat fee, a buyout. Which was okay with me because I now saw the property as my opportunity to become a screenwriter. What was especially appealing was Carliner's assurance that should a TV series develop from the movie, I would be involved, creatively and financially.

I finished the treatment and delivered it to Carliner. He read it, called me, said, "This is the best treatment I've ever read from a first-timer," and flew off to Los Angeles with it.

Dan O'Shea and I continued to have what amounted to weekly lunches at a variety of Manhattan restaurants, usually joined by an assortment of people from the publishing world including Jack Pearl; Hans Ashbourne (I was still writing occasional pieces for his magazines); Jack's close friend, Claire Huffaker, when he was in town from Los Angeles where he'd forged a successful career as a screenwriter; Larry Freundlich, an editor at Doubleday with a wicked sense of humor and sizable intellect; Arthur Praeger, an adjunct professor at NYU who wrote a number of successful nonfiction books; Sam Post; Harvey Gardner, a delightful, cherubic editor at Fawcett who would go on to edit a number of my later books when he wasn't appearing in theatrical productions in Nyack, where he lived; Herb Alexander, who "invented" the paperback book; and others who came and went. I loved those lunches, which often lasted through the afternoon into the early evening. A lot of booze was consumed on those happy days, along with good conversation. Meeting and becoming friendly with these people was important to my professional career, and I took every advantage of it, traveling into the city one or two days a week when I wasn't at home writing. (This was after I'd left Peckham Productions.)

I asked O'Shea on a number of occasions about the CBS contract and why Melva, Jo Ann and I hadn't been given it to sign. He told me that the contract took rights that hadn't been agreed upon in the letter of intent, particularly merchandising rights, and that he was actively negotiating with CBS. I never pressed because my financial situation was solid at the moment, and didn't need the CBS money. Merchandising rights were important, I knew, because the book's popularity had begun to spawn all sorts of items bearing *Coffee, Tea or Me?*—coffee mugs, aprons, tee shirts and hats.

I heard from Carliner a month after he'd gone to L.A. He called to tell me that CBS didn't like my treatment, and that they were bringing in two other writers to work on it. I asked the obvious question: "Why aren't I being given a shot at rewriting it?" His answer: "I don't want to upset CBS." He eventually sent me the screenplay that had been approved. I thought it was humorless and told him so (shades of Dr. Louis Sunshine). What especially upset me was that spinning a series off it would be virtually impossible.

O'Shea expressed his dismay to me about the way things were progressing, but said there really was nothing he could do about protecting my interests as the screenwriter. "That's the way they do it out there," he said. I knew he was right. "Besides," he said, "I'm still trying to straighten out the contractual problems."

In the spring of 1973, I received a call from Stuart Glickman, who was with CBS's business affairs office in Los Angeles. He was surprisingly conciliatory. He expressed his disappointment in the way Carliner had handled things, and said he would see what he could do about the situation. I pointed out to him that I was certain nothing could be done at that juncture. The screenplay was completed and approved. The only thing left to be straightened out was the contract, and payment.

I received another call that same week from Glickman. This time he offered to fly me to Hollywood to be on the set during filming, and to meet the cast. I resented that call. They were trying to appease me by dangling the possibility of rubbing elbows with actors and actresses, and basking in the glitter of moviemaking. I told Glickman I had no interest in coming to L.A., but thanked him for the offer. I liked Glickman, and knew he was acting upon orders from others in the CBS hierarchy.

He called again the following week. This time, he informed me that the business office had been having difficulty dealing with O'Shea, whom he characterized as being non-communicative. It was out of Glickman's hands. He'd turned it over to the network's lawyers.

That summer, I heard through the grapevine that CBS had commenced production on *Coffee, Tea or Me?* Then, in late August, I opened *TV Guide* and saw a full-page ad for the movie. It would kick off the network's new season on September 10.

I placed an angry call to O'Shea, who promptly wrote a letter to CBS warning that they broadcast the film at their peril, and pointing out that no contracts giving them the right had ever been signed by the principals. CBS ignored the warning and the film aired.

I forced myself to watch it, and hated it, although my disgust with the machinations leading up to it had probably tainted my judgment.

Shortly after the film aired (and garnered a strong rating), I flew to Los Angeles with Jack Pearl. While there, I met with Glickman who continued to express his understanding of my feelings. It was during that meeting that I learned the basis upon which CBS decided to go ahead to make the movie, even though neither I, Melva or Jo Ann had ever signed anything. According to Glickman, the network had decided to proceed based upon Dan O'Shea's verbal agreement with the terms of the contract. His word as agent, Glickman told me, was as binding as a written document.

This was all news to me.

The failure to secure a contract led to the severing of my professional relationship with Dan O'Shea. It was painful. I considered Dan to be one of my best friends, and certainly wasn't assigning any ulterior motives to his role in the CBS fiasco. He'd been talking about getting out of the agenting business for some time, and undoubtedly had other things on his mind.

In October, a month after the film aired on CBS, I consulted an eminent attorney in the publishing and performing rights field, Ephraim London. He told me that I (we, including Melva and Jo Ann) had an excellent case against CBS. He needed one thing, however, before proceeding. The three of us had to sign on with him as one client, and the girls would have to give me authorization to speak for them in the matter. I understood; London didn't want to have to chase after three individuals, one in New York, one in California, and one in Mexico City, to get papers signed.

I contacted Melva and Jo Ann, told them I'd spoken with the attorney, and asked that they provide what he wanted. Melva was cooperative. Jo Ann, who was in the process of suing Eastern Airlines for a work-related injury, responded that she didn't want to get involved in another lawsuit and refused to go along with us. Even at that, London wrote a letter to CBS on October 12, 1973, in which he said he represented us, and demanded from the network the written agreement giving them the right to make the film. Because there was no such document, he received nothing. In December, London wrote me to say that unless I could pull together "the team," he was unwilling to go forward. Months later, I had to admit defeat and informed London of my failure to secure Melva and Jo Ann's full cooperation. He returned all the documentation I'd given him and ended his covering letter with, "I, too, am sorry the girls refused to cooperate. The case should not have been too difficult."

On my instructions, because I was considering legal action, O'Shea had not cashed the $12,500 check CBS had sent him. I told him to go ahead, and the shares were dispersed, bringing an end to the episode. I wrote Stuart Glickman in September 1974 as my formal acknowledgment that it was over. In it I said, among many things, " . . . (Mark Carliner), as disappointing as he turned out to be, contributed to that wonderful experience known as the learning curve. I'll be forever grateful, although not so much so that it would preclude me from popping him in the nose in public."

It was a learning curve for me. Everything is. And if I were to run into Mark Carliner again, I wouldn't pop him in the nose. I'd buy him a drink and see whether he was interested in making a movie out of one of my 80-plus books. Carrying a grudge has never been my style.

*   *   *   *   *

The second movie version of *Coffee, Tea or Me?* was a porn film.

For years, I joined a few dozen eclectic friends for lunch every day at The Jolly Fisherman, in Roslyn, Long Island, across the street from an office I'd taken. In September, 1984, one of these friends mentioned he'd been driving through Queens the day before and had seen *Coffee, Tea or Me?* on a theater's marquee. I called the theater that afternoon and confirmed that it was, indeed, showing a XXX film with that name.

A few days later, I went into a Times Square porn shop and bought a video of it for $99. Hot stuff. But who gave *them* permission to make a film of my book? The "them" was Cal Vista International, located in Van Nuys, California. I flew there with Renée, the woman who would become my second wife (my first marriage ended after 19 years), and we visited Cal Vista, a huge facility that took up a city block. I went inside, introduced myself as a writer looking for work, and asked the receptionist a lot of questions about Cal Vista. The wall behind her was filled with materials touting their films, not pornographic ones, but family fare, Disney-type movies. The X-rated stuff was produced in the back and distributed around the world (Japan was the biggest market, she told me).

I returned to New York and contacted an attorney friend, Dick Weiner, who agreed to institute legal action on my behalf as majority copyright holder against Cal Vista. He started by informing

CBS of this second movie version of *Coffee, Tea or Me?*, the rights to which they owned. Lawyers there declined to join the suit, but agreed to act as "friends of the court" should the suit progress to the point of litigation. Weiner had Cal Vista served with papers, and hearings were scheduled in New York (Cal Vista had a New York office). Two things bothered me, however. Weiner pointed out the first; getting a fair count of money earned from the film and video would be tough. The second problem was more personal. I was uncomfortable going after money earned by a pornographic version of my frothy, "boys chasing girls but no heavy breathing" book. I told Dick that I would be content to see Cal Vista cease selling the movie, without any monetary compensation. He broached that with Cal Vista's attorneys and was turned down. Legal documents and phone calls went back and forth until the filmmaker offered to pay $3,500 up front, and a dollar in royalties for each video sold thereafter. I agreed, with the stipulation that any monies earned by me would go to a charity. The papers were signed and I received the $3,500, less Weiner's cut. I never saw a cent in royalties after that, and wasn't about to spend any more time pursuing it. That seems to be the way most legal entanglements are resolved. One of the parties says the hell with it and moves on, which was the case with me.

The legal difficulties with the movie versions of *Coffee, Tea or Me?* represented a frustrating period of my life, nothing more. The book and its sequels sold for 17 years, and became my annuity. It bought me the freedom to become a full-time writer, and led to many other books, including three sequels featuring the "Coffee, Tea or Me Girls." The books injected the phrase *Coffee, Tea or Me?* into the public vocabulary. To this day, it is used in ads for a variety of products or services. The motion picture *George of the Jungle*, produced in the 90s, has the character, George, reading *Coffee, Tea or Me?* in order to learn about how to conduct relationships.

The book also has been used, at least once to my knowledge, as a tool of seduction. I was with a Peckham film crew on a plane from New York to Charleston, West Virginia a few years after the original book had been published. We were on our way to shoot scenes for a Union Carbide film. I had a window seat; Mike Ferrante, the cameraman, was next to me on the aisle. While the flight attendant served us drinks, Mike playfully asked whether she had read *Coffee, Tea or Me?*

She laughed, leaned closer and said, "Read it? I know the man who wrote it."

I sat up a little straighter.

"It wasn't written by two stewardesses, it was written by a guy. He was on this flight a month ago. He took me to dinner. He's writing a sequel and I'm goin' to be in it."

I pictured dozens of men climbing on flights, a copy of the book under their arms, using that line about a sequel to woo wide-eyed stewardesses. What had I done? What evil had I wrought?

I never said a word to burst her bubble.

Twenty years after the initial publication, Jim Grau suggested an updated version. He'd been introduced to two other flight attendants who wanted to be the Rachel and Trudy of their day. I thought it was a good idea, but editors and publishers didn't. As more than one said to me, "*Coffee, Tea or Me?* was perfect for its time. Flying was fun twenty years ago. It isn't fun any more."

How true. How sad.

It would have made a great musical.

CHAPTER NINE

"Did I Wake You? It Must Be the Time Difference"

During the time that *Coffee, Tea or Me?* was making its way on to bestseller lists and TV screens, I became involved in another book through Sam Post.

Sam called me at Peckham Productions in July of 1967 to ask if I'd be interested in collaborating with Veronica Lake on her autobiography. I'd just returned from a family vacation on Cape Cod and wasn't looking to take on another book at the moment. But over lunch, Sam convinced me to fly to Miami with him to meet with the former movie star. Sam, among many things, can be persuasive. He'd created a business entity, Beverly Hills Associates, through which he was pursuing the Lake project.

Veronica Lake had been a female star in the 40s, a beautiful blonde who was built like Babe Ruth (skinny legs, big chest), and whose lasting fame had as much to do with her hairstyle as her many screen roles. That hairstyle, long wavy blonde hair worn over one eye, became so popular that the War Department banned it on female defense industry workers during WW II for fear of having women catch their hair in machinery.

She'd become a star in 1941 at the age of 17 when she appeared in a World War II drama, *I Wanted Wings*, with Ray Milland, William Holden and Brian Donlevy. She went on to appear in 25 other films, including a series of movies with Alan Ladd that linked them forever in moviegoers' minds as a dynamic screen duo. She also starred in a couple of memorable comedies, *Sullivan's Travels* and *I Married a Witch*, arguably her best work. And millions of war movie fans remember the scene from *So Proudly We Hail* in which Veronica, playing a military nurse on Bataan, nestles a live grenade in her ample bosom and walks into the midst of Japanese soldiers to save her fellow nurses played by Claudette Colbert and Paulette Goddard.

Sadly, her life was mostly downhill after her relatively brief Hollywood stardom. I remembered reading that she'd ended up working as a cocktail waitress in New York's Martha Washington Hotel in the early 60s, and had been employed prior to that at a South Broadway factory where she pasted felt flowers on lingerie hangers.

Sam and I flew to Miami the second week in August. Veronica, who'd been born in Brooklyn and whose real name was Constance Ockleman—everyone called her Connie—was living at the time in a small apartment complex on the fringe of the Cuban section of Miami, near the airport. Peg Wessel, who owned the complex and occupied the apartment above Connie's, was allowing the former actress, her friend, to live there rent-free.

The afternoon Sam and I arrived, a party was in progress, attended by a dozen assorted characters including Veronica's son, Michael. There wasn't any food at the party, just booze, lots of it. I peeked in Connie's refrigerator at one point and saw only two leftover slices of pizza.

Sam and I took Veronica and Peg to dinner that night at a Black Angus steakhouse—the receipt indicates that Sam paid $15.50 for the four of us. The good old days. After dinner, it was back to drinking at the apartment. I never noticed that Sam eventually slipped away and took the last flight that night back to New York, leaving me alone with the former Hollywood star and her boozy companions.

Other writers had attempted to work with Veronica Lake on her memoirs. She'd fired some; others had thrown up their hands and walked away. I decided late in the evening that the latter group had demonstrated sanity, and that I would join their ranks. I found a pay phone outside the apartment complex and called Dan O'Shea.

"This is nuts," I told him. "I'm coming home."

"Give it a couple of days," he suggested.

I called my wife. "This is nuts down here," I said. "Sam's already bailed out. I'm coming home."

"Give it a few days," she offered.

I ended up spending a week with Veronica and her assorted hangers-on, and am glad I did. Although working with Veronica was exasperating, it also resulted in a book of which I'm extremely proud, and allowed me to become close friends with this Hollywood legend, a vulnerable, tragic woman who drank too much while attempting to survive in the truest sense of the word, and to maintain what dignity she had left.

My week in Miami was a lesson in non-productivity. Veronica was a late riser, and took hours, it seemed, to pull herself together to get on with the day. Because no one there seemed to eat much, I snuck out to local eateries for breakfast, and when it was possible, lunch. I ate in self-defense. The drinking would start in early afternoon; without food in my stomach, I could see the lining being eaten away. I carried a small tape recorder with me and tried to get Veronica—she was Connie to me by this point—to answer questions. She'd start responding, but invariably cut it short, saying, "We'll get to that later." By the time I left Miami, my small notebook contained a hundred "get to it later" notations.

The people who showed up every day to drink with Veronica were an unsettling lot, in my opinion. There was a predatory quality to them, men and women with nothing else to do in their lives but freeload off this former movie star. Peg Wessel was a pleasant exception. She seemed to sincerely care about Connie. I slept in Peg's apartment during that week; she stayed downstairs with Veronica.

One night, Peg asked me if I'd enjoy going to a gay bar.

"Sure," I said, assuming she meant a happy bar. I'd not heard the term "gay" applied to homosexuality before. The bar at El Carol was in the shape of a horseshoe. Women congregated along one side, men the other. There was a pool table in the back to which I gravitated, and spent four nights in El Carol playing pool with male homosexual patrons. Never once did any of them make a pass at me, which either means they respected my obvious heterosexuality, or found me unattractive.

Either way, time spent at the bar was pleasant and uneventful, until my next to last night in Miami. I was standing at the bar with Peg and Veronica when another woman joined us and made a pass at Connie. Peg responded the way a husband might with a man making a pass at his wife. She belted the woman and decked her, sending her to the floor at my feet. I'd never seen anything quite like it and wasn't sure how to respond. The woman got up, dusted herself off, and rejoined friends at the other side of the bar as though nothing had happened.

The next night, I decided to get away from the scene. I rented a car and drove to Miami Beach where I had a quiet, peaceful dinner alone and walked through some of the beachfront properties. On my way back to the apartment, I stopped in at a little bar where I nursed several drinks until I figured everyone would be asleep. I'd had enough of them for that week.

The next day, with my notebook and tape recorder filled with "get to that later" items, I happily boarded a National Airlines plane for New York.

Sam Post's deal on the Veronica Lake autobiography was with a British publisher, W.H. Allen, headed by a classy gentleman, Mark Goulden. As I started researching and writing, I dealt primarily with Goulden's son-in-law, Jeffrey Simmons, and an editor assigned to the project, Irene Slade. My time with Veronica was haphazard. I never returned to Florida, but she came to New York on a few occasions, which gave me further access to her. At the same time, I spent considerable time at the Library of the Performing Arts at Lincoln Center going through newspaper and magazine clippings that chronicled her Hollywood career. I'd come to the conclusion that everything Veronica told me had better be double-checked for accuracy. While she had a good recall of anecdotes, the factual aspects of them were shaky, and I verified everything I could through the library's extensive sources.

I worked on the manuscript through the fall of 1967 and into the winter, juggling that project with what was a busy time at Peckham Productions. I traveled a lot, particularly for an ambitious film we were making for Union Carbide. When I wasn't on the road, I developed relationships with some of Veronica's close friends, including Nat Perlo, editor of the *Police Gazette*, who'd demonstrated many acts of kindness toward Connie during her difficult days in New York; Courtney Wright, a devoted fan who'd collected many photographs of Veronica over the years and supplied them for the book; and Bill Roos. Roos and his companion, Dick Toman, lived in a penthouse apartment on Park Avenue. Aside from being Veronica's trusted friend, Roos had begun acting as her manager. She always stayed with Roos and Toman at the apartment when she was in New York, and it became clear to me that of everyone in her life, they represented her truest friends, giving to her without asking for anything in return. God knows she needed people like them.

I finished the manuscript on January 24, 1968, and gave it to my typist (this was long before computers entered my life). I'd found it difficult hiring a part-time typist through a temp agency because I worked at home after leaving Peckham. It was against the policy of most temp agencies to send a female to a man's house for fear of sexual shenanigans. I literally ended up pleading: "Look," I said, "I'm married. My wife and two daughters are here. I have three dogs. I'm not a rapist or sexual nut. I really need somebody *to type*."

They relented and sent a woman who I judged to be in her 70s. No matter how high I turned up the thermostat, and no matter how many blankets she wrapped herself in, she complained of being cold, to the point of saying she could no longer work for me. The temperature in my office when she was there reached, I was sure, 100 degrees. I was happy to see her go. Olsten sent a couple of others who didn't work out for various reasons until Donna Pelini arrived. Donna was a no-nonsense gal who was married to Luigi, an Italian-American soccer fanatic who went on to become involved in a professional indoor soccer league. Donna worked with me for many years, and became a good friend. She not only typed like a madwoman, she offered lots of good editorial advice from her perspective as an avid reader.

I switched from a typewriter to a computer sometime in the mid-70s. Does a computer make you a better writer? I think so, although there are purists who disagree, citing the tactile joy of punching balky typewriter keys, or the fluid pleasure of a number two pencil flowing over a yellow legal pad. If those low-tech approaches work for other writers, that's good . . . for them. For me, the computer represented freedom, encouraging me to rewrite, to change and then change again sentences, paragraphs, whole chapters, and complete manuscripts. When I was using the typewriter, I often decided that what had been set down was good enough because the contemplation of retyping that page was too labor intensive. I never hesitate to rework my pages these days because the computer makes it easy. It wasn't always so.

*   *   *   *   *

Jack Pearl, who went on to write many books including the original biography of General George Patton, wrote a novel, *Callie Knight*, about a strong-willed woman in a small upstate New York town patterned after a real town, Lordville, where our family spent a few weeks each summer in a house and bungalow we owned.

Jack's agent, Ted Chichak (I was not Ted's client yet) had been urging Jack to try his hand at what was becoming a popular genre, the historical romantic novel, and was impressed with Jack's ability to create such a compelling female character in *Callie Knight*. Jack reluctantly took Ted's advice and wrote a novel under the pseudonym, Stephanie Blake. The first book was a big success, and Jack wrote many books under that byline, becoming financially comfortable as a result. One last note about Jack Pearl becoming rich as Stephanie Blake. He received hundreds of fan letters over the course of the series, including a marriage proposal from a wealthy older physician in Texas. This lonely gentleman promised Stephanie the moon if she would come to Texas and marry him.

"Go," I told Jack. "You'll never have to write again."

He didn't, much to the relief of his wife, June.

The publisher of the Stephanie Blake series was Playboy Press. Despite its connection to the men's magazine, it functioned with editorial independence within the Hefner empire, employing good editors and signing up a wide variety of books in many genres. Jack's editor was a bright young man, Bob Gleason, with whom I became involved through Jack and his historical romance series.

Gleason called me one day in 1977 after we'd become friends, and after I'd written other books for him. He asked if I wanted to try my hand at an historical romantic novel. It was the furthest thing from my mind at the time, but I was between books; doing something in a genre completely foreign to me was appealing. Besides, I was sure it wouldn't take more than a few months to write. I signed a contract with Gleason and Playboy Press and started work on *Daughter of the Sand*, under the name Pamela South. Gleason had only one bit of advice for me: "You have to take it seriously, Don," he said. "These are serious books to the readers."

Because I'd spent that year in Saudi Arabia as an Air Force officer, I decided to set the book in the Middle East, at least the first part of it. The story I came up with involved a Scottish physician, Angus Campbell, unhappily married to his second wife, who decides to spend a year in Arabia dispensing medical care to the impoverished citizens of that area, a conscience-clearing mercy mission. He takes with him his ravishing 18-year old daughter, Heather, who detests her stepmother, to function as his nurse. Shortly after they set up shop in Arabia, a fierce local sheik, Ibn-Kashan, raids the encampment and kidnaps Heather.

After brutally raping her, Ibn-Kashan finds himself falling in love, takes her as his bride, and they have a crippled son together.

It isn't long after that, however, that he notices a dramatic change in her behavior (not surprising under the circumstances, but puzzling to the sheik). He learns of a physician in Vienna, Sigmund Freud, who treats hysterical young women, and takes Heather to see the eminent psychiatrist. (I swear, I kept Gleason's admonition—take it seriously—in mind every step of the way.)

Freud urges Ibn-Kashan to leave Heather with him, which her Arab husband agrees to do.

Freud takes her to New York with him on the only trip he ever made to the United States. While there, she's kidnapped again, this time by a Prohibition gang lord named Monk, who sets her up as a speakeasy hostess until she makes her escape from him, aided by a rum-running midget. She's ultimately saved by a handsome young medical student, falls in love with him, and they set sail for England where they will be married.

No snide comments, please, about the plot. *Everything gets used.* Right? I used my experience in the Middle East, as well as a lifelong interest in psychology, as the basis for the story.

I gave the manuscript to Donna Pelini for a final typing. When she returned it to me, I asked what she thought.

"I enjoyed it," she said. "The only problem I have is, what ever happened to Ibn-Kashan and the kid?"

My heart sank. She was right. Once I had the sheik drop off Heather in Vienna, I completely forgot about him and their son. Those characters were never resolved.

This was pre-computer days. To properly resolve Ibn-Kashan, I would have to go back into the manuscript and add scenes explaining what had happened to him and the boy. Frankly, I wasn't in the mood to do that, not in a typewritten manuscript. Had I been working on a computer, it would have been a breeze.

I took the easy way out. As Heather and her fiancé stand together on the deck of the ship that would take them to England, I have Heather muse, "I wonder whatever happened to Ibn-Kashan and my son."

That was it.

I retyped the final page and sent the manuscript to Gleason, expecting an exasperated phone call from him. He did call, but he wasn't upset. Instead, he said, "Great ending. Sets up a perfect sequel when she goes back to Arabia to find the Arab and the kid."

There was no sequel. I'd had my fill of trying to write historical romantic novels, although I did write another in 1982 for Jove under the name Lee Jackson (*The Eagle and the Serpent*), and ghosted a Stephanie Blake for Jack Pearl in 1987 (*Texas Lily*), when Jack became ill and couldn't fulfill his contract for the book. I have no recollection of why I did the Lee Jackson book or how it came about. I do remember (aided by a fast read while working on this autobiography) that both books turned out pretty good. For some reason, maybe the settings and the strong historic material, I found them easier to take seriously than I had the first one.

* * * * *

It's always frustrating for a writer to finish a manuscript and then wait as the editorial, production and marketing processes take over. Dan O'Shea once told me after I'd delivered a manuscript, "The easy part's over. Now we've got to work like hell to get the publisher to pay attention to the book."

Words of wisdom.

The publishing industry moves painfully slow. Despite technological advances, it still muddles along at what seems a snail's pace. The average time between submitting a manuscript, and seeing the book in bookstores, is eighteen months, often longer. There are some valid reasons for this. Copies must be sent to reviewers months in advance of pub date. The back and forth time between author and editor can be lengthy, depending upon the shape the manuscript is in when submitted. I'm a firm believer in delivering to my editor the cleanest manuscript possible. Like most writers, I hate giving up a manuscript because I always know that I can make it better, cleaner, more perfect. But there comes a time when you have to let go, and be content that you've done your best.

The value of delivering a clean manuscript is both practical and psychological. Today's book editors are busy. Staffs have been cut, and an increasing number of books are farmed out to freelance editors. The easier I can make my editor's job, the less likely he or she will find things to change. My reputation with them will be that of a true professional, which will certainly hold me in good stead the next time my agent pitches a project on my behalf.

I've known writers, and have worked with a few, whose attitude is that they're responsible only for a book's creative ideas and input; cleaning up sloppy grammar and syntax, misspellings, poor word choices, out-of-whack time sequences, unrealistic dialogue and everything else that goes into a novel "is the editor's problem." I suppose there are those literary giants, and writers whose very name means bestseller, who can get away with this. Most professional writers can't, including this one. That attitude is pretentious, amateurish, and arrogant, and any patience I might have had with writers who deal this way evaporated years ago. More than anything, I wish to be considered a pro, a writer who understands and respects editors as well as the editorial process. *This is the most important thing I'll ever write, and it might be the last.*

Irene Slade proved an extremely capable, albeit demanding editor. She worked on the Veronica manuscript with a practiced eye, and her editorial suggestions contained in a series of letters from London were on-target, contributing to a better book. There was one major conflict between us, and that had to do with the lack of sensationalism in Veronica's story. Connie was not interested in doing the typical Hollywood tell-all, although she certainly had plenty of experiences upon which to base such an approach. She'd dated many of Hollywood's top leading men and assorted other famous gentlemen—Howard Hughes, Aristotle Onassis, and the oft-married Tommy Manville who offered her $100,000 if she would marry him for four hours—and had been subjected to plenty of casting-couch incidents. But she wanted to avoid that, opting instead to tell the story of her rapid rise to stardom, how she turned her back on Hollywood at the height of her career, and what her post-Hollywood life had been.

Ms. Slade summed up her feelings in a March 25, 1968 letter to Jeffrey Simmons.

"Mr. Bain is such a delightfully convincing writer that anything he writes is a pleasure to read. I hope one day he may write a book for us on a subject that is more exciting than VERONICA.

"Mr. Bain is marvelously cooperative, but I'm not sure there is much he can do to inject a story into a book which just hasn't got a story. I think he's done his best and we all appreciate his professional handling of the subject.

"I do see his point about VERONICA'S life being a change from all the usual sensation of sex and squalor that generally emerges from these Hollywood biographies. This is true. But it is also true that violence, misfortune and sensation *do* make for exciting reading whereas less-eventful, but nevertheless faithful to life, stuff doesn't."

I'm sure Irene Slade was right. But I wasn't interested in having to inject sensation into Veronica's story. As far as I was concerned, it was wrenching and compelling just as it was without having to artificially hype it. But that represents me. Because I agreed with what Connie wanted to convey in her life story, I was her perfect collaborator. Other writers might have been more in tune with Irene Slade's feelings, and persuaded Veronica to allow them to juice things up. Each writer approaches a project with certain beliefs, strengths, weaknesses, and his or her own particular likes and dislikes.

I've always enjoyed smaller stories within the larger ones, "back stories" in Hollywood jargon. Because I'm a boxing fan, I would like to write a novel about the sport. But my interest isn't in wealthy world champions. My novel would be about the tank fighters, those brave guys who fight week after week for a couple of hundred bucks a night.

Veronica, despite her brief fling at stardom—she was once the highest paid female star, $4500 a week, and the hottest female box office draw—was a tank fighter who walked away from Hollywood and never looked back. While her glamour years are inherently fascinating, and are covered in detail in the book, it was a romance she had with a merchant marine seaman, Andy Elickson, who met her when she was waitressing at the Martha Washington Hotel in New York, that captured my heart and attention. The big, gruff sailor provided her with perhaps the truest happiness of her life, and his premature death from cancer was a brutal blow to this already emotionally battered woman. I've always felt that their relationship would make a wonderful book and film on its own, a gem of a smaller story.

*   *   *   *   *

I had a similar response to a smaller story in 1977 when I wrote a novel under my own name, *Club Tropique.*

I'd received a call from Joe Elder, an editor at Fawcett Books, who asked whether I'd be interested in doing a novel based upon Club Med, that hedonistic, sexually free (at that time) vacation phenomenon that had become so popular with young singles. I told Joe it didn't hold any interest for me.

"We'll pay all expenses for you and your wife to spend a week at one of the Club Med villages," he said, "and the advance will be good."

"Not interested," I said. I didn't elaborate. My pale Scottish skin and the sun are enemies. I dislike heat; Club Med villages were in hot climates. And I don't swim. Add to that the Club Med philosophy, feeding upon the sexual revolution of the 60s and 70s, which didn't interest me as a subject.

"Why don't you at least submit a budget?" Elder suggested.

I agreed to do that and pulled together some figures. My final item was $300 for suntan lotion. I really didn't want to do the book.

My budget was approved.

The week at Club Med's village on Martinique was interesting. I've always enjoyed researching background for my novels, and loaded a notebook and two cassette tapes with observations to use once I got back home and started writing. The novel reflected the highly charged sexual atmosphere of the village, hundreds of young, attractive singles playing the mating game, their inhibitions left at home. The sex scenes were plentiful, graphic, and appropriate. But within that setting emerged two characters who seemed very much out of place at Club Med. One was a big, burly, middle-aged truck driver with a large gut who guzzled beer day and night, and who expressed disdain at the antics of the younger men and women. The other character was a middle-aged woman with broad shoulders, heavy thighs and small breasts, nothing like the hundred nubile tanned young women who proudly displayed their trim bodies on the nude beach. Although these real characters never seemed to connect during the week I was there, I created a romance between them in the novel, finding each other with real affection in the midst of all the posturing and disingenuous affection displayed at Club Med. Their "smaller story" was without doubt the least sensational one in the novel, but they were my favorite characters. I named them Barney and Marie, and like the romance between Veronica and Andy Elickson, their story could stand-alone as a novel or film.

*   *   *   *   *

Numerous complications arose between the time I submitted the Veronica manuscript to W.H. Allen, and when it was finally published on January 20, 1969, not the least of which was a claim by Walter Minton of the publisher, G.P. Putnam & Sons, that he had paid Veronica $5,000 a few years earlier as a down payment for the exclusive rights to her autobiography. When I called and asked her about it, she confirmed that Minton had paid her the money, but said it had been only for a one-year option. According to her, she'd split the $5,000 with a writer named Ed Seaver. This legal imbroglio was eventually resolved when W.H. Allen gave G.P. Putnam & Sons first crack at the American edition of the book. Walter Minton declined the offer, and he eventually dropped his claim, which allowed the British edition to go forward.

Another problem that developed had to do with a poignant scene in the book. Although I'd checked virtually everything for accuracy that Connie had told me, some things slipped past, especially when an anecdote she'd related was highly detailed. That was the case with Richard Maibaum, writer and coproducer of *I Wanted Wings*. Veronica had made a point of being critical of Hollywood friendships and how they were seldom genuine. She used Maibaum as an example. She said that after the film had launched her to stardom, she learned that he was very ill and decided to visit him. Here's what the book says regarding that incident.

"His mother answered the door and led me to a small Spanish terrace in the back of the house. Dick sat there with his mother and we talked about *I Wanted Wings* and what I'd been doing lately. He brought up my elopement with John (John Detlie) and I recalled with warmth how Dick had come to my dressing room to offer his congratulations. He was so nice and comforting to a very young and scared girl in her first major role. A fine person . . . I didn't stay much longer. Dick was in pain and grew quite weary. I got up to leave and went over to give him a kiss. He took my hand in his and said, 'You know, Ronni (another name she was known by), you're the only one who's come to see me. The only one. I left before the tears did more than just well up in my eyes. He was dead of cancer not long after my visit."

Shortly after the book was published in England, Richard Maibaum walked into the publisher's office to announce that he was very much alive, despite what Veronica Lake had said in her autobiography. Fortunately, he wasn't the litigious type. All he asked for was a correction in subsequent editions. "Having people think I'm dead is bad for business," he said.

Whew!

Mark Goulden wanted Veronica to come to England to promote the book, which she agreed to do. But before that, Britain's BBC tracked her down in Florida and said it wanted to do a documentary on her life. I was contacted, too, and asked to participate in the production, which would be shot in New York. Veronica called to inform me that she was flying to New York and would be staying at the New York Hilton. The BBC had told me that it was not paying any of her expenses. I asked her about it.

"National Airlines is paying for everything, flights, hotel, everything, in exchange for plugs on the show," she said. I accepted what she said. I had no reason not to.

When I picked her up at the hotel the first morning of shooting, I was surprised to see that she was staying in one of the penthouse suites. She'd arrived the night before, and it was obvious from all the bottles of liquor and trays of food that a party had taken place. I didn't dwell on it because we were running late for the first set-up at Bill Roos' apartment.

It was a hectic day of filming around Manhattan. When I delivered Connie back to the Hilton early that evening, there were a half-dozen of her friends in the penthouse. They'd ordered up more booze and food from room service, and Connie happily joined the festivities. I begged off and went home to Long Island to get some sleep in anticipation of another busy day with her in the city. We were also to meet with Mark Goulden and his wife the next night at an apartment the British publisher maintained on Park Avenue. It would be the first time Veronica would meet him.

The following morning, partygoers were sprawled on couches

in the suite when I arrived. It took some doing, but I eventually got Connie out of there and to the next set-up where the BBC crew waited. At the end of that second day, I brought her back to the suite to change clothing before heading for Goulden's apartment. The party was still in progress, and Veronica insisted upon having a few drinks before leaving. I was concerned about two things: her drinking—she'd been drinking at each stop during the day and was already inebriated; and time. It was raining hard outside, which would make finding a cab difficult. But I didn't have any choice but to have a drink myself and wait for her to get ready.

For Connie, getting ready consisted of downing a few glasses of vodka, slipping out of her dress, and passing out on a couch wearing a bra and panties. I was in the process of trying to wake her when I was told there was someone from the hotel who wanted to speak to Miss Lake. I went to the door and was confronted by a young man who asked me to step into the hall. He introduced himself as an assistant manager, and explained why he'd come to the suite. When Veronica had checked in, she'd told the manager on duty that National Airlines was picking up the tab for a suite. They believed her. But now, after a couple of days in which the room service tab was mounting, someone decided to call the airline to confirm what she's said. No one at National knew anything about the alleged arrangement.

"Someone has to pay for this," the assistant manager told me. "Unless we're paid immediately, everyone has to leave. Now!"

I thought it was pretty stupid of the hotel to check in a guest without verifying that someone else was paying, but that really wasn't the issue at that moment.

"Look," I said, "Miss Lake is due at a very important meeting with her British publisher. We're already late. I'll instruct everyone inside to pack up and be ready to leave the minute we get back, which should be in a couple of hours. I'll give you my credit card, and you can put all the charges on it."

He agreed.

I returned to the suite and made my announcement, got Veronica to her feet, slipped a yellow rain slicker on over her underwear, plopped a yellow rain hat on her head, and herded her out the door.

Getting to Goulden's apartment was as difficult as I'd anticipated. There weren't any taxis to be found, so we walked there in the rain. My wife, who'd been invited to join us, was at the apartment when we arrived. Mr. and Mrs. Goulden, who were extremely proper, greeted us at the door. I introduced Veronica to them, and Mrs. Goulden offered to take Connie's coat.

"If you do," she replied, "you'll see my fucking undies."

It was a tense evening.

Veronica, my wife and I returned to the Hilton by cab. No one in the penthouse had taken seriously my announcement that we were leaving. I started yelling, which brought about some reaction. People grabbed unfinished liquor bottles and uneaten food while I packed some of Veronica's possessions in a suitcase. We left the suite in single file, more than a dozen of us, me at the head of the line holding up Veronica who'd managed to down some vodka while we were preparing to leave, my wife bringing up the rear carrying a large bouquet of flowers someone had sent Connie. We must have been quite a spectacle marching through the crowded lobby, under the watchful eye of the assistant manager.

It was still raining, and the line waiting for cabs beneath the hotel's expansive canopy was long, at least 50 people. I pushed to the head of the line and opened the rear door of the first cab that pulled in. People started yelling while I tried to maneuver Connie into the taxi. As I struggled with her, she slipped down through my arms, causing the yellow slicker to ride up to her neck. All I could think of was whether all those people around us realized that the woman on the sidewalk, wearing a bra and panties, was the famous movie actress, Veronica Lake. Someone from our contingent helped me get her into the cab. I climbed in with her and slammed the door shut against the rising voices outside.

"Get her out 'a here," the cab driver said.

"Why?" I asked.

"She'll throw up all over the cab."

"She hasn't thrown up in years," I said. "Come on, get going."

We went to Bill Roos' penthouse apartment, where we were joined by my wife and a few others who'd been at the hotel. As I came to learn would be the case with Veronica, she sobered up quickly and thoroughly enjoyed the rest of the evening.

I'd paid the hotel bill on my credit card—I don't have a clear recollection of how much it was, although I do know it was more than we had in our checking account. I got Veronica to agree that the publisher would reimburse me out of her share of proceeds from the book. That became a pattern. Connie would call me from various places she was staying (people would be charmed by her her and offer to put her up) to ask for money.

"Hello?"

"Don. It's Connie. Did I wake you?"

"Yes. It's three in the morning."

"It must be the time difference."

I was in New York. She was calling from New Jersey.

I ended up lending her a considerable amount of money, and did it willingly, although there were times when my inclination was to balk. "Give it to her," my wife would say, and I would. Despite the frequent frustration of dealing with Veronica—dealing with someone who drinks too much is always frustrating—there was a decent, human quality to her that transcended any difficulties she might have caused me. I liked her, and respected the survival mode she'd been in for a very long time.

Connie did travel to England to promote the book, but not without incident. The publisher had booked her on a highly rated TV show hosted by Eamonn Andrews, who had arranged to pay all her expenses, including air fare, hotels and meals. She never showed. She sent a telegram a few days later claiming she'd taken ill at a friend's house, and that there was no phone there. It was to be the first in a series of missteps that marked her first trip to Europe.

When she finally did arrive, she immediately asked Mark Goulden for spending money. He advanced her $500. She came back the next day to report she'd been mugged and that all the money had been stolen. She needed more.

She missed some appointments and bookings, but remarkably did a decent job overall of promoting her book in Great Britain, appearing on many TV and radio shows, and generating extensive feature articles in major newspapers. When she returned, she gleefully told me of the many fans and friends she'd met while touring England, and wanted very much to go back one day. In the meantime, W.H. Allen sold American publishing hardcover rights to Lyle Stuart's Citadel Press, and softcover rights to Bantam Books.

Lyle Stuart and I have been friends for many years. As anyone who follows publishing knows, he's the ultimate iconoclast, a stand-up guy who's always bucking trends and taking on controversial projects no other publisher would touch. Some of his books have been morally questionable, and I've expressed my dismay to him about them. We spent many hours together on Long John Nebel's all-night radio show in New York discussing the controversies that seem always to surround him, along with myriad other subjects in which we have a mutual interest. I've written books for Lyle, some of which are the subject of subsequent chapters. Allan Wilson, who edited the books, is one of the most gracious gentlemen I've met in my long career; one of the pleasures of writing those books was time spent with Allan, often at a favorite haunt of his, the bar at the Gramercy Park Hotel.

Lyle took a no-nonsense approach to Veronica when preparing for her to promote the U.S. edition in the States. He laid down the law, and it seemed to work. She showed up on time for appearances, and aside from a few awkward moments with interviewers when she'd been drinking prior to meeting them, things went relatively smoothly. I was on to writing other books and only heard reports from Lyle and his publicists on how things were going. The one time I did become directly involved with one of Veronica's appearances remains etched not only in my mind, but in the minds of thousands of listeners to Long John Nebel's all-night show.

Lyle had persuaded Nebel to book Connie on the show, and I was asked to appear with her. It was the first time I'd appeared on Long John's show, and couldn't know at the time that I would go on to become a regular on the program, appearing more than 200 times; become one of his closest friends; write his biography and that of his last wife, the famous model Candy Jones; and deliver the eulogy at his funeral.

This night, however, turned out to be a disaster. Connie had been drinking and displayed a belligerent side to Nebel's producer as we sat in the green room at WNBC waiting to go on at midnight. The atmosphere was uneasy, at best. I would learn later that Nebel had a hidden microphone in the Green Room, and could hear everything being said as he sat in his office waiting for the show to begin.

The opening ten minutes on the air went okay. Then, just before the first commercial break, Nebel asked Connie a question that she considered offensive (it wasn't). She leaned toward him and said, her words slow and slightly slurred, "You want to match wits with me? Go ahead."

Nebel paused, smiled, and replied, "Did you bring them with you this evening, Miss Lake?"

He signaled the engineer and a commercial began to play. Nebel politely told Veronica and me to leave. The interview was over. The tape of that brief exchange became one of Nebel's favorites in his archives of treasured on-air moments, and he played it on many occasions over the ensuing years.

Veronica and I stayed in touch for the rest of her life, sometimes when she'd call for money, most times just because she wanted to say hello. Whenever I saw her, she always had a small gift for me or someone in my family.

She'd returned to England for a brief period, staying in Ipswich with a retired British gentleman she'd met during her promotion tour. I visited her one day at his home, a pretty cottage on the water. I took a train from London, and a cab to the cottage. When I arrived, she was busy ironing his shirts; he was away on a trip to the Continent. I'd picked up lunch on my way, and we had a pleasant few hours together. She was happier than I'd ever seen her.

She'd done some acting after the book, a couple of low-budget horror movies filmed in Canada, dinner theater in Florida, and an impressive performance of *The World of Carl Sandburg* in Boston. While the book had been a critical success despite its lack of sensationalism, it was a failure at the cash register.

One day, I heard through Bill Roos that Veronica had married for a fourth time, her new husband a Florida commercial fisherman who called himself Captain Bob. A few months later, Roos told me she'd left Captain Bob to live with a sculptor friend in the Bahamas. Then, in late June, 1973, Connie was flown to Burlington, Vermont where she was admitted to a special alcoholism ward at the Medical Center of Vermont. Her liver and kidneys were failing, and the prognosis was grim.

I touched base there with a doctor who graciously kept me informed about her condition. In early July, he informed me that she was terminal and had only days to live. I made a decision after that phone conversation. Although I didn't know this Captain Bob, I was uncomfortable having whatever material possessions Veronica had go to a man with whom she'd spent only a few months, husband or not. Bill Roos had been Veronica's best friend, in my judgment, and I felt it only right that he be her beneficiary after all he'd given to her over the years.

I called a good friend, Joe McCartney, an attorney, film buff, and community theater actor who'd also appeared as an extra in dozens of movies. I asked Joe whether he would be willing to fly to Vermont with me and have Veronica execute a bedside will, leaving everything to Roos. He readily agreed. I booked two tickets for the next morning on a flight to Burlington. That night, I contacted Connie's physician in Vermont again to tell him of my plans.

"She's gone into a coma," he said. "She won't be coming out of it."

We cancelled the flight.

Veronica died July 7, 1973, of acute hepatitis. She was 51 years old.

I reached her mother in Brooklyn and informed her of her daughter's death. She told me she wasn't interested. I received basically the same message from one of Connie's two daughters; I couldn't locate the other. I called Bill Roos, and we decided to hold a memorial service for her in Manhattan. On Thursday, July 12, we gathered in a room at the Universal Funeral Chapel at Lexington Avenue and 52nd Street. My wife and I sent flowers; so did Roos. Those were the only flowers there. Whenever she was at Bill's apartment on a Sunday morning, she would tune in a radio evangelist; a Dr. Barker, whose sermons she enjoyed. I got hold of him and booked him to deliver a eulogy with a religious flavor for twenty-five dollars. I would give non-religious comments.

The night before the service, I received two phone calls. The first was from Captain Bob. After introducing himself as Connie's husband, he said he wanted to hold a memorial service for her in Florida.

"Great," I said.

"Well," he said," the problem is I'm a little short of cash. I thought maybe since you wrote the book with her that you'd send me some money so we could have a fitting tribute to her."

I told him that was out of the question and ended the conversation.

The second call was from Veronica's son, Michael. He'd come from Hawaii with his girlfriend to be at his mother's funeral, which he'd assumed would be held in Vermont. That's where he was. Could I send him some money for them to fly to New York?

"No," I said.

"You want me at my mother's funeral, don't you?" he said angrily.

"I don't care whether you're here or not," I said.

He showed up the next day wearing torn jeans, a T-shirt, and rubber thongs on bare feet. His girlfriend was very pregnant and dressed similarly. There weren't many people at the service, more press than mourners, including all the leading tabloids. Dr. Barker gave a canned eulogy that had nothing to do with the deceased, took his twenty-five dollar check, and split. I talked about Connie, not the movie actress, but the human being, Constance Ockleman. Michael sold a story on the spot about his mother to one of the tabloids in attendance, in return for a hotel room for a couple of nights and Lord knows what else. I didn't care.

Afterwards, some of us went to a local restaurant. Because I'd agreed to pay for the service, people chipped in—a hundred dollars each from McCartney, Sam Post and a singer, Joe Garri, and a hundred and twenty-five from Nat Perlow. I promised to reimburse them should any money come in from future book sales.

Two sources of money did surface. The first was Veronica's Social Security death benefit, $225. Captain Bob had put in for it as her husband, but I fought to receive that money as the one who'd paid all her burial expenses, as well as $300 to the Corbin & Palmer Funeral Home in Burlington where Connie had been cremated.

I won my battle with Social Security. And the American Federation of Television and Radio Artists (AFTRA) sent $359.73 from its George Heller Memorial Special Welfare Fund. I paid everybody back and that was the end of it.

Until, in March 1976, Bill Roos called. Veronica's ashes had remained at the Burlington funeral home, and he wondered what we should do about them. She'd always said that when she died, she wanted her ashes "strewn over southern waters." He and Dick Toman were heading for Florida and thought it might be a good time to fulfill her wish. I called the funeral home. Two hundred dollars was still owed on the bill. I sent them a check, and they sent the ashes to Bill and Dick, who went out on a boat off Florida and laid Veronica Lake to her final rest.

CHAPTER TEN

"DAMN! THE TAPE IS BLANK!"

If I thought I'd been busy in 1967, it was nothing compared to what 1968 and 1969 held in store.

With the Veronica Lake manuscript delivered in January 1968, I huddled with Dan O'Shea trying to decide what book would be next. Actually, one was already in the talking stage. Sam Post at Bartholomew House informed us he wanted to do another book in the *Coffee, Tea or Me?* vein, but not a direct sequel by Rachel Jones and Trudy Baker. (Those would come later, three of them, with a different publisher.)

When we met, I suggested applying the same lighthearted, frothy, humorous formula to nurses. Sam liked the idea. I then added another dimension to the concept: "Let's make them military nurses," I said.

Based upon Sam's assurance that a contract and a sizable advance were forthcoming, I informed John and Peter Peckham that I was leaving their production company to pursue a full-time freelance writing career. They were sorry to see me go, which mirrored my feelings. Peckham Productions was a good place to work, the atmosphere congenial, the films produced of the highest quality. The company, now based in Westchester, continues to turn out good work under Pete and Wally's stewardship. John died six years after I'd left the company, and I joined a number of people at the hospital the night he succumbed to lung cancer. Once, when he'd drifted back into consciousness, he asked me to come back to work for him. I agreed, of course. He also said we should buy uniforms so that we all were dressed alike. A good idea, I told him. He passed away a few hours later, a talented man gone too soon.

When the contract and advance from Bartholomew House didn't come through after a month, we queried Sam about it. There was a problem. Before signing the contract, Sam's boss, Fred Klein, wanted to personally approve the two military nurses who would front the book. We didn't have two such female creatures. We'd intended to find them after the book had been written.

This set off a mad scramble to find young women with backgrounds as military nurses, who would be interested in promoting the book as its ostensible authors. Dan made contact with a distant family member who had access to military records, who in turn gave us the names and backgrounds of a dozen women, each of whom had either previously served on active duty, or were currently in the service. We interviewed six or seven in New York, none of whom worked out, either because we didn't want them, or because they decided getting involved in such a venture was a dumb idea.

The search took us into May when Dan and I flew to Los Angeles to interview a pretty, vivacious young Air Force nurse named Diana. (The agreement with the two women stipulated that their identities would remain secret; I'll only use first names.)

We met Diana at O'Shea's father's Beverly Hills apartment where the walls were covered with original costume and set designs from *Gone With The Wind*. Her fiancé, who accompanied her, was a serious young man who expressed concern that she would be portrayed in the book as immoral. We assured him that wasn't the case; the subsequent agreements drawn with the women contained a clause protecting their moral images.

From Los Angeles, we flew to Atlanta to interview Nancy, a tall, attractive blonde Air Force nurse with a charming drawl. She, too, expressed concern that her moral image might be sullied. We gave her the same assurances we'd given Diana, and she signed on to the project.

Fred Klein kept insisting that he personally meet with our two young women, but was eventually convinced that it was too difficult logistically, and settled for photos of them. The contract and advance ($10,000) finally came through for a book, *Tender Loving Care*, by Joni Moura and Jackie Sutherland—and dedicated to me, of course. Bill "Call me William" Wenzel agreed to lend his no-knees style to the illustrations. And Rachel Jones and Trudy Baker of *Coffee, Tea or Me?* fame provided a glowing quote for the cover: *"What a book! And we thought airline stewardesses were the biggest swingers."*

* * * * *

The period from January through May 1968 wasn't devoted exclusively to finding our two nurses. I had long been interested in the growing conflict between the rights of the commercial airlines, and private pilots, more important the safety risk private pilots posed for airline passengers in congested airspace surrounding major cities. I'd done my flying in the relatively empty skies over Indiana and Cape Cod. But once I'd moved back to New York, I stopped flying because I didn't have the time to become sufficiently proficient to safely navigate that busy airspace.

I wrote a proposal, *The Case Against Private Aviation*, and Dan submitted it to Bob Meskill at Cowles Book Company, the book publishing division of Cowles Communications, publishers of LOOK Magazine. Cowles bought it; the advance was $7,500 for the hardcover edition. There was an unusual provision in the agreement that I hadn't seen before, nor have I seen since. Cowles insisted I take out a life insurance policy on myself, with Cowles as the beneficiary, to be paid in the event I died in an aircraft accident. My insurance agent tacked on a rider to an existing policy, which satisfied them.

My work was cut out for me. Besides having to write *Tender Loving Care*, I was now up to my ears in researching the aviation book. I accessed all the usual resources (this was pre-Internet days), and began a series of trips to Washington to interview people at the Federal Aviation Administration (FAA), the agency responsible for aviation safety, and the National Transportation Safety Board (NTSB), which investigates aircraft accidents. The FAA has always had a questionable reputation, the primary charge that it places airline profitability above safety considerations. I made a dozen trips to Washington, always staying at the Hotel National, a haven for foreign students, where I paid $7.50 a day for the best room in the place, a one-bedroom suite.

I haunted the FAA without much success in getting to interview its top people. Then one day, I received a call at the hotel from Ralph Lovering, special assistant to the assistant administrator for general aviation affairs. (His answers to my questions turned out to be as long and convoluted as his title.) He would meet with me the following morning. The focus of my interview had to do with near-misses between aircraft. In that year alone, there would be 2,230 such incidents reported by pilots.

Lovering was a tall, distinguished gentleman whose office was huge; two of its walls were floor-to-ceiling windows overlooking the Mall. I plopped my small tape recorder on his desk and started citing statistics about near misses. Lovering was gracious enough at the start of the interview, but grew visibly impatient when I failed to acknowledge that his long, twisted responses made sense. In frustration, he got up from behind his large desk and told me to follow him to one of the windows. It was a beautiful morning in Washington, sunny and with a pristine blue sky. He pointed out the window. "See any airplanes out there, Mr. Bain?"

"No, not at the moment."

"Then where's the problem with near misses? There's a lot of sky out there, plenty of space for everyone."

He smiled. That was it. It didn't matter that pilots of both commercial airliners and private aircraft were reporting near miss incidents every day. The problem didn't exist as long as this bureaucrat couldn't see it out his window.

I worked day and night on the book and continued to set up interviews, including members of Congress who'd taken a position in the matter. One such interview was memorable for the wrong reasons.

I caught an early morning American flight from LaGuardia Airport in New York to interview Westchester Congressman Richard Ottinger in his Washington office. His schedule was tight, I was told. Be there promptly. We taxied out and got into a long line of planes waiting to take off. I kept checking my watch; I'd be okay if we got off the ground soon. The captain announced we were now second in line, and should arrive in Washington close to schedule. I breathed a sigh of relief . . . until an anguished male voice wailed behind me, "Washington? I'm going to Boston!"

To my shock, and everyone else on board, the captain, after being informed by a flight attendant of the confused passenger, elected to get out of line and taxi back to the gate to let him off. I didn't know who I wanted to strangle more, the passenger or the captain.

Fortunately, Congressman Ottinger found time for me when I finally arrived. It was a good interview, filled with useful information for the book. I went to a coffee shop when it was over and turned on my recorder. Blank! It hadn't worked. I spent the next hour frantically trying to resurrect what Ottinger had said, and getting it down on paper. I learned a lesson that day. Ever since that morning I've become a belt-and-suspenders interviewer, running two recorders whenever possible, and stopping the interview now and then to be sure they're working.

The *Case Against Private Aviation* received considerable attention when it was published on November 13, 1969, thanks in part to an aggressive marketing campaign by the folks at Cowles. Robert Serling, former aviation editor of UPI, said this about it: *"The Case Against Private Aviation is a gutty book with the enormous virtue of being hard-hitting and fair at the same time . . . As one who has worked and written in the field of air safety for nearly 30 years, I found uncomfortably little in Bain's book with which to disagree . . . Bain's book deserves to be widely read—and heeded."*

Other reviews were equally as positive, except for some that appeared in publications sympathetic to the private aviation industry (more commonly known as general aviation), and particularly to the Aircraft Owners and Pilots Association (AOPA), an aggressive lobbying group for general aviation pilots.

Cowles scheduled an ambitious national promotional tour, which I looked forward to although it came at such a busy time. Prior to my embarking on it, AOPA took out a full-page ad in *Broadcasting* Magazine, claiming that the book was filled with distortions, half-truths and scare tactics. The ad put every radio and TV talk show on notice that if I was booked as a guest to promote the book, someone from AOPA should be there to set the record straight.

My initial media appearances were in New York, starting with the Martha Deane radio show on WOR. That's when the trouble started. Max Karant, AOPA's chief spokesman, showed up and appeared with me. The program had no sooner started when Karant, a stocky, gruff talking guy, delivered a telling blow. He cited the cover of the book on which the following line appeared: *"The half million noncommercial aircraft now using the airways have created a new and perilous problem."* As he read it, his voice thick with scorn, I immediately realized the problem. Whoever had written the cover copy had mixed up statistics. There were a half million private *pilots*, not aircraft.

"Even the cover is wrong," said Karant. "How can you trust anything in the book when even the cover lies?"

I spent the entire show defending myself and blaming the publisher for the mistake. Needless to say, it was an ineffective defense, but there was nothing I could do about it. I traveled the country appearing on local radio and TV shows, and Karant, who flew his own twin-engine plane, showed up at every one, pointing out the mistake on the cover, and thoroughly dashing my credibility.

As a result of the book, I was invited to testify in November 1969 before a Congressional committee on airline safety, a heady experience. The book, and perhaps my appearance before the committee, contributed to needed rule changes at the FAA, including a prohibition on drinking before flying. The existing rule said only that thou shalt not fly when under the influence of alcohol or drugs. The airlines all imposed their own strict standards about drinking and flying, but private pilots were free to down a few at the airport bar and then take off in their small planes, competing in the same airspace as commercial planes loaded with passengers. Who was to determine when they were "under the influence?" I felt good having played some role in improving flying safety; *The Case Against Private Aviation* was my Ralph Nader shot in life.

Another plus that came out of having written *The Case Against Private Aviation* was to become a close friend to one of the most remarkable men I've ever known, Long John Nebel, the king of late night talk radio in New York. I was booked on the show to discuss the book. With Nebel was his attorney at the time, Kenneth Knigin, a bombastic guy who slashed at me for six hours as though I was under cross-examination. Which I was in a sense. I evidently held my own because I received a call a week later from Nebel's producer, Anne Lombardo, asking if I'd like to join the show as a regular panelist. I did, and went on to appear on more than 200 shows with Nebel, write his biography and that of his controversial wife, former model Candy Jones, and end up delivering one of two eulogies at his funeral. The Nebel years were among the most interesting of my life and career; they deserve a chapter of their own later in this book.

*   *   *   *   *

While researching, writing and promoting the aviation book, I continued to work on *Tender Loving Care*. The writing went smoothly; dealing with our two military nurses didn't. I received two letters in early March. The first was from our southern belle, Nancy, responding to the page proofs of the book that I'd sent for her perusal. She said among other things: *". . . after reviewing the book, I feel very strongly that my moral interests have not been protected in writing it, it being my feeling that the book includes numerous passages which reflect unfavorably upon my moral character."*

I found her stance to be confusing as well as amusing. What could she possibly find offensive in a book intended to be humorous and lighthearted? The sign still hung over my desk: **Boys chasing girls but no heavy breathing**.

My reaction didn't matter, however. The second letter was from her attorney. Nancy with the laughing face and prolonged drawl was history. Fortunately, Diana contacted a friend, Linda, who agreed to take Nancy's place, and we were able to go forward.

Finding a replacement for Nancy proved to be an academic exercise. When *Tender Loving Care* was published in March 1969, there were ambitious plans to send Diana and Linda on tour. But Diana had married her caring boyfriend who'd expressed concern at how she would be portrayed in the book, and become pregnant, which prompted legal concern at the publisher about touring her in her delicate condition. Too, advance sales of the hardcover were running at a pace in excess of *Coffee, Tea or Me?* Although Mark Greenberg, VP of marketing at Bartholomew House, never said so, O'Shea and I were convinced that the publisher had cut back on plans to tour the nurses to save money.

None of it mattered. *Tender Loving Care* was a big success in bookstores, and ended up on a number of bestseller lists around the country. Dozens of reviews were favorable, with only an occasional bad one. One reviewer compared the writing to the humorist, Max Shulman, which thrilled me. I'd always been a Shulman fan.

Ralph Daigh of Fawcett bought the paperback rights for $50,000; that the subject matter didn't lend itself to Indians on the cover presumably made it easier for him to make that decision. And Hollywood came calling, including my old buddy, Mark Carliner, who tried to option the book for either a 90-minute made-for-TV movie on CBS, or a half hour pilot for a sitcom series. Producer William Dozier, and the Spelling-Goldberg organization also attempted to cobble together performing rights deals, but they never worked.

Fawcett launched its softcover edition with an initial printing of 315,000, and went back to press a week later for an additional 50,000 copies. (Eventually it would print almost a million books.) *Tender Loving Care* continued to sell well into the early 70s, which made everyone happy. Although Diana and Linda weren't called upon to do much, they collected their respective ten percent of all monies earned until the book finally went out of print. Diana and her family became friends after that, and we kept in touch for many years. She was an exemplary young woman, and I assume she and her family are doing well.

*   *   *   *   *

My *Coffee, Tea or Me?* saga lasted 17 years. At least that's how long the original book and its three sequels continued to spin off royalties.

I wrote the first of the sequels in 1969. It was titled *The Coffee, Tea or Me Girl's 'Round-the-World-Diary,* and was published in 1970. Sam Post had wanted to produce a sequel at Bartholomew House, but Fred Klein vetoed the idea for reasons known only to him. Alan Barnard at Bantam Books, who'd published the paperback version of the original and saw it on every bestseller list in the nation, including the hallowed *New York Times,* brought us together with editors at Grosset & Dunlap who offered a three-book hardcover contract, with Bantam committed to publishing the softcover editions.

The second sequel, *The Coffee, Tea or Me Girls Lay it on the Line*, came out in 1972. And *The Coffee, Tea or Me Girls Get Away From it All* was published in 1974.

All in all, the four books by Rachel and Trudy were translated into a dozen languages, and sold more than 5-million copies worldwide.

Not bad for the punch line of an old airline joke.

CHAPTER ELEVEN

HAVING FUN AND
MAKING MONEY

Although I was now firmly entrenched in a writing career, other interests kept creating new opportunities too appealing to pass up.

I was doing a lot of playing on weekends, including a nine-month run of Friday nights as a drummer at a jazz club in Huntington, Long Island; and later, a year of Fridays on vibes at Bill's Steak House on the Island's south shore, the quintet led by jazz clarinetist Charles Nostrand. I would play hundreds of gigs with Nostrand over the course of my life, even as recently as 2001 when we performed jazz concerts in Long Island parks.

But music wasn't the only activity I managed to work into the writing schedule.

I received a call one Friday morning in 1969 from my former boss and mentor at American Airlines, Red Sutherland. He was now gone from American and enjoying life in his house in West Hampton Beach, which he'd personally designed and helped build. Most days, you had to use ship-to-shore to reach him on a 35-foot commercial fishing dragger he'd bought and refurbished. He was no weekend sailor. His favorite time to go out on the water was early morning when the fog had rolled in and kept everyone else at the dock. He enjoyed the challenge of using sophisticated navigation equipment to reach a destination, anchor, cook himself a hot breakfast in the galley, and spend the day on the water working on a novel he was writing.

"'Morning, Kid. How goes it?'"

"Things are good," I said. "What's up?"

"How would you like to have some fun and make money, too?"

"Just tell me how."

The next morning, Saturday, I drove to West Hampton Beach where Red outlined the project over breakfast. Willis Player, American Airlines' vice president of public relations, a man for whom Red and I had the greatest respect, had left American to head up Pan Am's PR efforts. He'd taken with him Gayle Williams, another highly regarded PR pro who knew as much about airline operations and marketing as anyone in the business.

A new era in commercial aviation was on the horizon, spearheaded by Pan Am and the Boeing Company. The airline and Boeing had developed what would become the world's first jumbo jet, the huge 747. Player was putting together a team to promote the new aircraft, including outside consultants to augment his excellent PR staff. Sutherland was the first person he'd called, and I was the first person Red asked to join the team.

Although I knew the project would be time-consuming and involve lots of travel, I didn't hesitate to sign on that morning. The money was good. More important, it was an opportunity to work with Red again, and to be involved in commercial aviation.

The launch of the 747 was an exhilarating time. Aside from countless planning sessions at Pan Am, I found myself deeply involved in two particular aspects of the promotion. Red designated me the cockpit commentator on dozens of promotional flights we made with one of the early aircraft. I rode in the cockpit jump seat as we crisscrossed the country taking local press, politicians and business leaders up for introductory rides. I used the aircraft's PA system to inform the hundreds of invited guests in the rear about the aircraft—it could be configured to carry as many as 490 passengers, although Pan Am's version accommodated 370 passengers. It was twenty feet wide; four times around the passenger cabin was the equivalent of walking a half-mile. I proudly spoke of the plane's technological sophistication; it had three internal navigation systems of the type used in NASA's space flights, one controlling the plane's route, a second checking on the accuracy of the first, and the third a backup. Sixteen first-class passengers had access to a lounge and bar in the distinctive "bulge" on the aircraft's second story. All in all, the 747 was a truly remarkable aviation achievement, a monument to Pan Am's commitment to the future.

Sitting up front with Pan Am's consummate pros, a captain, first officer, and flight engineer, was a privilege. One day, the crew shot hands-off instrument landings at Kennedy Airport, all the controls moving without the aid of human hands, the captain taking the yoke only a few feet from the runway. Red had been right; I was making money, and having the time of my life doing it.

My other primary responsibility was to handle the press in Roswell, New Mexico, where Pan Am had entered into an agreement to use an abandoned military base with a long runway to train pilots transitioning from the 707 to the new jumbo. I spent many weeks in Roswell, a town that had fallen on hard times when the Air Force pulled out years earlier. (More recently, it's been home to the flying saucer crowd.)

Members of the press arrived almost daily. Each morning at five, the reporters and I climbed aboard one of the 747s designated for training and spent hours with each crew as it became familiar with the aircraft, shooting takeoff and landing after takeoff and landing, the instructor pilot killing engines immediately after liftoff to create emergency situations; performing airborne maneuvers while flying over the rugged landscape that surrounded Roswell. I was constantly surprised at how quickly these veteran pilots made the transition from the much smaller 707. Their biggest problem, they often said, was depth perception; the 747's cockpit is located on the upper level of the plane, 35 feet off the ground, considerably higher than the 707's.

I spent a total of six weeks in Roswell. That phase of the project was an unqualified success, although a problem did emerge at the end of my stay.

At the time, Pan Am's president and CEO was Najeeb Halaby, a handsome, charismatic Arab-American whose daughter, Lisa, would marry King Hussein of Jordan in 1970 and become Queen Noor of Jordan. Her father had been many things—lawyer, Navy test pilot, a JFK Democrat, and former administrator of the Federal Aviation Agency (FAA). He'd been brought in to run the airline by its founder Juan Trippe, who'd begun huddling with Boeing as early as 1964 to develop a jumbo jet to accommodate what Trippe was certain to be an explosion in air travel, which ultimately didn't happen, at least not soon enough to pull the airline out of its increasingly desperate financial situation.

I was told during my second week in Roswell that the airline had decided to make its training facility there permanent, and was instructed by New York to make that announcement. The citizens of this depressed town were ecstatic. Pan Am's presence would mean jobs, and an infusion of money into Roswell's stores and services. Local politicians were so happy, they declared "Pam Am Day." All schools and business were closed, and a parade was held up the main street featuring school bands, local service groups, and anyone else capable of walking.

The day after the parade, I received a call from Sutherland. Najeeb Halaby himself was coming to Roswell: "Roll out the red carpet," Red instructed.

I not only arranged for a red carpet in front of the town's best restaurant, I planned a luncheon in it for Halaby and Roswell's leading citizens.

Halaby arrived by Falcon executive jet at eleven in the morning. I was at the airport to greet him. He stepped off the private jet with a sweater casually slung over one shoulder, his "uniform" when making public appearances. After much fuss at the airport, a limo whisked him to the luncheon; he was scheduled to leave Roswell at two. After he'd entered the restaurant, I was approached by reporters from a local TV and radio station, who asked me during an interview whether Halaby had come to officially announce the airline's plans to make Roswell a permanent training base.

"I assume so," I replied. I said a few other things, too, like "We're looking forward to a long and mutually beneficial relationship between Pan Am and Roswell." I said it because that's what I'd been told by corporate headquarters in New York.

I went inside to join the luncheon. Halaby got up and made a few brief remarks over coffee and desert. I couldn't believe my ears. He announced that at the end of the initial 747 training program, only a few months away, Pan Am would be pulling out and establishing a permanent training base elsewhere. There was stunned silence as he tossed his sweater over his shoulder, strode from the room, and was gone.

Leaving me there as Pan Am's spokesman.

I stayed a few more weeks, but my enthusiasm was no longer what it had been. I was now the enemy instead of the popular young man who'd brought good news to Roswell. I couldn't wait to leave. Sutherland flew in a few days before I was scheduled to depart, having stopped on his way in Dallas to pick up a pair of custom cowboy boots and a Stetson.

"Cheer up, Kid," he told me. "A hundred years from now, nobody will remember."

I'm sure he was right, although roughly 30 years later, I still remember it as though it had happened yesterday. Seventy years to go.

The 747 launch project garnered a Silver Anvil award from the Public Relations Society of America (PRSA). I shared the pride of everyone at the dinner when Willis Player got up to accept the award. But it wasn't the last project for Pan Am with which I'd become involved.

*   *   *   *   *

In 1980, Pan Am merged with National Airlines, which had started as an intra-state Florida airline in 1934, expanded to a national airline 10 years later, and eventually became an international carrier. Pan Am wanted to merge in order to create a domestic route structure to feed into its vast international operations.

Willis Player sought to gain public support for the merger in advance of any government anti-trust decision. Red Sutherland was called upon again to aid that effort, which brought me into the picture. My proposal was to create teams of Pan Am flight attendants to go out across the country and make the case for the merger, stressing how it would benefit local communities. I conducted hundreds of interviews in a dozen cities and chose ten young women for their poise, intelligence, and potential as media guests. After three weeks of training, they were sent out in five teams of two, making radio and TV appearances on talk shows, giving interviews to the print press, and delivering speeches before local civic and fraternal groups. We won that battle; the merger was approved. But the "war" was another thing. Like the introduction of the 747, what should have been a boost to Pan Am's fortunes backfired. The airline's large fleet of 747s took off day after day only half full. And the marriage of Pan Am and National proved to be virtually impossible to make work. The two airlines' pilots unions fought over seniority and work rules, and the aircraft in each carrier's fleet were so incompatible that cross training of crews, and maintenance of the planes, turned out to be a nightmare. Our PR project succeeded. The merger was a failure.

*   *   *   *   *

The third major project in which I became involved came a few years after the merger effort. Once again, Player wanted to mount a national campaign to boost the image of Pan Am, whose fortunes continued to sink. Management's bad decisions, coupled with some bad luck, was taking its toll on the airline that had opened the world to air travel and become synonymous with American aviation innovation.

I met with Red and presented an ambitious plan. Whether we could sell it to Player and his people was conjecture. It was worth a try. We would pull every flight attendant's personnel record and cull those who held private pilot's licenses. Out of thousands, I was certain there would be at least a few dozen. Once we chose a crew of three, we would dress them in designer jumpsuits and train them for media appearances. The key was whether we would be successful in persuading a private plane manufacturer, like Piper or Cessna, to lend us a plane that we could paint white, and put the familiar Pan Am blue ball on its tail. If we pulled that off, we'd send the three pilot-rated flight attendants off on an old-fashioned barnstorming tour, flying from town to town and city to city, carrying the Pan Am message.

It worked. One of the reasons was an advocate we found in Jim Arey, a PR executive at Pan Am, who guided our effort through management minefields. Jim and I worked closely together throughout the project; he was one of the nicest, brightest men I'd ever met. I introduced him to Dan O'Shea, who sold a book Jim had written, *The Sky Pirates*, a history of skyjacking.

With Arey's unflappable help, we found our high-flying threesome, got Piper to give us the plane, trained the gals, and off they went. It was wildly successful. A team of us traveled ahead to drum up local interest in their arrival, which proved easy. Hundreds of people, including media, showed up at the airports when they made their pass overhead, landed, and stepped out smartly in their sky blue jumpsuits. They wowed the crowd and interviewers; I'd never seen a PR project generate so much press. Our flying emissaries were attractive, bright, and personable. And they were good pilots. I got to fly with them on a half dozen legs of their cross-country trips, and was constantly impressed with their professionalism at the controls.

My memories of those months with Pan Am's own "Amelias" are numerous and wonderful. But it ended up another example of a PR project succeeding (it won another Silver Anvil award from PRSA), while the larger goal failed. As most people know, Pan Am sold off many of its holdings in a valiant attempt to remain in business, including selling its Pacific routes to United. In advance of the sale to United, and to celebrate the 50th Anniversary of having opened up the Pacific to air travel by sending its "China Clippers" across the ocean, Pan Am recreated that adventuresome journey by flying a 747 to all the stops made a half century ago. Jeff Kriendler, Pam Am's PR spokesman at the time, asked me to write the script for the trip, which included a dozen stops at which speeches were to be made. It was one of many writing assignments given me by Kriendler over the years, each one of them enjoyable because of his pleasant professionalism.

My Pan Am experiences ended with the airline's bankruptcy. Much of the work I did for it was paid in barter; I would be called to write a speech for a top executive, state my price, and that amount would be credited to an account at the airline. Whenever I wanted to travel overseas, I simply called and was issued first class tickets, their worth deducted from my account. I should have taken greater advantage of it. When the airline went belly-up, I had $17,000 in my account, all of which instantly disappeared. But I never really cared. The privilege of working with the dedicated people of Pan Am, and being allowed to put into motion those three major PR projects, was payment enough.

But what I especially loved was working with R.H. "Red" Sutherland." He could be arrogant, even bullying at times, but I've never known a man so willing to stand behind his convictions. Once, during the flying flight attendants project, Red called a meeting of everyone involved to discuss a problem. The meeting was scheduled for nine o'clock one morning at Pan Am headquarters in the Pan Am Building. Red wouldn't physically be there. He sent me to represent him, and told me to place a call to him on his boat after everyone had gathered.

There were those in Pan Am's PR hierarchy who disliked Red's brashness and brusqueness, and who held a similar view of me by extension. I was Red's boy. And Red was Willis Player's "boy."

I sat in the conference room with a dozen blue and gray suits, including Jim Arey who found Red's approach to things to be amusing, and effective. He was squarely in our corner even though it was awkward for him with some of his colleagues.

The ranking executive, Harvey Katz, placed the call to Red's dragger, anchored somewhere in the Great South Bay.

Red answered. "Hello."

"Hello, Red," Katz said. "We're all here and ready to go."

"Yeah, well get back to me in ten, fifteen minutes. I'm just getting breakfast off the stove."

He hung up.

Everyone looked at me; I squirmed in my chair and avoided their disbelieving eyes. I couldn't believe it either. Here were a bunch of highly paid executives being told by someone who didn't even work there to cool their heels while he ate breakfast.

Arey intervened and brought up other issues to kill time until the second call was made. This time, Red had finished eating and was ready to talk.

Jim Arey died of pancreatic cancer. Red died, too, of cancer. He checked into the VA hospital in Manhattan for tests, and was scheduled for surgery the following day to biopsy spots on his lungs. I spent the afternoon with him at the hospital. I was getting ready to leave at five when he said, "Know what I did last night, Kid?"

"No What?"

"I had a couple of belts. Bourbon."

"Good for you," I said.

"I'm scared."

"I know," I said. "I'd be, too."

The next day, as I was about to leave with my family for a Cape Cod vacation, Red's wife, Mabel called. She was the perfect wife for Red, almost as large as he was, and with a sense of humor necessary to live with him.

"Red had the surgery," she said.

"Great. How did it go?"

"It went fine. But he died a few minutes ago in the recovery room. The cancer was everywhere, even some shoots of it into his heart."

I cried.

"Just as well, I suppose," she said. "The doctors said he wouldn't have had much time anyway. Better to go in his sleep like this."

I could only agree.

I saw Mabel a few weeks later when I provided the band to play Red and Mabel's daughter's wedding in Westhampton Beach. Red had asked me months earlier to provide the music. We told Red Sutherland stories during intermissions, and laughed a lot.

But I feel a pervasive sadness to this day that he's no longer here. No one's called me "Kid" since he died. I really miss that.

CHAPTER TWELVE

BACK IN THE SADDL AGAIN

By the time 1970 rolled around, I'd established a reputation within the publishing industry as a writer who could turn fluff into gold. Well, maybe not gold, but certainly sterling silver. The success of the light, frothy, sometimes silly books about stewardesses and nurses had publishers contacting Dan O'Shea to see whether I wanted to write more books in that vein. I did.

I was still working as a consultant for Pan Am, playing jazz gigs on weekends, and appearing with some regularity on the Long John Nebel Show from midnight til six in the morning, but there was plenty of time—or seemed to be—to sit at the typewriter and add to my publishing credentials. I came up with the idea of a *Coffee, Tea or Me?* type of book featuring office temporary workers, "temps" as they're called. Dan sold it to Harvey Gardner, senior editor at Fawcett, and we huddled over a few lunches to come up with a title and approach. Kelly Girls was the biggest temp agency in the country. Why not call it *The Kelly Girls?* Dan knew Bob Hayes, the New York manager for Kelly Services (O'Shea seemed to know everyone, in every business). If we could get Kelly Services' management to bless a book with its corporate name as the title, there would be built-in promotional opportunities through their hundreds of offices.

Hayes liked the idea. He saw it as a win-win situation. The books would receive publicity, and so would Kelly Girls. He arranged for us to meet someone from top management named Cosgrove at Kelly Service's corporate headquarters in Detroit, and Dan and I flew there early one morning. The meeting went well; we returned to New York confident we had a deal.

We were wrong.

Not long after our meeting, I received a certified letter from one Cedric A. Richner, Jr., director of Kelly Girls legal department. It was a long, awkwardly written letter (why do all lawyers think they can write?). The letter was filled with clumsy legal jargon, as well as threats making it clear that if anyone in the book so much as whispered "Kelly Girls," I could count on Sing Sing as my next residence.

Okay. Who needed Kelly Girls? I named the fictitious temp agency in the book *Girlpower*, made it the title, and started to write. The premise was simple. Because office temps find themselves working in different businesses and industries every week, the book's two "authors" would analyze the men in those diverse business settings, and weave their tales about what it was like to work for them. (I always thought it was a perfect premise for a television sitcom.) The names I used for the two office temps, and authors, were Kathy Cole and Donna Bain. Donna Bain is a favorite cousin of mine and I was confident she wouldn't sue.

But I couldn't resist making an editorial comment about Kelly Girls in the book. Here's part of what I wrote in the foreword.

"Girlpower is our creation. To our knowledge there is no office temporary agency named Girlpower. We decided to use a false name because the management of Kelly Girl, a real agency, got uptight when we asked them if we could use *their* name.

"They took the time and corporate effort to write us a letter. That was thoughtful; who ever said big business doesn't have a heart? It was sent Certified and Registered . . . The mailman made us sign papers and forms and cards and slips so that Kelly Girl would know we received their letter. The letter said, in part:

"'. . . we wish to affirm our verbal admonishments regarding the use of our proprietary and exclusive rights in and to the terms 'Kelly,' 'Kelly Girl,' 'Kelly Girls,' 'Kelly Services,' and any abbreviation or derivation thereof as used in the temporary help business we conduct . . . .'"

"*Whew!*" I wrote as Kathy Cole and Donna Bain. "It's a good thing neither of us are named Kelly or we'd be in big trouble putting our names on this book."

In retrospect, it was silly of me to take a shot at Kelly Services that way, and probably foolhardy, considering there was a Cedric A. Richner, Jr. lurking out there. But it seemed right at the time.

Girlpower was published in 1971, with a blurb on the cover from Rachel Jones and Trudy Baker of *Coffee, Tea or Me?* fame: "If you liked our book about girls in the air, you'll love this one about girls who really fly in the office!" Because my name was on the cover, albeit as a female, I saw no need to dedicate this one to me.

The book took off. Big Wilson, who did the morning show on WNBC in New York, provided a quote: "Everybody, especially secretaries, will love this book. Here's office intrigue, office sex, and office asininity as seen by a pair of sharp-eyed, and well-stacked, lovable and able kids from GIRLPOWER."

O'Shea and I signed up two delightful young women, Lynn Leggett and Ingrid King, who'd worked as office temps, to assume the identity of the authors; they did a 15 city promotional tour during which they appeared on many radio and TV shows. Suzette McKiernan, an outside publicist hired to assist Phyllis White, Fawcett's PR director, put together a solid promotional package that paid off. Notes from Harvey Gardner and Ralph Daigh indicated that Fawcett kept going back to press to meet consumer demand.

It was another winner, and not a lawsuit in sight.

Until a letter addressed to "The Misses Kathy Cole and Donna Bain" arrived from London. It was from one Ann Petrie, who informed The Misses Cole and Bain that there was, indeed, a temporary employment agency called Girlpower, and that the same Miss Petrie had founded it in 1966. According to her, it was a household name in Great Britain, and had been bought by the large international agency, Manpower, in December 1970.

"Although I would not dream of suing you for using my name, I am absolutely amazed that the company I 'married' (Manpower) did not," she wrote.

I sent her a letter apologizing for this inadvertent mistake, and never heard a word from her again.

I continued writing books of this ilk into 1971 and 1972. There were the *Coffee, Tea or Me?* sequels, and *If It Moves, Kiss It*, a follow-up to the military nurse book, *Tender Loving Care*. And then there was a book that led me into one of the most unusual promotional situations I've ever experienced.

I don't know who came up with the idea of a book in which the sexual proclivities of stewardesses from each major airline would be analyzed—how did the sexual antics and attitudes of Air India stewardesses differ from those of TWA, or Lufthansa, or Delta?—but someone from our weekly luncheon crowd did. I know it wasn't me. All I remember is that Harvey Gardner at Fawcett signed it up through O'Shea, and I went to work writing it.

Actually, working on *How to Make a Good Airline Stewardess* proved to be pleasurable and easy. It was as silly and wacky as previous books in that genre, and took me only a few months to finish. Bill Wenzel signed on to provide the illustrations, and shared the byline with a fictitious Cornelius Wohl. Once the manuscript had been turned in to Fawcett, O'Shea, Gardner, and I spent time together trying to figure out how to promote it. Unlike previous books, the publisher declined to put up any promotional money. It would have to make its own way in the marketplace unless we came up with a way to publicize it.

It was O'Shea who hit upon the answer one day at lunch at the Lambs Club. "The best way to promote a book," he said, "is to attack it. So, we'll attack it."

And so the Stewardess Anti-Defamation Defense League (SADDL) was born.

Although I'd worked in public relations and publicity, I knew that this project would need the hand of someone with a different, slightly skewed approach. That person was Sanford Teller. I'd met Sandy on the Long John Nebel Show, and we went on to become the best of friends. He'd worked for a major PR agency early in his career, but soon ventured out on his own to become one of the most effective and highly regarded one-man PR practitioners in the business, providing sage counsel to a variety of large and small corporations. He was also fond of offbeat ideas to promote a client's services or products; Sandy has never been known to walk away from a whimsical project.

We got together and planned the campaign, which was intended to be mercifully brief but hard-hitting. The first step was to take one of those rent-'em-by-the-week mail drop offices in the name of SADDL in the Pan Am Building. Next, we had an impressive letterhead printed, and Sandy wrote a press release announcing the formation of SADDL. Its first paragraph read:

"A new organization to combat negative image of airline stewardesses was announced today by the organization founder and president, Ms. Joanna Chaplin. Called the Stewardess Anti-Defamation Defense League (SADDL), the group plans to wage a campaign to restore to the stewardess the dignity and stature she possessed before the publication of such vile books as *Coffee, Tea or Me?*, its numerous sequels and, most recently, an infuriating publication by Cornelius Wohl and Bill Wenzel, *How To Make a Good Airline Stewardess*."

The name Joanna Chaplin was pulled out of the air; no such person existed. We chose it because it had a pleasant ring to it.

The release quoted Ms. Chaplin: "Cornelius Wohl, the author of *How to Make a Good Airline Stewardess*, is particularly offensive

. . . he defames everyone, especially the girls who are painted as brainless, whorish sexpots."

She went on to call for every airline stewardess to band together through SADDL to restore their dignity and honor.

Sandy arranged for the distribution of the release to newspapers and wire services, and we sat back to await the results. We weren't expecting much. All we hoped for was the release to run in enough newspapers around the country to convince Ralph Daigh and Fawcett to put money into advertising the book.

Twenty-four hours later, I stopped in at the Pan Am Building to check with the telephone operator handling SADDL's calls. There were more than 40, and they'd come from media all over the world. Associated Press had run a long piece on its international wire service. The *London Times* wanted to interview Joanna Chaplin. So did TV stations in New York. The *New York Times* wanted in on the action, as did media from every corner of America.

O'Shea, Teller and I held a quick meeting in a favorite bar. What now? There was no Joanna Chaplin.

"I know somebody," said O'Shea. "She's a former TWA stewardess who's eight months pregnant and can use some extra money."

She agreed, and the deal was struck. She would function as Joanna Chaplin and return the media calls.

She was interviewed live on two New York TV stations the following day. When she returned home, she called me and said, "I can't do this. I'm eight months pregnant. I'm exhausted."

Another emergency meeting.

"Look," said Teller, the only way to get around this is to handle the media in one shot. We'll hold a press conference." He had a wicked gleam in his eye.

There was no gleam in my eye by this time. I was convinced the whole idea was crazy and would backfire on us, especially on me. I argued against holding a press conference, but O'Shea and Teller prevailed.

We scheduled SADDL's press conference for a week later in an elegant Italian restaurant that was a particular favorite for all of us, Antolotti's, on East 49th Street. The Antolotti family agreed to open up in the morning and serve coffee, juice and Danish. Every news organization that had shown interest received a telegram in those pre e-mail days.

In the meantime, we launched a letter-writing campaign, and it began to show results. We'd written to the president of every major airline asking for support in this fight against stewardess slander. Most wrote back with basically the same message. They shared SADDL's and Joanna Chaplin's outrage over the way stewardesses were depicted, but cautioned that to attack these books would only help to sell them.

The gleam was back in my eye.

We received another letter, one we hadn't solicited. This came from a law firm in New York that had 20 names on the letterhead and was signed by one of the partners, Samuel Gottlieb.

Mr. Gottlieb pointed out that his firm was counsel to the Anti-Defamation League of B'nai B'rith. It was a long and very legal letter, the thrust of it being that if SADDL didn't drop "Anti-Defamation" from its name, we would all end up in jail, or worse. O'Shea, who was a lawyer by training before becoming a literary agent, decided to ignore the letter. B'nai B'rith didn't own the phrase "Anti-Defamation."

Journalist Judy Klemesrud wrote a personal note asking for an interview with members of SADDL. A letter came from an outfit in Chicago called Rent-A-Stew, that sent out former stewardesses on temporary assignments at trade shows and for corporate aircraft. They thought SADDL was wasting its time. Besides, they thought the book was hysterically funny.

Other things were happening at a frantic pace as we prepared for the press conference. When Ralph Daigh heard of the media interest, he immediately agreed to put up some money to support our efforts. We hired two young women from a temporary agency, put them in rented stewardess uniforms and sent them out on the streets of New York to hand out "Wanted: Dead or Alive" leaflets. Caricatures of Mr. Wenzel and Mr. Wohl were on the poster, and people were encouraged to call SADDL if these two scoundrels were seen. The sketch of the fictitious Cornelius Wohl was based upon the face of my editor on the book, Harvey Gardner.

There were snags to that aspect of the project. The young women were arrested at noon on Fifth Avenue for violating the Fifth Avenue Association's rule against handing out things on their precious street. Fawcett's Joe Elder and I went to the precinct and arranged their release. "Look," I said to them, "we're paying you for the day and it's only 2 o'clock. We'll work the commuters at Grand Central Station." We did. An undercover cop dressed like a bum arrested them for the second time. We got them out of that, too, gave them a cash bonus and promised never to call again.

Not only did Harvey Gardner agree that his face could be that of Wohl, he also agreed to appear that week as Wohl on the all-night "Long John Nebel Show" on WMCA (Nebel, with whom Sandy Teller was very close, was in on the scam). Teller did some telephone interviews with radio stations posing as Wohl, and I made a quick trip to Chicago to appear on a TV show there, wearing a bow tie and heavy horn-rimmed glasses with clear glass in them, parting my hair in the middle, and in general looking like a fool.

Things had fallen beautifully into place, as Sandy promised they would. Now, all we had to do was get through the press conference at which more than 30 of New York media representatives had pledged to attend. I wrote a long statement for Joanna to use to open the press conference, and we spent hours briefing her on how to answer questions that might come up.

The day before the press conference, I checked with our telephone operator to see if there were any last minute additions to the media list. There were. More interesting, however, was that three young airline stewardesses had come by the office wanting to meet Joanna Chaplin. They were the founders of a new, legitimate organization called "Stewardesses for Women's Rights." They claimed they had 60 members, and wanted to "join hands with Joanna Chaplin and SADDL in this worthwhile fight."

We invited them to join us at the press conference. They were thrilled at the media exposure. But having these "legit" women's rights advocates of the sky on the dais with our bogus Joanna Chaplin made me nervous, I kept thinking of what Teller repeatedly said whenever my confidence flagged: "Trust me." What choice did I have?

The press conference went off without a hitch. Media heavies read over the printed copy of Joanna's opening statement, made copious notes as questions were asked and answered, and the television cameras recorded every moment.

When it was over, we were giddy about how successful it had been. That night, like members of an opening-night cast waiting for the reviews, we watched television and saw these four young women stand up for the rights of airline stewardesses on what seemed to be every TV station in town. The next morning, the papers were filled with photographs and lengthy stories—full-page articles and photos in the New York *Daily News*, Chicago *Tribune*, Houston *Post* and dozens of other major papers around the nation. Laurie Johnston wrote a lengthy piece for the *New York Times*. UPI and AP had been there, and papers overseas carried the news that America's airline stewardesses were "mad as hell and weren't going to take it anymore."

The Nebel show went well, too. Harvey, an excellent actor, played the role of Cornelius Wohl, the ultimate male chauvinist pig. I was on the show, too; so was Sandy. The phones rang off the hook for six hours with furious women calling to denounce Wohl. It was a romp.

The final meeting was to decide how to get Joanna and SADDL offstage.

"Easy," said O'Shea. "Joanna had the baby and is now too busy as a mother to devote her time to SADDL."

Sandy Teller sent out another release announcing that Joanna Chaplin had given birth to a bouncing baby boy and was stepping down as president of SADDL. No one ever asked whether the organization would continue without her. We closed up the office in the Pan Am building and went back to our separate endeavors. For me, that meant another stewardess book with Bill Wenzel called *Fly Me,* a collection of old gags reconstructed to apply to stewardesses.

I considered resurrecting SADDL for that book but didn't bother. It was over. The age of the stewardess book had come to its natural demise, although in 2003, Penguin brought out a new edition of *Coffee, Tea or Me?,* affording the traveling public another opportunity to read about air travel when it was actually fun to fly.

It had been a great run for me, climaxed by SADDL and the insanity surrounding it. Today, flight attendants have every reason to rail at the image portrayed in my books. These men and women are on the front line of airline security, dealing with drunks, people carrying on steamer trunks to put in the overhead bins, whining kids and abusive adults, air rage—and the threat of terrorism.

It was time to move on.

CHAPTER THIRTEEN

Movin' On

I've done a lot of "moving on" in my career, figuratively and literally.

Every writer has a favorite place in which to work. I'm no exception. In fact, I plead guilty to being obsessive-compulsive when it comes to my working surroundings. I read about novelists writing their books in longhand on lined legal paper while commuting to day jobs and am impressed. I couldn't do that, and never have.

I need order around me when I work, everything in its place. I can't even start a book without having the title page printed and in front of me, nor can I write out of sequence.

I wrote my first book, *The Racing Flag*, in a corner of the kitchen of the house we rented on the horse farm in Old Westbury. We bought our first house not far from there, a modest tract home in Carle Place where I worked in the unfinished basement. I finished that basement myself; one look at the result proves that carpentry is not in my genes.

We moved not far away to another house, large and more interesting than the one we'd left. The basement became my studio again, and I was content until my wife decided having me home all day wasn't good for our young daughters, Laurie and Pamela. "They don't need two mothers," she declared after returning from finding me office space for $150 a month in Roslyn, a picturesque village on Long Island's north shore. "You go to work and I'll be the mother."

She was right. The household ran better with me gone during the day, and I quickly adjusted to the fifteen minute drive each morning to my new working digs, a large, airy room in the Lincoln Building, directly across from Roslyn's landmark clock tower in the center of town. The clock tower didn't hold any particular interest for me, but two restaurants across the street did, the Lake Tower Inn owned by a bigger-than-life guy, Nick Vasile, who would become a dear friend and collaborator on two books; and a superb seafood restaurant, the Jolly Fisherman.

My routine in those days was different from the way I've lived and worked for the past ten years, and those two restaurants in Roslyn were the reason.

Nick Vasile's Lake Tower Inn was a quiet restaurant during the day. At night, it became a dimly lit nightclub frequented by cops and wiseguys, politicians and hustlers (hard to tell them apart), and bored housewives out for a little excitement. There was live jazz six nights a week; I played there a few times. I started going to the Lake Tower Inn for lunch with Jack Pearl. Jack and I pretty much shared the same writing schedule. We were early risers, and on most days had turned out our requisite ten pages by noon, leaving us free for the rest of the day to hang out at "Nick's place."

My writing routine hasn't varied over the past thirty-five years. I try for ten double-spaced pages a day—2500 words—and begin the next day editing the previous day's work. This gets me back into the scene and establishes the momentum I need to continue. There was a period during which I dictated large portions of whatever book I was working on at the time. Sometime in the early 80s I was introduced to Ruth Lazzara, who began working for me in a variety of capacities, including transcribing my dictation. I found dictating especially useful when writing scenes involving action, and lots of dialogue. I would act out the characters, pacing my office holding a small recorder to my mouth. The pages pile up fast when dictating, although there's always plenty of rewriting to do once Ruth has put my words on paper. Recently, I purchased a voice recognition system which I use sparingly, more fascinated with my spoken words appearing on the computer screen than actually producing much of value. Ruth, whose husband, Frank, is a retired FBI special agent, is still with me; she defines indispensable.

At first, Jack and I were among only a few people who lunched at the Lake Tower Inn. Daylight highlighted its obvious decorative flaws, and the food was filling if uninspired. But Nick was a genial host, and soon others started showing up. I decided we should form a luncheon club. Borrowing from my experience with SADDL, I came up with the Writers' Anti-Defamation Defense League (WADDL), and began inviting publishing friends and writers to join us at a monthly luncheon. The "membership" soon grew to more than 20 people; at times we had in excess of 30 at these gatherings. I'd become friendly with Richard M. Dixon (real name James LaRue), a former Disney animator who was making his living at the time doing impersonations of President Nixon, including walking on stage at the end of rock concerts, flashing Nixon's V-for Victory sign, and being hit in the face with a pie, all for a thousand bucks a night. Jack introduced another impersonator and look-alike to the group, actor Bob Sachi, who was Humphry Bogart incarnate and did Bogie dialogue throughout lunch. There was a printer, Phil Gullo, horseman Ray Hoey, writer Ed Linn, Harvey Gardner, Dan O'Shea, Sam Post, a few local reporters from *Newsday*, Bob London, an iconoclastic psychiatrist, and a dozen others, including a British actress, Joan Wood, with whom I eventually did a book. They were raucous, high-spirited lunches that sometimes lasted into the early evening.

Gullo printed a membership certificate I wrote, which said in part:

"This certifies that _____, having displayed the necessary personality defects which have led to, or resulted from having written anything, and having further demonstrated social instability by accepting money for such writing, is hereby granted membership in the WRIT-ERS ANTI-DEFAMATION DEFENSE LEAGUE, with permanent headquarters at the Lake Tower Inn of Roslyn, L.I., N.Y."

Nick eventually sold the place, leaving us without a steady watering hole. That problem was quickly resolved when we moved down the street to the venerable Jolly Fisherman. It had a welcoming bar manned by a consummate professional, George Watson, whose right-of-John Birch political philosophy made for some lively discussions with those of us leaning the other way. It didn't take long for WADDL to establish itself in its new quarters, but it took on a new name in honor of our regular waitress, Carol Gensheimer, who had the quick wit and casual temperament to deal with this eclectic band of malcontents. Our little club was renamed "Carol's Cult." Membership cards printed by Phil Gullo became a hot item in town, and the Jolly's bar was hopping every weekday.

I eventually gave up my office in the Lincoln Building and rented an historic house on Main Street in Roslyn, only a couple of hundred feet from The Jolly. But shortly before that, I'd spent six weeks dog and house sitting for Gary and Bettie Kraut, friends in Greenwich, Connecticut who were off on an extended European trip. My wife and I had separated after 19 years and I was trying to decide where to live. My experience at Gary and Bettie's was memorable for a number of reasons.

I'd signed a contract with Lyle Stuart to write a coffee table book on the subject of caviar. My coauthor was Gerry Stein, president of Iron Gate Products, the 21 Club's fancy food purveyor, and a leading caviar expert. I'd made the deal with Lyle over ice cream sundaes (Lyle was an ice cream fanatic; no contract talk over martinis or long lunches for him.) I wrote most of *Caviar, Caviar, Caviar*, an oversized book that sold for $75, while in Greenwich, interrupted only when the Krauts' magnificent collie, Cagney, decided to chew on my socks (while still on my feet), and then when Ted Chichak called with a proposition. Dan O'Shea had gotten out of the agenting business, and I'd signed on with Ted at the Scott Meredith Agency.

Ted's call was interesting for a number of reasons. The Italian actress, Gina Lollobrigida, was in town to peddle a novel based upon her life in Italy during the war, and Ted wanted me to collaborate with her. He suggested I stop by the agency the next afternoon and pick up a thousand dollars in cash with which to squire Ms. Lollobrigida around town for the week. I was to meet her and the agent-packager, Bill Adler, at the Four Seasons Restaurant. Adler, a noted idea guy in the publishing business, and I would become increasingly involved over the years, including a book that led me to sue a collaborator for the only time in my long ghostwriting career.

It was quite a week. Gina was certainly beautiful, and her story that unfolded over a succession of lunches and dinners was inherently fascinating. She tended to be pouty, which was annoying at times but I've always been good at smiling through prolonged pouts. Our final dinner together was at Antolotti's, my favorite New York City restaurant, where we'd held the press conference for SADDL. When we arrived, Gina was treated like royalty. Every waiter had brought with him a camera to snap photos of the Italian star, and we were given the prize table, occupied almost every night by Truman Capote when he was in town at his U.N. Plaza apartment. Truman, whom I'd met at Antolotti's a number of times, was visibly annoyed at having been relegated to a lesser table. Talk about pouts. But after enough drinks, he decided to join us. It turned out he'd worked on a screenplay for an early Lollobrigida film and they were suddenly best of friends. I sat with them until things got sloppy; Capote was nibbling on her earlobe and saying, "Yummy, yummy, yummy." I excused myself and spent the rest of the night in the kitchen chatting with the Antolotti family.

Gina left town the next day and I wrote a proposal for the novel.

Ted Chichak sent it to Larry Freundlich at Doubleday, who promptly responded with an advance offer of $125,000. I was ecstatic, until Ted reported that Gina had turned it down. The reason, according to Ms. Lollobrigida? "Sophia got more for her book."

Sometimes you eat the bear, sometimes the bear eats you. I felt as though I'd been chewed up and spit out by this gorgeous Italian bear, although I really can't complain. I got to eat at fancy restaurants with this voluptuous, famous female creature on my arm, compliments of the Scott Meredith Agency. It could have been worse.

The historic house on Main Street was a lovely place in which to live and write. The only problem was that its driveway came down to the road in such a way that you couldn't see to your left, which resulted in some spectacular near misses. When I tired of having to leave the driveway before sunup in the hope of seeing headlights to my left, I rented another house, this in Port Washington, ten minutes away from where I seemed to be spending half my life, the Jolly Fisherman.

There was a period when I decided I wanted to be in the city. I sublet a studio apartment in Tudor City and commuted to it every day for a year. When the one-year lease was up, Dan O'Shea offered me space he'd taken as an office on the second floor of an Irish bar on Second Avenue. I would share part of the space with Larry Freundlich, the Doubleday editor who'd wanted to publish Gina's novel. I painted my portion of the space, laid a wall-to-wall carpet, moved my typewriter, books and supplies in, and went to work. I wasn't there a week when Dan informed me that Freundlich wasn't happy. Larry had wanted the office as a place to escape from Doubleday, somewhere he could put his feet up and relax from time to time. "It's not going to pan out with Don," he told O'Shea. "He's actually using it as a *working* office."

I told Sandy Teller the story, and he offered me an office in a five-room suite he had on Lexington Avenue, four of which were vacant.

I moved from over the Irish bar into Sandy's space, laid a new carpet, hung pictures, and got to work again. I was there for an uneventful month until one Friday night when I left my coffee pot plugged in and took the train home. I realized after arriving on Long Island that I hadn't turned it off, and pictured my carelessness causing a fire that would burn down the whole building. I unsuccessfully tried to reach Sandy, who lived in Manhattan, and couldn't come up with a number for the building management. I eventually called Long John Nebel, who solved the problem. He called a friend at NYPD who dispatched a squad car to the building, where two officers went to the office and unplugged the pot. I don't know if they'd trained for that at the Police Academy, but New York's finest accomplished their mission.

A week after the police had saved the building, Sandy came into my office. "Don," he said, "you've got to leave."

"Because of the coffee pot?"

"No. I've got a book I've been meaning to write for a long time; I just never seem to get around to it. I can't stand hearing you in the next room typing, writing a book. It's driving me nuts."

I didn't argue with Sandy. He was too good a friend and still is. I packed up and went home, minus two carpets and committed to never leaving home again in search of a more interesting setting in which to write.

Of the moves I've made during my career, one did not involve finding a new place in which to write. This move was decidedly more traumatic.

There came a time during my writing career that I became depressed, not because the career wasn't going well, or because of domestic problems. I was tired of working alone, and missed the action of a busy PR department. Or maybe it was so-called "writer's block." I never have figured it out. If it was writer's block, it was because I'd lost faith in myself as a writer. I don't know of any other reasons for writer's block to occur. Sustaining one's faith as a writer is never easy. You work alone for months, in some cases years, writing a book and eventually hand it over to an editor who may or may not be helpful and encouraging. A year later, your work is published and sits on bookstore shelves until, or if, someone decides to buy it. In most cases, the publisher won't spend any money promoting it until it begins to sell, which has always seemed to this former PR and marketing guy to be a backwards approach. Your family and friends have read it and assured you it deserves a Pulitzer, at the least. But then some reviewer reads it and decides he or she doesn't like it, often for skewed reasons that completely miss the point of the book. If you're lucky enough to be sent on an author tour, you sit with talk show hosts who haven't read it and prove it by the dumb questions they ask. And, of course, for unexplained reasons, your books never make it to the city where you're appearing, guaranteeing a lack of sales.

All of this, coupled with how practiced publishers are at finding reasons to not pay when payment is due, can kick the pins out from under a writer's confidence. Maybe that's what happened to me.

It wasn't as though I lacked for companionship. There were the daily lunches at The Jolly, and I was doing the Nebel show with greater regularity. Maybe it had to do with having written so many books in the *Coffee, Tea or Me?* vein. They'd become a blur. Harvey Gardner and Joe Elder at Fawcett kept coming to me with proposals I simply couldn't turn down. There was *We Gave at the Office*, a follow-up to *Girlpower*, and *Teachers Pet: Once you Get to Know Them* (get it?) about teachers—same stories, different uniforms, and dedicated to me. There was also a book I wrote for Dell, *Wall Street and Broad*, which came about when I received a call from John Boswell, who introduced himself as an editor at Dell: "Are you the Don Bain who wrote *Coffee, Tea or Me?*" he asked.

"Yes."

"How would you like to do a similar book about women on Wall Street?"

It seemed he had a friend, a female stockbroker, who wanted to do for brokers what Rachel and Trudy had done for airline stewardesses.

Why not?

I wrote *Wall Street and Broad* . . . and quit writing.

CHAPTER FOURTEEN

"Every Midget Has an Uncle Sam Costume"

My hiatus from writing lasted approximately eight weeks. It didn't involve walking away from the typewriter and contemplating the meaning of life while painting the house, or planting an award-winning rose garden. It was a lot more tumultuous than that.

At the end of the eight weeks, I happily went back to writing books. Years later, I told the story of what happened during those weeks to an editor at *Advertising Age*, who found it sufficiently interesting and amusing to suggest I write about it for his publication, which I did. Here's what happened, as I basically reported it in *Ad Age*.

*   *   *   *   *

In the summer of 1972, after successfully pretending to be an airline stewardess for four years by virtue of *Coffee, Tea or Me?* and its sequels, I got lonely writing books in my basement. It occurred to me one morning that if I didn't start interacting with people again on a daily basis, I would become a serial killer in my own home. Woman and children first. Dogs and cats next.

My three years as a public relations executive with American Airlines before going it alone had been happy ones, so I called my old friend, Dave Frailey, who'd become vice president of public relations for the airline, and informed him I was thinking of returning to the real world. He told me my timing was good; American's hotel division, Flagship Hotels, was looking for a vice president of PR, and Dave offered to call the hotel division's president, Jim Heimbaugh. Frailey got back to me the next day to report that Heimbaugh was interested in talking to me.

I set up an appointment, moved buttons on the only corporate suit left in my closet, and met with Heimbaugh at ten o'clock on a hot August morning. I knew I'd get the job because, by this time, I didn't want it. I said all the wrong things during the interview, but the more I said them, the more Heimbaugh seemed interested in hiring me. I went back a second time and was introduced to the chairman of the division, Carter Burgess, a big, blustery southerner with physical and vocal similarities to Lyndon Johnson, although I don't think Burgess spent much time dwelling upon great societies.

Heimbaugh called a few days later: "Welcome aboard, Bain."

My wife, children and four-legged animals had been spared.

I hit the ground running, in corporate parlance (highly proactive). There were two major projects I was expected to throw myself into with the zeal of a cornered honeybadger. One was a lavish Las Vegas type cabaret show, "Catch a Rising Star," that was set to open in the Royal Box, a nightclub in New York's Americana Hotel. Flagship had bought the Americana, which led to the second major project, changing the name of the company and all Flagship Hotels around the world to Americana Hotels. That event would take place on Halloween, which proved prophetic as time went by.

First, I had to settle into my office, get to know others on the staff who had chosen the boardroom as an antidote to committing domestic mayhem, and get out a release with accompanying photograph announcing to the trade press that a new vice president

had been born. I started work on a Monday; the release and photograph went out the following Friday; I handed in my resignation
that Friday afternoon.

"You've got to be joking," Heimbaugh said as I sat in his office.

"No, I'm not. Look, I'm really sorry but I realize I made a mistake. I think I took this job because I was running away from
something instead of running towards something."

Heimbaugh wasn't much into existentialism. "I suggest you
think about this, Bain," he said.

"Sure," I said, silently praying he wouldn't throw his large desk
model of a 727 at me.

"Give it a week."

"Okay," I said.

I used the weekend to assure the two-legged and four-legged animals with whom I shared a house that my killer instincts had
abated, and that they need not fear for their lives once I returned
to the basement.

I spent the first half of the following week hanging around
rehearsals for Catch A Rising Star, directed by a manic German
from Las Vegas named Wolfgang or Helmut. The show wasn't very
good in my opinion, but what did I know from Las Vegas? My idea
of showbiz was the last set at Eddie Condon's.

I also tried to make peace with Dave Frailey. Although he told
me he understood and not to worry, he undoubtedly viewed me
as one large, failed flake.

That Friday, two weeks after I'd started, I made sure Heimbaugh
had gone to lunch before dropping another letter of resignation
on his desk. I went to lunch, too, indulging in what I assumed
would be my last free and unlimited eating and drinking binge in
the Americana's bar and restaurant.

Because I couldn't relate to Helmut or Wolfgang's show, I
decided to leave most of the publicizing of it to a hyper freelance
flack we had on retainer, Milton Karle, a human speech-compres-
sion machine who assured me he knew Earl Wilson personally.

Wilson was the most influential gossip columnist of the era. That left me free to use my remaining days to help promote the hotel chain's name change. Heimbaugh had asked me to stay until the end of October, which I agreed to do, not because I wanted to but because I thought it might head off his taking billboards to announce to the world at-large that I was a man not to be trusted, to say nothing of being un-American.

I'd inherited a bright and talented young man named Tony Tedeschi as my assistant in the PR department. He hadn't been there much longer than I had but knew his way around enough to be invaluable in the massive public relations project the name change entailed. He'd also had enough run-ins with Carter Burgess to be able to clue me as to when to talk to the chairman and when not to. Of course, Burgess saw me in the same light Heimbaugh did, only worse. He knew a lame duck when he had one in his sights. He was also a man of action. He'd walked through the Americana lobby one evening, saw some attractive young women sitting around who he assumed were prostitutes, and issued an immediate order that all furniture was to be removed from the lobby so the hookers wouldn't have a place to plop. Of course, neither did hotel guests. Eventually, new lobby furniture was installed, ordered from a firm noted for designing chairs as comfortable as a broken bicycle seat. He was also known to prowl through the offices at night, spot what he considered a messy desk, and toss everything on the floor, leaving a surprise for the desk's owner the next morning.

The plans to promote the name change from Flagship to Americana were elaborate. Every hotel in the system, from Korea to New York, from Mexico to the Fiji Islands, would simultaneously hold a party the night of October 31. Tony and I wrote a script for Burgess to film, and to be beamed by satellite to all these parties.

Locally, it was my responsibility to put together the bash at the Americana in Manhattan. We had it under control until Tedeschi informed me that he was going into the hospital for elective surgery.

"Now?" I asked, incredulous.

"What better time?" he replied with a laugh that was, at once, infectious and devious.

Still, even with his absence, we'd done enough together so that the party looked as though it would come off with minimal hitches. A cast of thousands had said they were coming—travel agents, writers, and hundreds of secretaries and girlfriends who became "editorial assistants" on such occasions.

I was feeling pretty good a week before the party. Then, Burgess called me into his office and shut the door. "Bain," he announced, "I've come up with an idea that'll put the New York party over the top."

"What's that, Mr. Burgess?"

He sat back in his big chair and a contented smile washed over his face. He leaned forward and said, "We get ourselves a couple 'a midgets, put 'em in Uncle Sam costumes and have 'em run around the party yellin' 'Call Americana! Call Americana!' Just like that little fella Johnny did for Philip Morris."

"A midget?" What else could I say?

"Not one midget, Bain. *Two* midgets."

I'd managed to contain myself until escaping his office. But in the sanctity of my own office, I started to laugh. A half hour later, I called Tedeschi at the hospital where he'd had his surgery that morning. He'd just come out of the recovery room. "Tony, how are you?"

"Okay. I hurt but I'm okay."

"Good. I have to tell you something." I started to recount Burgess' request for midgets. I didn't get far before uncontrollable laughter hit me again, and I could hear a mixture of laughter and pain on the other end. Tony muttered something about breaking his stitches and hung up.

It now occurred to me that maybe I was the victim of a joke. Maybe this was Burgess' way of sticking it to me for the embarrassment I had caused him, Heimbaugh, and the whole company. That had to be it.

I went into another vice president's office. "Jack," I said, "let me bounce something off you." I told him the story, ending with, "He's not serious, right?"

"He's serious. He told me about the idea, too, and that he'd given you the assignment."

"He's serious."

"Yes, he's serious." I looked across the desk and saw a sober face. No laughter from this vice president. There would be midgets in Uncle Sam costumes running between guests' legs at the party.

Where do you find two midgets?

I started making calls, beginning with a public relations guy with Ringling Brothers I knew through the Long John Nebel Show. "We stopped using midgets a couple of years ago," he told me. He gave me the name of somebody else to try, which brought about the same result. Another suggestion of someone to call, then another, each call widening my network of midget-hunters.

Eventually—and I have no idea who this was—I reached a person who told me that finding two midgets in New York for such an assignment was easy.

"Really? How so?"

He gave me the name of a rundown hotel on Manhattan's West Side, and its phone number. "It's a midget colony," he told me. "There's got to be thirty, forty midgets living there, and they book themselves out for showbiz jobs, things like that."

I thanked him, drew some deep breaths and dialed the number. A voice that answered, belonged, I assumed, to the head midget. I introduced myself and said, "I need two midgets for two hours on Halloween night at the Americana Hotel. It's for a promotion party."

"Okay," said the little voice. "No problem."

"Ah, how much will it cost?"

"A hundred-and-a-quarter for one, two bills for two."

"A volume discount, huh?"

"Right."

I hesitated before saying, "Look, there's a problem."

"What's the problem?"

"Well . . . well, they have to wear Uncle Sam costumes."

He never missed a beat: "*Every midget has an Uncle Sam costume*," he said.

I was speechless.

"I'll send up six to audition," he said.

"No, no need for that."

"It's better you choose the two you want. I'll have them to you tomorrow morning. What's your address?"

I reluctantly gave it to him and we arranged for them to arrive at eleven.

My secretary entered my office the next morning. "Don, there are six dwarfs in the reception area to see you."

"They're not dwarfs, they're midgets," I said wearily.

A dozen questions were written on her face.

"I'll tell you later," I said. "Send them in."

"*All* of them?"

"Yeah, I guess so."

A moment later, she appeared at the door with one snappily dressed midget. "Where are the others?" I asked.

"It's better to see us one at a time, less confusing," he said. Was he ready to tap dance, sing, jump into my lap, or into my wastebasket and pretend he was about to be shot out of a cannon? I'd told the head midget what they had to yell as they ran through the party: "Call Americana!" Maybe that's what he was about to do.

"Well?" I said.

"Anything special you want me to do?"

"No, you look great. You'll do just fine. You do have an Uncle Sam costume?"

He looked at me as though I'd asked whether he had trouble with the length of hotel beds.

"I appreciate you coming in," I said. "Thanks. Please send in the next."

One by one they paraded past my desk, six nice little guys who seemed to expect me to give some stage directions, to hand them a script, or to turn to a piano player and say, "Hit a chorus of 'When It's Apple Blossom Time in Orange New Jersey, We'll be a Peach of a Pear.'"

After they were gone, I called the head midget and told him I wanted the first two who'd "auditioned." Each of them had left his card (no Sleepy or Grumpy, just Edward, Morris and Joe). I could have chosen any pair just as long as they carried themselves in their Uncle Sam costumes with the dignity befitting the event.

Two days before the party, I was summoned into Carter Burgess' office. "Cancel those midgets," he told me.

"Cancel them?"

"Yes, I've changed my mind. Pay 'em off but I don't want any midgets runnin' around my hotel."

His decision saddened me because, by now, I was looking forward to the party and seeing my two miniature Uncle Sams ducking through legs shouting the name of our new hotel chain. The party was dull without them. I would have enjoyed getting to know them a little better.

It was my last day on the job.

*   *   *   *   *

I was happy to be back in my basement, writing another book. Of course, everything gets used. That episode in my life resulted in a screen treatment I wrote, *Suzie and the Seven Midgets*, an updated version of *Snow White and the Seven Dwarfs*—young girl runs away from her Westchester home and her evil stepmother, ends up wandering the mean streets of Manhattan until she's rescued by seven midgets who wear Uncle Sam costumes and live in a west side hotel. It never sold, which was okay. My biggest disappointment was not succeeding in providing seven plum movie roles for my newfound little friends. I hope they're all doing well.

(While doing a final edit and rewrite on this book, my friend, Pete Peckham, called after reading an earlier version. He told me that when his production company was shooting commercials for Nobody Beats the Wiz, a Christmas spot called for two elves. He, too, was put in touch with midget headquarters in the west side Manhattan hotel, and was assured that every midget had an elf's costume. "The two guys we booked did a great job," he said.)

CHAPTER FIFTEEN

"Could We Make it 'Magnificent' Charlatan?"

I first met Long John Nebel in December of 1964 when I was a PR exec with American Airlines. I suggested to WNBC's head of publicity, Jim Grau, that the station do a remote broadcast from American's terminal at JFK Airport. Grau agreed, and lined up Big Wilson to broadcast his popular morning show from there, and to do Mimi Benzel's lunchtime celebrity chitchat program from the Astrojet Room restaurant. The only hitch was that Grau wanted to include Long John Nebel's midnight-till-six talk show. I balked. I didn't want Nebel because of his reputation as a no-nonsense interviewer, abrasive and rude. I pictured the conversation turning to flight delays, lost baggage, and even the tragedy of aircraft accidents, an airline PR man's nightmare.

But Grau was firm in his insistence that Nebel be part of the package. Long John had recently come over to WNBC from WOR, and Grau wanted to publicize the switch.

Everything went well, to my relief, although Nebel did nothing to ease my fears prior to the broadcast. He was arrogant and aloof.

But I'd been forewarned by Grau not to suggest to the king of all-night talk radio that he avoid any particular subject. To do that, according to Grau, was to ensure that he would make a point of introducing that very topic. After I became a regular panelist on Long John's nightly program, I learned that Nebel and his producers had installed a microphone in the Green Room where guests waited for the show to begin. Nebel sat in his office and listened to what they talked about, including comments to a producer about certain areas of their lives they preferred not be raised, guaranteeing that Nebel would bring it up.

Five years later, I again met Nebel when I was a guest on his show to promote *The Case Again Private Aviation.* That appearance led to a close friendship with this remarkable, enigmatic man and radio personality. I would eventually do approximately 200 shows with John as one of his many panelists, sitting in his studio from midnight until six in the morning talking with an eclectic array of individuals, many of them household names, others from more mundane walks of life but who received their own dose of fame with Nebel's millions of listeners a night in 35 states—WNBC was a 50,000 watt clear channel station.

Nebel was one of the more complex and quixotic individuals I've ever known. Being his friend wasn't easy. He could be infuriatingly demanding within a friendship, and you played by his rules. His magnetism was almost hypnotic; no small wonder that hypnosis was a consuming interest of his and would eventually lead to a book I eventually wrote about his last wife, the former top model Candy Jones, a highly controversial book involving hypnosis and its misuse by governmental agencies.

He openly wielded the power of his show and the exposure it offered hundreds of people, me included. He often talked about the lure of being on radio and television: "It's that hot mike and red eye," he would say with a high-pitched, contagious laugh that could render those around him helpless.

There are so many facets to Long John Nebel that it would take a book of its own to do justice to them. That's why in late 1971 I suggested to him that we collaborate on an autobiography. His response surprised me. "Why don't you write my biography? I'd prefer that."

I assumed the Nebel need for control would get in the way, and braced myself for it as I started preparing a proposal for Dan O'Shea to use to sell the book. But John was the model of cooperation. He provided me with a list of more than 200 names of people he thought I might like to interview, including former wives and girlfriends, a gutsy move.

Both before he became a radio personality and after, Nebel's life was rich with anecdotes. He was born in Chicago in 1911 and dropped out of school in the eighth grade to join a circus as a substitute clown. From there he sold housewares door-to-door, managed a Wurlitzer piano store, and headed for New York at the age of 16 where he became an usher at the New York Paramount Theater. He left there to become an assistant manager at the Winter Garden but decided he wanted to be a performer. He bought a used banjo, took a few lessons, gathered seventeen musicians around him, found a booking agent, and hit the road as the John Nebel Orchestra. Tired of the travel, he abandoned the band and got a few jobs as a male dancer in Broadway revues. But always, he turned to selling to supplement his income, including gadgets of dubious worth on the streets of New York.

There was Chinese Corn Punk, nothing more than small hunks of cheap yellow laundry soap wrapped in pieces of a Chinese newspaper and billed by Nebel as "A miraculous cure for all your foot ailments, the original, therapeutic and extremely rare Chinese Corn Punk."

He was especially fond of peddling the Miracle Juice Extractor, a serrated device, which when inserted into an orange released its juices while Nebel squeezed the fruit. What his customers didn't know was that John had used a hypodermic needle to inject water into the oranges before hitting the street, causing them to gush forward with orange liquid. "You squeeze a little, you get a little," he would intone to the crowd—the "tip"—gathered around him. "You squeeze a lot, you get a lot."

He was soon recognized as one of the best "talkers" on the street, a role model for fellow pitchmen.

There were other careers. He became a photographer for leading fan magazines, and managed a camera store in New York. Another brief fling at leading a band occurred when he met a large orchestra that had come to New York from the Philippines at the urging of a booking agent, who promptly abandoned them. Included in the musical aggregation was a Siamese twin dance act. Nebel took over as leader and managed to nail down a few bookings in Chinese restaurants to entertain the lunch crowd. "I bought a new tux and the longest baton I could find," he said, "and bullshitted everybody." I have a prized 1931 publicity photo hanging over my desk of John wearing that tux and wielding that baton.

He eventually became an auctioneer at various New Jersey auction houses where his fame as a talker spread. Long John—he picked up that name because he was six feet, four inches tall and reed thin—could sell anything, to anyone, it was claimed. It was at one of these auction houses that his radio career was launched. An executive from WOR stopped in on his way home from work and was mesmerized by this tall, skinny pitchman who had the crowd in the palm of his hand. He gave Nebel his card: "You ought to be on the radio," the exec said.

Nebel called and was hired. In February 1956, Long John Nebel made his radio debut, and went on to forge one of the most impressive careers in radio history, which lasted until his death from cancer on April 10, 1978, more than twenty years in front of a microphone probing the philosophy, beliefs, and often misdeeds of countless men and women, famous and infamous.

In early 1972, O'Shea called with good news. Bruce Carrick, an erudite young editor at Macmillan, a respected publishing house, wanted to publish the Long John Nebel story. A contract was signed, and I got to serious work on the research phase, necessitating spending even more time with John than appearing on the show entailed.

Being a panelist and friend meant a considerable commitment of time to Long John Nebel. I found myself appearing on the show as frequently as three times a week, and loving every minute of it. Most nights, I joined John at his favorite restaurant, Antolotti's, where Truman Capote feasted on Gina Lollobrigida's ear. Despite the restaurant's superb Italian menu, John's dinner choices never varied—shrimp cocktail, a steak, and soft drink. On other nights we had dinner at Ho-Ho, a Chinese restaurant near Rockefeller Center. After the show ended at six in the morning, everyone headed for Sarge's Delicatessen, only a few blocks from Nebel's East Side apartment, where his table was always set for him.

But researching his biography upped my commitment of time. We sat together for hours in his apartment, my tape recorder going as he weaved tales from his childhood and early career. Doing a biography of a great talker makes life easier. His memory for details was remarkable, and his recreation of the spiels he delivered on the streets of New York, and in the Jersey auction houses, were laced with all the colorful language used by him and other sidewalk salesmen.

I became predictably close to John Nebel during this period, and was privy to his most ebullient moments and darkest depressions. He often threatened suicide, particularly when one of his many romantic relationships wasn't going well (according to his definition), and was "rescued" a few times from the roof of the RCA Building when he was poised to jump. He never did take the leap, of course, and would be talked down, usually by psychotherapist and show regular, Dr. Hanna Kapit, who would be summoned from home to intervene. Nebel would go on to do that night's show as though nothing had happened. The show was the most important thing in his life—it *was* his life—one of the reasons it was so successful.

I interviewed everyone on the list he'd given me, plus others I sought out on my own. Everyone respected his success and the power he wielded in New York. Many expressed deep affection for him. Others spewed hatred for this controversial character. I took it all in on tape, and began writing the book.

My agreement with John was that I would show him the finished manuscript to allow him to point out factual errors, but nothing more. I delivered the manuscript to him some time in early 1973, and waited for his response. I'd titled the book *LONG JOHN NEBEL: Radio Talk King, Master Salesman, and Charlatan.* I knew that the word charlatan was harsh, but I didn't intend it to be critical. I chose it to indicate that Long John Nebel wasn't always what he seemed to be.

He called a few days later.

"It's great," he told me, "but there's one change you have to make."

"What's that?"

"The word 'charlatan' in the title. I don't like it."

His objection didn't surprise me. I started to suggest that I would be happy to remove it from the title, but he cut me off. "Could we make it *magnificent* charlatan?"

That's the way it was published in 1974 to wonderful reviews— *LONG JOHN NEBEL: Radio Talk King, Master Salesman, Magnificent Charlatan.*

Besides having had a superb subject for a biography, Long John's wide circle of famous friends made easier the process of garnering quotes, blurbs, to be used on the book's cover and in advertising. Best-selling author Jacqueline Susann, whose *Valley of the Dolls* was one of the decade's biggest sellers, and who was rumored to have had an affair with John, offered, "Long John Nebel is part fiction, part hero, part con man, and part legend—and I love every part of him." I interviewed her for the biography. We sat on a couch in her living room while her husband, Irving, dozed in a chair across the room. He never stirred until I asked whether there was any truth to the rumor that she'd slept with Nebel. "No truth at all," *he* muttered, never opening his eyes.

Publisher Helen Gurley Brown gave us, ". . . It's a genuine love story about John's love affair with the industry, with his wife, with life. I loved it."

Famed film and stage director Elia Kazan said, "Long John Nebel is unique, a phenomenon. A beautiful story."

Best-selling author Irving Wallace wrote, "I could not have invented a character like Long John Nebel. He's simply too unbelievable . . . a remarkable and fascinating book about a remarkable and fascinating man."

There were dozens of such accolades from well-known personalities. But the real coup was having the introduction to the book written by actor-comedian-TV star Jackie Gleason. Gleason ended his long, glowing intro with, "Chances are I'll live and die without anybody trying to inject fluid into my brain to make me a different person. But if I had to have fluid from another brain, I'd be willing to have just a squirt or two from the brain of Long John Nebel."

The Tonight Show's Ed McMahon, himself a sidewalk salesman (in his case a boardwalk pitchman in Atlantic City), wrote, "Reading Bain's biography of one of the greatest talkers of our time was nothing but a delightful reading romp. Long John Nebel—the public personality and the man—knocks me out, and so did this book."

Although the publisher supported the book with advertising, and John and I did book signings in stores around Manhattan, sales were disappointing nationally. Still, having written the life story of a man who had become my close friend was personally rewarding and satisfying. I continued to be a panelist on the show, appearing with such luminaries as comedy writer Bob Orben; gossip columnist Earl Wilson; playwright Robert Anderson; sportscaster Marv Albert; big band arranger Sy Oliver; Elia Kazan; comedian Phil Foster; jazz great Errol Garner; psychiatrist Herb Spiegel, arguably the world's leading expert on medical hypnosis and who would play an important part in the book I would do with Long

John's wife, Candy Jones; and a hundred other fascinating individuals, doctors, lawyers, politicians, actors and actresses, movie producers, cops and wiseguys. Some became close and enduring friends—Jack and Reiko Douglas; John's producer Anne Pacurar, who married one of the show's engineers, Victor Lombardo; husband and wife psychoanalysts Hanna and Milton Kapit; and, of course, Sandy Teller, one of Long John's best friends.

One day, John received a generous gift from Danny Bergauer, who was part of the family that owned Manny's Music in Manhattan where professional musicians bought their gear. Danny had delivered to John's apartment a brand new set of Musser vibes, the concert series. The Musser vibes I'd been using since buying them from Hank Tracy in Saudi Arabia was a good set, but the concert model was far superior. John took the cover off his gift, learned to play the first eight bars of *The World is Waiting for the Sunrise*, put the cover back on and didn't remove it again for years.

"Why don't you sell me those vibes?" I suggested one afternoon as we sat around his apartment.

"Six hundred," he said.

I paid him, took the vibes home, and have been playing them ever since. Not only is it a superb instrument, I think of John every time I set them up for a gig.

Long John Nebel's funeral was as tumultuous as his life had been. He and Candy Jones had separated, and he'd moved into a hotel around the corner from the WMCA studios from which he now broadcast, after having left WNBC in that station's campaign to attract younger listeners. Management had brought in a brash new talent from Cleveland, Don Imus, to do the morning show, and felt a younger overnight audience would be a better lead-in to Imus's show. I enjoyed a couple of lunches with Imus while researching the Nebel biography, and he trashed WNBC's management for getting rid of Nebel, terming them stupid, inept and other unflattering terms. I was impressed with his candor, especially since he'd just gone to work for that same management. But

I received a call a few days after our final lunch from Imus's lawyer, who told me Imus had never said those things to me, and that if I quoted him, I'd be on the wrong end of a lawsuit. The I-Man evidently had second thoughts about telling it like it was.

It was during Nebel's tenure at WMCA that he was diagnosed with prostate cancer, and it had spread. Despite the acrimony between him and Candy—he'd brought her on as a cohost shortly after their marriage—she functioned in that capacity night after night. Nebel had become frail and weak, yet did the show every night until the day he died in his hotel suite. Controversy surrounded his death: Had he taken his own life, or had the cancer claimed him? Only a few people know, and we're not talking.

The night before his funeral in Manhattan, in April 1978, I joined a small group of friends at Antolotti's. John had asked me to deliver a eulogy when he died, and I was anxious to go home and get some sleep before having to be back in the city the following morning. It promised to be a tense day. Fans had already begun lining up outside the funeral home; thousands were expected to pass the casket and view the man whose voice had provided them comfort all through the night for more than twenty years. What complicated the funeral arrangements was that Candy, John's widow, had decided that I might ignore her during my eulogy, or even say something uncomplimentary. She arranged for her own eulogist to speak fondly of the loving, brave woman John left behind. When Lyle Stuart, never one to mince words or stifle strong emotions, heard this, he threatened to grab the microphone and denounce Candy, or worse. While many of us shared Lyle's anger, we managed to cool him down, and the service went smoothly.

My "Nebel Years" remain etched in my mind and gut. Long John became a potent influence on me personally and on my career, joining Jack Pearl and Red Sutherland as primary forces in my life. I'm just happy I was alive, and had the energy, to pal around with the king of New York late-night radio for as long as I did.

CHAPTER SIXTEEN

STRANGER THAN FICTION

"It has been almost two years since I was first invited to hear portions of tapes that had been recorded in the cramped East Side apartment shared by John Nebel and Candy Jones—Mr. and Mrs. Nebel. I recall sitting there on a hot and sticky August day in 1974, a drink in my hand, a yellow legal pad on my lap and a tightening knot of uneasiness in my stomach.

"'I don't understand,'" I said. I was to say that many times during the long afternoon.

"'Is it all right if I play this one?'" Nebel asked Candy, referring to another cassette. He was to ask her that many times.

"'If he's to be told any of it, he might as well be told all of it,'" she replied.

"That was the beginning of my involvement with The Control of Candy Jones."

*   *   *   *   *

These are the opening words of the introduction I wrote to this strange, frightening tale of a 12-year portion of Candy's life in which she was a subject of the CIA's infamous mind control experimentation. The book was published in early 1976 to a flurry of reviews, denials by the CIA, a six-week promotional tour with Candy that was a test of my stamina and patience, and a substantial film deal with 20th Century Fox that bought the rights to the story as a vehicle for Jane Fonda. Twenty-five years later, this bizarre tale continues to generate controversy. Anti-government groups point to *The Control of Candy Jones* as proof of the CIA's evil misdeeds; as recently as 2001, a half-dozen independent film producers were pursuing the film rights (20th Century Fox, after three screenplays by top screenwriters, never made the movie but has refused to sell the rights back to me, or to others interested in actually making the film.) The hardcover, which sold for $8.95 at publication, has achieved cult status, copies of it being sold on the Internet for as much as a hundred dollars.

The project was sold to Bob Gleason and Ed Kuhn at Playboy Press, based upon a long proposal I wrote. Playboy's book division operated independently of the Hefner magazine empire, employed some top book editors, and published many substantial books that in no way reflected the sexual thrust of the magazine and clubs.

I was between agents at the time. Dan O'Shea had packed it in, and Jack Pearl introduced me to Gleason and Kuhn who, in turn, suggested I discuss representation with the Scott Meredith Agency. It didn't take Meredith and one of his vice presidents, Ted Chichak, long to decide to take me on as a client. I'd already sold the project to Playboy for an advance of $50,000, which meant the Meredith agency picked up a quick $5,000 in commissions simply for negotiating the final contract. Those were the days of 10 percent commissions, with every postage stamp and phone call deducted from the writer's share. Fifteen percent is the standard commission now, with higher rates for overseas representation.

The Meredith agency was big and powerful, and I remained with them until Scott Meredith's death, at which time Chichak, Russ Galen and Jack Scovil left to form their own agency. Chichak eventually branched out on his own to operate a boutique literary agency representing just a few writers, including me. It's been a mutually lucrative relationship for more than thirty-five years.

Candy Jones was one of America's leading models in the Forties and Fifties. In one month she was featured on the covers of 11 magazines, including *LIFE,* and starred in a successful Broadway play, *Mexican Hayride.* She married Harry Conover, cofounder of the Conover modeling agency; his partner was a young male model in New York, Gerald Ford. When Ford returned from the war, he got out of the modeling business and eventually went on to become President of the United States.

In 1960, Candy fell on relatively hard times and was receptive, at least financially, to a CIA overture that she act as a courier during her many travels. She served the agency for 12 years. But simple courier assignments soon turned into her becoming a human guinea pig in the CIA's now well-documented experiments in using drugs, behavior modification, and hypnosis in an attempt to create the perfect courier, messages locked in the brain and released only to those knowing how to unlock the control exercised over the subject.

Those of us who attended the wedding of Long John Nebel and Candy Jones on New Year's Eve, 1972, at the apartment of Nebel's attorney, Ken Knigin, realized that there was something strange about Candy. More than 40 of Nebel's friends were at the apartment; Candy's only guests were her mother, and someone who worked for Candy who attended more as a companion for the mother. Having a conversation with Candy was difficult. One moment she was open and smiling, not so much a beautiful woman as a handsome one. Within seconds, her face would change and become hard and distant, and her voice deepened and darkened, almost as though another person had slipped in to take her place. It was disconcerting, to say the least.

Nebel would later describe to me their wedding night at the Drake Hotel. "One minute she was the Candy I loved and married," he said. "Then, she would return from the bathroom a different person, cold and bitter, her deep voice having the slicing effect of a razor. A minute later, she was warm and loving again."

This transition in personality occurred with regularity, and Candy suffered insomnia. Nebel, who'd received some informal training in hypnosis, began hypnotizing her in an attempt to help her relax and to sleep. She was an excellent hypnotic subject, a "Five" on the Hypnotic Induction Profile (HIP) developed by one of the leading voices in the use of medical hypnosis, Dr. Herbert Spiegel, a friend of John's and a frequent guest on his show. The scale runs from One to Five. Few people even approach the Five stage in which it is possible to manipulate such a subject to do many things. It was during these innocent hypnotic sessions that different personalities began to emerge from Candy, and the story of her twelve-year ordeal with the CIA came out in bits and pieces. Nebel was shocked and confused at first. But after he began making a habit of turning on a tape recorder whenever inducing a trance in Candy, a fuller picture of this tormented woman and her experiences began to fall into place. He would draw this chilling story from her over the course of more than 200 hours of taped sessions. Those tapes formed the basis for the book.

The amount of information on the tapes was too unwieldy for transcription from the originals. A literal transcription would have resulted in thousands of single-spaced pages. Instead, I devised a system in which as original tapes were played through earphones, I recorded on to another tape recorder my "play-by-play" of the events on the original. In addition, I used a stopwatch and called out the passing of minutes during individual half hour segments. The built-in digital counters on the many recorders I used for the project were calibrated against minute counts. Thus, I was able to go to any point on an original tape, no matter what machine was being used, by relating minutes to digit counts. My transcriber,

Donna Pelini, transcribed my comments as opposed to the original tapes. Even at that, the condensed transcripts (my comments) numbered over 700 single-spaced pages. In addition to the tapes, I conducted approximately 60 recorded interviews with John and Candy.

Because we were concerned at what the CIA might attempt to do once the agency knew such a book was in the works, I duplicated every tape, a time-consuming but necessary process. The originals were secured in large safe deposit boxes at John's bank in Manhattan, with the two of us as cosigners, and I rented large boxes at my local bank in Roslyn, on Long Island. I would be at the bank when it opened at nine, bring the tapes back with me to my office in the Lincoln Building, and work on them until a few minutes before three when I would return them to the bank vault. It was an awkward way to work and slowed things down, but the peace of mind was worth it.

There's a tendency to retell the Candy Jones story in this autobiography, but that would take up the entire book. Suffice it to say, *The Control of Candy Jones* was published in early spring, 1976, generating hundreds of reviews, virtually all of them favorable, but many raising a question about the book's credibility. Could this compelling story have been fantasized by Candy during her hypnotic sessions with John Nebel? Based upon independent research I did through Herb Spiegel, who wrote a provocative, supportive foreword for the book; psychiatrist Bob London; psychiatrist Barbara DeBetz; Dr. Frederick Dick, an internist with a deep understanding of hypnosis; and digging into files released about MK-ULTRA, the CIA's top secret mind control program, the answer is a resounding no. I attended medical hypnosis seminars around the country, including weeks soaking in Dr. Spiegel's impressive seminars at Columbia-Presbyterian Hospital in New York City. I constantly compared material from the Nebel tapes to facts garnered from this independent research, and came to the unshakable conclusion that these horrific things had happened to

Candy Jones. There were gaps in the story, to be sure. There were times when I felt Nebel was leading her in a direction he wanted to go. But for me, the story held up, and I took to the road with Candy on a six-week tour with confidence, a trip not without incident.

After doing TV shows in Cleveland, and waiting to catch a plane that same day to Los Angeles, I suffered a bout of heavy sweating that literally soaked through my suit. I hadn't been feeling well when we left New York and was certain the flu was coming on.

Upon arrival in Los Angeles, Candy and I gathered with publicity people hired by the publisher to choreograph the West Coast portion of the tour. We were staying in the Beverly Hills Hotel, and met for drinks that night in its Polo Lounge. I mentioned I was feeling poorly, which resulted in the insistence that I go to the emergency room at Cedars-Sinai Medical Center to get some medication before we started making media appearances the following day.

I took a taxi to the hospital and told the doctor on duty why I was there. During his questioning of me, I mentioned my sweating incident in Cleveland earlier that day. My comment prompted an EKG. I watched the physician's face as he read the readout. Not good, his expression said. A second EKG was performed. No better.

"You had a heart attack this afternoon," I was told.

"That's crazy," I said. "I have the flu."

My diagnosis was dismissed and I was told that if I didn't check into the hospital that night, the ramifications could be serious. I stopped arguing. I'd barely turned forty and wasn't ready just yet to drop dead of a coronary.

I spent the night wired up to machines watching my heart rhythms on a monitor over the bed. It was a sleepless night, my life flashing before me, a wife and two teenage daughters back in New York, no more tennis, a cardiac cripple like my father had become.

The next morning, a young cardiologist, Steve Rubin arrived and reviewed my EKGs with me. An irregularity said to him that

I had suffered a mild heart attack the previous day. I asked him to call my internist in New York, Fred Dick, with whom I'd had an EKG earlier that year. Dr. Rubin reached Fred and told him of the blip on my EKG. Fred assured Rubin it represented my usual EKG. I'd played in a basketball league one night a week that year and had taken a severe shoulder to my chest, resulting in a bruised heart muscle and permanent marker on any EKG I would have. After stern advice that I carry a copy of my EKG with me at all times, I was released and met up with Candy for our first radio appearance.

The tour went well, although being with Candy day after day was unnerving, at times downright unpleasant. She was a true multiple personality, with a woman named Arlene the dominant second person. Arlene would come out at the damndest times, in a restaurant, a cab, or on a plane heading for San Francisco. At times, her emergence was so sudden and dramatic that it frightened me. It happened on shows, too, but I developed a skill at rapidly shifting attention from her to me until Arlene disappeared as quickly as she'd arrived.

I would like to chalk up all of Candy's unpleasant behavior to her psychiatric abnormalities, but I can't. Sure, they contributed. But I came to believe that Candy Jones, my friend Long John Nebel's new wife, was an unpleasant, argumentative woman, as well as a bigoted one.

One night, after we'd had a serious argument, I called Nebel who was doing the show in New York and told him what I thought of Candy. He agreed with me, which was small solace. I still had to spend weeks with her until the tour ended. I played the good soldier throughout and we finally got on separate planes for flights back east, Candy to New York, me to Philadelphia where Bob London, who'd become a good friend, had arranged for me to attend the annual American Psychiatric Association convention where Bob, Barbara DeBetz and Herb Spiegel would be major participants. What happened there was, I suppose, a fitting end to the trip.

There were two high profile physicians involved in the CIA's manipulation of Candy Jones, one of whom who had many Hollywood celebrities as patients. Because the lawyers at Playboy Press were concerned that there wasn't enough independent corroboration of this particular doctor's involvement, they insisted I use a fictitious name, which I did. Corroborating certain aspects of the story was a problem from the beginning. The CIA is, of course, good at covering its tracks, and keeping secret the identities of physicians who participate in its experiments. My research not only verified that this doctor had conducted numerous experiments on Candy, it linked him to the suicide of Hispanic actor Freddy Prinze, and to Sirhan Sirhan, Robert Kennedy's assassin. But I could never prove these allegations to the satisfaction of attorneys, and therefore wasn't able to include such material in the book.

The name I gave this physician was Marshall Burger. I eventually learned through various sources that the real doctor knew I'd based the Burger character on him, and made it known that he was unhappy about it. To my surprise, "Dr. Burger" was in Philadelphia attending the convention. I was even more taken aback on the first day when he sought me out during a coffee break, introduced himself, and suggested we have lunch together, an invitation I readily accepted. He was friendly, telling me jokes and kidding me about thinking he could possibly be involved with the CIA and its experiments on innocent citizens. It was toward the end of lunch that he confided in me that he was friendly with a couple of very attractive young women in Philadelphia, and suggested we go out with them together that evening. Bells and whistles went off in my head. This guy was trying to set me up in some sexual blackmail scheme. I declined *that* invitation and we went our separate ways that afternoon. But he didn't give up. He cornered me at various times during the convention to repeat his offer to fix me up with a woman.

I never saw the good doctor again after the convention. I read his obituary years later, a long and detailed one in which his impressive medical career was chronicled. There was not, of course, any mention of his CIA involvement.

Working with Long John and Candy Jones was a fascinating experience for me, often frustrating, challenging, a lot of hard work, and ultimately satisfying both professionally and personally. That *The Control of Candy Jones*, retitled *The CIA's Control of Candy Jones*, has been reissued by Barricade Books, is gratifying. I believe it is an important book, whose subject matter should be of interest to every thinking person. Continuing interest in it on the part of Hollywood might result in a motion picture version, bringing Candy's tale to an even wider audience.

As noted film producer David Brown commented after reading the manuscript, "An utterly fascinating and haunting book. Truth in this case is certainly stranger than fiction."

He gets no argument from me.

CHAPTER SEVENTEEN

You Can't Tell a Man by His Cover

_____

Although the Long John Nebel biography, and *The Control of Candy Jones* represented significant commitments of my writing time during the 1970s, I wrote a number of other books as well, some of which have already been mentioned.

A popular TV show of that era was *Toma*, starring the actor David Toma. A series of "Toma" paperback books was launched to capitalize on the series' success, and Jack Pearl wrote a few of them. He approached me to do some, and I wrote in quick succession *The Airport Affair*, and *The Affair of the Unhappy Hooker*, relatively easy paydays.

At one of the monthly luncheons of WADDL at Nick Vasile's Lake Tower Inn, Sam Post arrived with an attractive, young British actress named Joan Wood. Sam, who by then was a publishing consultant through his Beverly Hills Associates, thought there might be a *Coffee, Tea or Me?* sort of book about the trials and travails of an aspiring actress seeking stardom in New York City. Sam sold a proposal I wrote to Walker & Company for a hardcover, and I began work on *The Casting Couch and Me*.

Joan was a willing and helpful collaborator. She'd experienced numerous casting couch situations in her young career, and was forthcoming in relating them to me. The problem was that as the manuscript developed, the tone became serious and dramatic rather than frothy and comic, as in *Coffee, Tea or Me?* Would Nancy Yost, my editor at Walker, accept this significant departure from what she'd originally expected when signing a contract based upon my proposal for a light comedy?

I never had a chance to find out because Post arranged a meeting with Fawcett's Ralph Daigh before I turned in the manuscript to Walker. Prior to a lunch at the Harvard Club, Sam asked me to send the manuscript to Daigh, who arrived having read it. The purpose of the lunch? Sam wanted Ralph to commit at that early stage to a sizable paperback offer.

Daigh offered $50,000 for softcover rights to *The Casting Couch and Me.—provided* I rewrote the book to better conform to the *Coffee, Tea or Me?* style.

I said I wanted to think about it, although the lure of that much money at that point in my career was strong. Sam and I talked about it after Daigh had departed, and I agreed, reluctantly, to rewrite. I hated to do it. The story that had evolved was strong, compelling and poignant, funny at times, but a real departure from all those other lighthearted comedies I'd been doing.

I rewrote *The Casting Couch and Me.* Nancy Yost at Walker accepted it, and planned an impressive launch for the book. Of course, knowing that Fawcett had promised to purchase softcover rights for $50-thousand had obviously boosted her enthusiasm.

But then Daigh called me at home to announce that he wasn't going to buy the rights. No explanation, no apologies, except some vague comment about Fawcett shifting its editorial focus. Everyone involved shared my disappointment. Walker published the hardcover in 1975 to a resounding lack of interest. Pocketbooks published a softcover edition, paying a fraction of what Fawcett had promised, and Peter Elk published a British hardcover. As it turned out, I would have been better off sticking with my original manuscript, a much better book in my opinion. But that kind of retrospection doesn't accomplish anything. Understandably, Daigh's retraction of his offer was upsetting to me, but it didn't taint my view of him personally or professionally. He was too much of a gentleman for that to happen.

There is a lesson for every writer to learn from my experience. H.G. Wells once said, "No passion in the world is equal to the passion to alter someone else's draft." There are people in publishing who blithely have writers do revisions of works that haven't been sold, even though they have little or no intention of buying the book. These same people will encourage writers to write proposal after proposal, eating up countless creative hours without any hope of it resulting in a contract. I don't include Ralph Daigh in that group. I believe he was sincere when he asked me to rewrite Joan Wood's book in anticipation of a large advance. Others aren't so genuine.

A major problem faced by writers is the natural tendency of people to suggest changes. Give a manuscript to forty people and you'll receive forty suggestions on how to revise it. That makes it imperative to have a small group of people—professional editor, astute family member, literate and candid friend—whose reactions to a manuscript can be trusted, read it. As I said earlier in this book, a good editor is worth gold, and I treasure suggestions from those in whom I have such faith. But to run a work past countless eyes is to ensure confusion and ultimately failure. Those who praise everything you write because they don't wish to offend aren't providing any favors. On the other hand, people who fall into the group cited by H.G. Wells will kick the skids out of whatever confidence you may possess by criticizing every page you've written.

Too much self-editing can also be counter productive. I've never seen a page of prose that couldn't be changed, often for the better, sometimes not. I enjoy editing my own work, and believe that all good writing is rewriting. But there comes a point when a writer must let go of a manuscript and submit it to others for their judgment, and suggestions for editorial change.

A word here about collaborations.

I'm often asked to define what makes for a good collaborator and collaboration. It's not an easy question to answer. I've worked with a wide variety of individuals, the majority of them good and pleasant people who sincerely want to contribute to their book's success. What becomes nettlesome is when they want to contribute too much, in effect looking over my shoulder at every page and refusing to allow me, the writer, to use my experience and skills to their fullest. Obviously, if I'm using someone's life experiences as the basis for a book, I need all the input they can give. But once they've delivered the factual aspects of their story and life, it's time to exhibit faith, walk away, and let me, the writer, do what I do best, shaping their material into a publishable book. Some collaborators with whom I've worked possessed the wisdom to do just that. Others, consumed by their egos, can't let go, which makes for a more difficult and less successful endeavor.

I once signed on to collaborate on a nonfiction book with a leading New York acting teacher. He was a charismatic guy whose acting studio was immensely successful. His students, hundreds of aspiring young men and women seeking to triumph on the stage and in front of the camera, paid plenty to participate in his classes, undoubtedly money they'd earned working as waiters or waitresses, or doing other nontheatrical jobs while awaiting their breakthrough.

This particular teacher's approach to teaching acting was highly psychological and confrontational. He worked with his students as though they were patients in a behavior modification therapy group, attacking them verbally to shake out of them their most traumatic life experiences that could, according to his theory, be put to use on the stage when plumbing the depth of characters they might portray. The sessions were often brutal, with many of his students breaking down in tears, or worse. I spent a lot of time at his studio taping sessions and interviewing students. And, of course, I conducted hours of taped interviews with him.

The book's premise was that the techniques he employed to develop actors and actresses could be put to use in everyday life, a self-help book of the sort that was so popular in the sixties and early seventies. The proposal I wrote was strong enough to induce G.P. Putnam's Sons, a major publisher, to offer a sizable advance, and I enthusiastically set to work on the manuscript. Although his methods with his students often caused me discomfort, I enjoyed the subject matter. I've had a long fascination with psychology, and sincerely felt that the lessons in the book could help readers navigate some of their life problems.

After having written approximately a third of the book, I sent it to my teacher-collaborator. He called and asked that I come to his apartment that afternoon to discuss the pages, and where to go next. I arrived at four and was buzzed in to a large, expensively furnished and decorated apartment. The teacher greeted me wearing a floor-length silk robe, and said he was about to take his afternoon bath. "Please wait," he said.

Being told to cool my heels after I'd arrived on time while he took a bath was annoying enough. But as time passed, and after hearing poorly sung operatic arias coming from the bathroom, my anger increased. After what seemed an eternity—it was about forty minutes—he emerged dressed and ready to go. I shelved my pique and began to discuss the book.

"Wait," he said in a stentorian tone, dramatically holding up his hand. "We have a serious problem here."

I asked what it was.

He went on to tell me that I obviously didn't understand him, and that it would be necessary to bring in another person to "translate me to you."

"Translate?"

"Yes, translate." He said a young psychologist, a friend, would be arriving shortly. She would do the translation of his inner self for me. My anger returned, but I continued to keep it in-check. A few minutes later, an attractive young woman came through the door, warmly kissed and embraced the teacher, and joined me on the couch. The teacher suggested we get to know each other and disappeared from the room.

She was a pleasant young lady with a ready smile, who seemed interested in everything I had to say. It didn't take long for her to reveal that she wasn't actually a psychologist—she was in her second year of undergraduate study at a city college—and it was obvious that she was more than just a friend of the acting teacher.

He returned to announce that a portion of the advance would go to the pretty thing sitting next to me on the couch for her translating services. It was over. I excused myself—another engagement—said I'd get back to *them*, went to a phone and called my agent: "Enough craziness," I said. "I'm sending back my portion of the advance."

Which I did.

A friend of the teacher eventually finished the book. That it ended up, as Long John Nebel would say, a "secret service book"— published without knowledge of the book buying public, with sales to reflect it—didn't give me any particular pleasure. I was just glad to be free of it, and had gone on to other projects, most of them pleasurable and profitable.

But not all of them.

This might be a good time to talk about another collaboration that didn't work, and that plunged me into the only legal action with which I've been involved in my 35-plus year writing career.

Ted Chichak, my agent, called me early in 1978 to see whether I'd be interested in ghosting a novel for a major figure in the magazine publishing industry. (Documents signed when we resolved our legal problems prohibit me from using his name.)

It was a Bill Adler project. Adler, you'll recall, was and is an "idea guy" within the publishing industry, someone who dreams up book ideas, puts together the necessary parties, and "packages" the finished product for major publishers. He was at the center of the aborted Gina Lollobrigida project, and would be instrumental in a novel I would eventually do with former congresswoman and award-winning TV reporter Marjorie Margolis-Mezvinsky, as well as a long-running collaboration on a series of novels carrying the name of a well-known person that I continue to write to this day.

I met with the magazine publisher and Adler at seven one morning in the publisher's lavishly appointed office. He was a charming man to whom I took an immediate liking. His secretary delivered coffee on an impressive sterling silver tray, the sugar in the bowl flattened to perfection with a wooden tongue depressor. After a pleasant and productive hour, it was agreed that I would write a proposal for a contemporary novel about men and women in the highly competitive and stressful magazine business that would carry the publisher's name. We tossed around many ideas about the story and characters, focusing primarily on the male protagonist who, in many ways, would mirror my collaborator. I suggested that this character be divorced to give him more latitude in his romantic and sexual life, to which this titan of magazines enthusiastically agreed.

Shortly after writing a 10-page proposal in July and sending it to Chichak, who was still with the Scott Meredith Agency, a meeting was scheduled with Michael Korda at Simon & Schuster, a large and influential publishing house. Present were my collaborator, Chichak, Bill Adler, and me. Korda strode into the room late. He was dressed in riding gear and carried a short whip. He sat behind his desk, propped his highly polished black boots on it, picked up my proposal, glanced at it, then tossed it into the air over his shoulder. That arrogant bit of action wouldn't have bothered me as much had the proposal missed the wastebasket. But swish, it landed squarely in it. A few minutes later we were dismissed. I was happy to be gone. Pomposity is always so suffocating.

A call from Chichak a week later was heartening. Another publisher, William Morrow, had offered an advance of $101-thousand for the book, which my collaborator and I quickly accepted. We met with an editor who'd made the decision to buy the book, Ellis

Amburn, and walked away from that meeting brimming with confidence. Amburn was unabashedly enthusiastic about the project, and so was I.

I worked on the manuscript through June of the following year, and delivered 180 pages to Chichak, who passed them on to Amburn. There was a significant payment due at the delivery and acceptance of the first half of the novel. The contract called for a 400-page, double-spaced manuscript; 180 pages fell short of half. But Amburn responded to Chichak with praise for the writing, and a check. He said in his letter accompanying the check, "Although the pages are short of half the manuscript, I'm paying anyway. The main thing is, what a novel! I'm spellbound."

During the period from late 1978 through July 1979, I spent considerable time with the magazine publisher. We met frequently for lunch, and a few dinners. One night, I accompanied him to Studio 54 to attend some sort of promotional party. I remember it well because after a half hour of being assaulted by the disco's insanely loud music, I opted to leave. On my way out, I bumped into radio talk show host Barry Farber, whom I knew, and we laughed about the need to escape the din. We parted on the street and I walked a block to Jimmy Ryan's jazz club where I sat at the bar and basked in the sweet, acoustic jazz being played by the club's regulars, some of whom I knew personally.

Everything was going smoothly. Amburn's positive reaction to the 180 pages I'd submitted fueled my enthusiasm as I continued to work on the novel. Equally important was the relationship I'd forged with my collaborator. I looked forward to our get-togethers. He was a man I both respected and liked, a wonderful conversationalist and compatible dining companion. Aspects of our personal lives emerged during our lunches. I was in the process of a divorce; he was happily married and spoke often of his wife, never in detail, but said on a number of occasions that he was married to a wonderful woman. My progress notes to Ted Chichak and Ellis Amburn almost always mentioned how my collaborator was a joy with which to work, and that my hopes for the novel were elevated each day. It had "bestseller" written all over it.

On September 24, I delivered to Chichak the finished manuscript, 441 pages. He told me he loved it and was sending it to Amburn. Twelve days later, Scott Meredith, whose literary agency bore his name, received a letter dated October 5 from Amburn. After saying how much he liked all the people involved with the project, he stated that the manuscript was unacceptable, that Morrow was not going forward with it, and that the $50,000 advanced to date would have to be paid back. He suggested that we try to find another publisher, whose advance would help defray what was owed Morrow.

The letter was, of course, devastating news. It was also revealing. Amburn indicated that even if the authors wished to meet with him to discuss revisions, he didn't feel a revamped manuscript would ultimately be acceptable. This flew in the face of customary publishing procedure. Authors are almost always given a shot at revising a manuscript to satisfy a publisher's concerns and incorporating suggestions into a revised version. Amburn's refusal to entertain this said clearly to me, my collaborator, Ted Chichak and Scott Meredith that Morrow was backing out for reasons having nothing to do with the manuscript. (We would later learn that Morrow was undergoing an internal upheaval and was jettisoning a number of books, using the excuse that they were "unacceptable.")

Every publishing contract contains a "delivery-and-acceptance" clause, under which a publisher can refuse to pay the "D&A" payment due if it decides to not formally accept a manuscript. Unfortunately, this clause has been misused by too many publishers for the purpose of avoiding making that final payment for reasons other than a manuscript's quality. I've seen it occur when an editor leaves a publishing house, and his or her replacement doesn't wish to work on projects brought in by the departing editor; or when a publisher decides to shift emphasis and no longer publish certain types of books. It's a cruel, cynical way of backing away from financial obligations to writers who've worked for months, perhaps years on a book, have met the editor's expectations and fulfilled what the proposal and outline promised, and are counting on the D&A payment to survive.

There wasn't much time to stew about it, however, because Chichak and Meredith quickly sought, and found, another publisher for the book, Jack Geoghegan of Coward, McCann & Geoghegan. He agreed to pay a $50,000 advance, ten of which was paid on signing, the remaining $40,000 to be paid on delivery and acceptance of a completed manuscript. My collaborator and I met with Geoghegan, who wanted certain changes in the existing manuscript. Working with Jack Geoghegan was one of the highlights of my writing career. He was the consummate gentleman, exposing rough edges when appropriate, but never losing focus on why we were there—to come up with the best possible book that would become a commercial success.

Geoghegan's major concern about the manuscript was that it wasn't hard-edged enough, the characters a little too sanguine. He summed it up in a letter to Meredith when he said, "(Magazine publisher) is obviously concerned with his fictional image. Bain, a most agreeable guy, finds it difficult to withstand these demands. (Magazine publisher) is inclined to give Bain the kind of story direction that blurs the very sharp edges the story requires—and which are now missing."

He was absolutely right. A major problem every writer faces when working with a collaborator, especially a high visibility one, is balancing the collaborator's image needs with the demands of a good fictional story. In retrospect, I realize I was too aware of my collaborator looking over my shoulder, making many suggestions that while satisfying his psychic needs, got in my way of producing a good story. Ghosting a novel places the writer in the untenable position of serving two masters, the publisher who wants a good book, and the collaborator who wants his or her image enhanced.

Numerous meetings ensued with Jack Geoghegan, and correspondence flowed suggesting revisions to the novel. My collaborator and I also met frequently. By this time, I'd decided that if the
project were to fulfill its promise, I'd have to stiffen my resolve
with the magazine publisher and write to satisfy Jack Geoghegan
and his publishing house. My collaborator acquiesced and told me
to run with it, to craft the sort of commercial novel that was
promised in the beginning. As he said to Geoghegan, "Don is
going to put claws into the story. It'll be steel-edged."

And Meredith reinforced that pledge in a November 6, 1979 letter to Geoghegan: "The problems arose because Don Bain was writing with one uneasy eye focused on (magazine publisher) at all times,
and his fear of embarrassing him or compromising him found its
way into the book, and weakened it. But (magazine publisher) now
understands how this has hurt the manuscript, and the necessity of
giving Don a free hand, and Don will now simply write the best
book he can, without worrying and sticking to your suggestions."

Meredith's support of me throughout the process was encouraging and appreciated. I forged ahead and delivered a completely
revised manuscript in the summer of 1980, more than 100 pages
longer than the original. The hard work and long hours had paid
off. Geoghegan wrote me in August: the book would be one of
Coward, McCann & Geoghegan's lead titles for spring 1981. A lead
title means a publisher will put extra effort and money behind it.
The $40,000 D&A payment was promptly paid, and all I had to
do was wait for publication and see the fruits of my efforts make
bestseller lists and generate big royalties. A stunning cover was
designed for the book; ads were created; the publicity blitz started
(a photo of my collaborator hunched over a typewriter "writing"
the book appeared in several newspapers); the manuscript spawned
competitive bidding interest at major magazines for first-serial
rights; and the publisher took a large ad in *Publishers Weekly*, the
publishing industry's leading trade journal, announcing the pend-
ing publication of an important novel. Having Ellis Amburn and

William Morrow jettison the book had turned out to be a good thing. The book and I were in good and capable hands at Coward, McCann & Geoghegan.

My pleasure was short-lived, however. My collaborator told Jack Geoghegan that he needed time to make final revisions in the manuscript. This dismayed Geoghegan, who expressed his displeasure to Scott Meredith. Going back into the manuscript at this late date to make revisions would delay publication, adversely affecting sales when it finally did come out. The manuscript had already gone into production. Pulling it would be expensive and counterproductive to everyone's best interests.

Geoghegan wrote my collaborator on February 12, 1981, informing him in stern language that he had until March 10 to submit his changes for approval. He missed that deadline and said he needed more time. To my surprise, and disappointment, Geoghegan gave him an extension. Pub date was put off a year, and the magazine publisher was given until September 1 to make his changes. On April 23, Ted Chichak sent a strongly worded letter to my collaborator, pointing out how uncooperative he'd been, and informing him that come September 1, the book would go to press. (The publisher's attorneys concluded that they had the right to publish with or without changes from the man whose name would appear on the book as its author.)

I received a call during this period from my collaborator, who wanted to meet for lunch at the University Club in Manhattan. What he said stunned me. According to him, the problems he was having with the manuscript had to do with his wife of many years. In the novel, I'd created a fictitious ex-wife for the divorced male character. My collaborator's wife in real life saw herself in that character, and accused her husband of having revealed to me unflattering information about her upon which the fictitious character was based. Nothing could have been further from the truth. The magazine publisher had never said a word about her except that she was a wonderful woman and wife. In a sense, I was flattered that I'd fashioned such a three-dimensional female character. But that was small solace. My collaborator told me that not only was his wife upset about the book, colleagues within the magazine industry to whom he'd showed the manuscript were critical of him for dredging up "inside dirt" about that business. There was a certain truth to this. My collaborator had suggested at the beginning that I come up with a phony credential that would allow me free access to his magazine empire and the people working for him. I had an old business card from a radio syndication company with which I'd been involved, Royyce Communications, and with my collaborator's blessing I told people at the magazines that I was researching a series of radio programs about their publications. I'd evidently been told too much "inside dirt," and had put it to effective use in the novel.

The bottom line at lunch was that this magazine executive's wife was threatening to divorce him if he went ahead and put his name on the novel as written. But he promised that he would make all his changes quickly and submit them to the publisher. What that meant to me, of course, was that the "claws" he'd said the revised novel would enjoy would probably be defanged. Hopefully, Jack Geoghegan would resist such changes and go with the story as it stood.

The next thing I heard came from Ted Chichak, who called to tell me that my collaborator had returned his share of the advance to the publisher and told them to "burn the book." I was shocked when they agreed to do just that. The reason, of course, was obvious. Because of my collaborator's stature in the magazine industry, he was in the position of buying lucrative first serial rights from book publishers. Too, I suppose, not having him publicly stand behind the book and promote it would have adversely impacted sales. All I knew was that I'd devoted more than two years of my creative life to the project, with nothing to see for that effort. Most of the advance had gone to pay back William Morrow. Any money to be made would come from royalties and subsidiary rights sales, magazine serialization, foreign rights, and performing rights. Based upon the novel's promise, those sums would have been substantial.

I was furious, and expressed it in a letter to my collaborator. But my anger really exploded when I received a letter from an attorney for Coward, McCann & Geoghegan demanding that I return any portion of the advance I'd received. I went to war with the publisher and its attorneys, as well as with a collection agency they'd retained. I pointed out in a series of letters that I'd written a good book that was enthusiastically accepted by a major publisher, had done all the revisions requested of me, and was in no way responsible for my collaborator's decision and that of the publisher to "burn the book." Scott Meredith and Ted Chichak were firmly in my corner, and expressed it in their letters to the parties involved. Their support pleased me greatly. Although literary agents represent the writers in their stables, and receive their money from a percentage of a writer's earnings, they often side with a publisher in such a dispute. The reasoning behind it is that while a writer might produce a limited number of salable books in his or her career, a publisher is in a position to buy many books from many writers represented by an agency. This certainly wasn't the case here.

I felt I didn't have any choice but to sue my collaborator. An attorney in the family into which I eventually married, Richard Nidel, took the case and aggressively pursued the magazine publisher. As happens in most such litigation, we settled. He paid me $40,000 with the stipulation that any copies of the manuscript "in my possession" would be shredded (there were a half-dozen copies in the hands of family members or friends that were never mentioned), and that I would not seek to publish the book with any other publisher. I agreed, took the money, and moved on. But to this day, a bitter taste remains in my mouth about the experience. This charming, successful gentleman, whose career was based upon encouraging writers and championing their cause, had turned out to be a major disappointment to me. The "cover" of himself he presented to me was certainly impressive. Unfortunately, his content didn't match up.

CHAPTER EIGHTEEN

"At Least With the Mob, You Can Believe When They Promise You Something"

Choosing a favorite out of the more than 90 books I've written is complicated by the fact that I believe some of my best work appears in a 25-book series of novels ghostwritten over the past 25 years for a well-known person. It would be professionally inappropriate for me to take public credit for this series, although I'm not under contractual obligation to conceal my involvement. Many of my written agreements as a ghost have contained a clause under which I agreed to not reveal that I'd written the book. But legal agreement or not, it's understood that unless given permission, a ghost is expected to remain silent in the background.

I believe in honoring this understanding, and have little patience with those ghosts who don't. In line with this, I'm always amused at writers who sign on to ghost a book with the understanding that their name will not appear on the book—and that the ostensible author will go out and promote the book—and then complain publicly about their lack of recognition. Literary agent Lucianne Goldberg is a case in point. She ghosted *Washington Wives* for

Maureen Dean, wife of Watergate figure John Dean. Mrs. Dean did what she was expected to do once the novel was published. She went out into the public and promoted her book, including giving an interview to the *Washington Post* in which she said, "Every morning I have to have Number Two pencils, very sharp. My housekeeper sharpens them for me. And I get a stack of legal pads and I write and write until I am exhausted."

This undoubtedly will strike many as hypocritical, perhaps even downright dishonest, creating a scenario of how she wrote the book when she hadn't written a word. But that was *the deal*. That's always *the deal* when a book is ghostwritten—the ghost writes, and the author-of-record promotes.

But Ms. Goldberg was angered at Mrs. Dean's efforts, terming it tacky. She went public and claimed credit for the book, which in my opinion was a tasteless breach of her obligation. *That* was tacky.

I sometimes wish I could take public credit for a successful book I've ghosted, especially when it ends up on major bestseller lists and receives sterling reviews. Of course, when a book I've ghosted doesn't succeed at the cash register, or receives a less than favorable review, my reputation is preserved; my collaborator whose name is on the book takes the heat.

I've had a few amusing moments when with a group of people who are discussing a book I've ghosted, and have no idea I'd written it. I remember one in particular, a black tie affair during which I was engaged in conversation with a half dozen people. One of my books became the subject, and a woman said she'd read it and didn't like it. She turned to me: "Have you read it?' she asked.

"Yes," I replied.

"What did *you* think of it?"

"I thought it was wonderful," I said, excusing myself to get a drink.

Is a book buyer cheated when buying a novel not written by the person whose name appears on the cover? Is it fraud? I don't think so, although my bias is understandable. For me, it boils down to whether the book is any good or not. In most cases, the consumer gets a lot better book than if the nonwriting collaborator had attempted to do it solo.

This sort of debate really revolves around the ghosting of fiction, not nonfiction. I think everyone accepts that professional writers are called in to write nonfiction books in collaboration with famous people. We all know that politicians deliver speeches crafted by their speechwriters, and that business leaders make numerous addresses written by their PR departments. That's all accepted, although some who enjoy the efforts of ghostwriters display hypocritical displeasure with the practice. I was once a guest on a network TV morning show discussing ghostwriting. The reporter displayed overt scorn at the practice, which I found remarkable. She sat there in the studio, her every uttered word written by someone else and scrolling in front of her on a Teleprompter.

But fiction, I suppose, is judged by a different standard than nonfiction. At least some book buyers thought so when they filed a lawsuit in 2001 after having bought a novel by best-selling author William Caunitz. Caunitz had just started his new book when he died in 1996, and his friend, Christopher Newman, was commissioned by the publisher to complete it. When *Chains of Command* was published in 1999, Caunitz's name was prominently displayed on the cover, with Newman receiving only a small credit on the title page. A few people who'd bought the book filed a class action suit against the book's publisher, citing fraud. The court upheld their action. Any damages suffered by these literary plaintiffs is purely conjecture—the price of a hardcover book? More important, did they enjoy the book? If so, what are they suing about?

I was interested in this case for two reasons. The first reason is obvious. I'm a ghostwriter. The second stems from possibly having been tangentially involved with this case ever having been brought.

I'd received a call in early 2000 by a producer from "CBS Sunday Morning" hosted by Charles Osgood. They wanted to do a segment on ghostwriting and asked me to participate. I did, and a correspondent from the show and her crew spent a day at my home taping interviews. When the show finally aired, the primary focus was on Chris Newman and his ghostwriting role in the Caunitz novel. I don't know whether that TV exposure played a role in prompting people to sue, although I suspect it did.

(My attorney, Frank Curtis, recently informed me that the Caunitz case had been overturned on appeal.)

* * * * *

My favorite book?

I'm often asked to name a favorite during question-and-answer sessions following talks I give, most notably on ships such as the QE2 and the Seabourn Sun, and am never comfortable doing it. The long-running ghostwritten series aside, there are many books that please me, either because I think they represent good work; because I enjoyed the people with whom they brought me into contact; or simply because I took pleasure in the actual writing of them. I've loved every one of the 29-book "Murder, She Wrote" series of murder mystery novels I've written, based upon the popular TV show starring Angela Lansbury. Again, I've been fortunate to work with wonderful editors at Signet, and to travel the world researching settings for this successful series. (More about that series in a subsequent chapter.) Even the nine westerns I wrote under the pseudonym J.D. Hardin were pleasurable, if only because it prompted me to learn about the history of the Old West and to build a substantial library on the subject.

But if pushed to the wall to come up with a short list, I suppose I can cite three books, one of which is *A Member of the Family* by Nick Vasile, a novel based upon a true story, which I ghosted in collaboration with friend and novelist Tony Tedeschi. (Because Nick, now deceased, always encouraged Tony and me to take public credit for our participation in the book, I'm not breaching any confidences here.)

Vasile, to whom I'd referred earlier in this book, and who died a few years ago, had been a Washington D.C. vice squad cop, was fired for allegedly having used excessive force (against the son of a political bigwig), opened a restaurant and nightclub on Long Island, and became a New York licensed private investigator. Jack Pearl and I chronicled his Washington years in *Sado Cop*, published by Playboy Press in 1976. That book, the first of two written with Vasile, was forgettable except for the role it played in a high profile mafia trial at which Nick was a witness.

His primary clients as a private detective were members of the Colombo crime family, one of New York's five major mafia families. Nick had grown up in the rough-and-tumble Red Hook section of Brooklyn, and went on to spend WW II as a combat Marine in the South Pacific where he was seriously wounded. After his stint as a D.C. vice squad cop, he opened his restaurant and nightclub in Roslyn, L.I., which is where we met, and where he'd earlier renewed a relationship with an old friend from Red Hook, Andrew Russo, allegedly a captain in the Colombo crime family; its reputed head was Russo's cousin, Carmine Persico.

In *Sado Cop*, Nick was brutally honest about how he and fellow officers would lie and plant evidence to put away known "bad guys." Cops in Washington D.C. during Nick's days on the force functioned a little like lawmen in the Old West—either get rid of bad apples by bending the law, or rough them up and put them on the next stagecoach out of town, in Nick's case the next Greyhound bus. Whether that's admirable or not makes little difference. That's what he told Jack and me, and that's what we wrote.

In 1986, ten years after the book had been published and gone out-of-print, Nick was the final witness in what was known in the press as the "eight-month mafia trial." Nick had been the chief investigator for the defense, and took the witness stand confident that he was prepared to handle any questions thrown at him during cross-examination. The direct examination by one of the defense lawyers went well. But as the prosecutor was about to get up to begin his cross, Nick saw him reach into a briefcase and pull from it a copy of *Sado Cop*. Nick admitted that the book was his when asked, and answered affirmatively when the prosecutor further queried whether Nick stood behind its contents. That was the end of Nick Vasile as a credible witness. The prosecutor cited paragraph after paragraph in which Nick admitted to having lied to superiors, judges, district attorneys and other government and court officials. He told me he'd never felt so uncomfortable in his life, and left the stand embarrassed, relieved when the ordeal was over.

But something good came out of that trial for me, the *real* story behind it that became the basis for the novel, *A Member of the Family*.

The events leading to an indictment and conviction of Andrew Russo and Carmine Persico took a long and convoluted route, and Vasile knew every twist and turn from the inside. Here's a bare-bones synopsis.

One of the FBI's top priorities was putting Persico away for life. He'd recently come out of prison after serving time on a truck hijacking conviction and was vulnerable. (I met Russo at a dinner Vasile had arranged for us at his Lake Tower Inn, the purpose to see whether I'd be interested in writing a book about how Persico had been framed by the feds on the hijacking rap. I wasn't interested. I was, however, impressed with Andrew Russo. He was no central casting Mafioso. He wore a blue button-down shirt, white cable-knit sweater, and was well read and conversant on a variety of subjects. It was an extremely pleasant, if occasionally awkward evening.)

The FBI caught a wise guy named Puglisi in a sting and cut a deal with him: Carmine Persico was being accused of evading income taxes. Puglisi was to go to him and claim he had a rogue IRS agent in his pocket who could fix Persico's tax problems. If they nailed Persico for attempting to bribe a federal agent, it was back to prison. Puglisi played out the FBI-choreographed scheme, Persico was recorded offering the bribe, was arrested, and was released on bail. Although Vasile never knew what eventually happened to Puglisi, it was assumed he went into the Witness Protection Program.

The FBI wasn't through with Persico. At the time of his release on bail, Russo's sister was dating a soldier in the family named Fred DeChristopher, who according to Nick defined lowlife. Like Puglisi, DeChristopher was also caught in an FBI sting for selling drugs and was offered a deal. "Marry Russo's sister and feed us information from inside the family," De Christopher was told, "or you're going away for a very long time."

The wedding reception was held at Vasile's Lake Tower Inn. Nick had taken an instant dislike to DeChristopher the first time they'd met, and told Russo repeatedly he didn't trust him. But Russo was happy for his sister and turned a deaf ear to Vasile's warnings.

DeChristopher spent three years providing damaging information to the feds as a member of the family—in both senses of the phrase. During that period, Persico, feeling the heat, fled. Where did he go to hide out? He holed up in the supposedly safe and secure home shared by Mr. and Mrs. Fred DeChristopher. It was an FBI dream come true. The agency allowed Persico to remain there while DeChristopher continued to help them build the case against the Colombo family leader. They went as far as to offer a $50,000 reward for information leading to Carmine Persico's arrest, even though they knew exactly where he was every minute of the day and night.

When an arrest was finally made, DeChristopher disappeared, and Russo and his attorneys hired Vasile to find him. He didn't surface until the pretrial hearing when the prosecution waltzed him in as their chief witness against Russo and Persico. His testimony put Carmine Persico away for more than 100 years, and sent Russo to prison, too, for a shorter sentence. Unlike Puglisi, who it was assumed had gone into the Witness Protection Program, DeChristopher's entry into that program was common knowledge, and he remains in it to this day unless he's dead, either from natural causes or at the vengeful hand of a Mafioso.

Nick related this story to me over many months as it unfolded, and I was spellbound with its layers of drama and the issues raised by it. How devastating it must have been for Russo's sister to learn that the reason DeChristopher had swept her off her feet and married her was to put her brother and cousin behind bars.

Like the debate surrounding the government using a sadistic killer like Sammy Gravano to put John Gotti away, getting into bed with a devil like DeChristopher to convict Persico and Russo haunted Vasile. Nick was a flag waver, a believer in law-and-order. He could have gone either way, wise guy or cop, and he chose the latter. His two daughters have gone on to impressive careers, one as an assistant D.A. in the New York area, the other chief investigator for a large New York City government agency. He was no apologist for organized crime, but he did respect the fact that he could depend upon Russo and Persico's word.

In early 1990, I suggested to Nick that Tedeschi and I write a proposal for a nonfiction book from Nick's insider perspective about how DeChristopher and the FBI collaborated to put away Russo and Persico. Nick agreed. When we'd finished the 25-page proposal, Nick felt he had to first run it past Persico. He took it with him to a federal prison where Persico was incarcerated and allowed him to read it. A few days later, Nick arrived at my home, obviously unhappy about something.

"What happened?" Tony asked.

"Carmine doesn't want it done. He's very serious."

"Why?" I asked. "You thought the book might even help him with his appeals."

"He doesn't see it that way," Vasile replied.

A week later, after discussing it with Tedeschi, we proposed to Vasile that we use the story as a basis for a novel rather than a nonfiction account, with fictitious characters, and set it in Washington instead of New York, a city I know quite well. And Nick's years as a detective in Washington provided an intriguing addition to the story. He was well versed in the rumored deal between J. Edgar Hoover and the mafia for the mob to stay out of D.C. in exchange for allowing organized crime to flourish in other cities, and we made good use of it in the novel.

After Nick agreed to go forward with the book, we went to work on *A Member of the Family*, a title Tedeschi came up with while we were traveling back to New York from Washington on Amtrak after having researched a book we'd contracted to write for a leading business leader. Bob Gleason, who'd been my editor at Playboy Press for *The Control of Candy Jones*, the series of western novels I'd written under the pseudonym J.D. Hardin, and my attempt at writing historical fiction, was now at St. Martin's Press. He liked the proposal and agreed to publish the novel under the TOR imprint headed by Tom Dougherty.

Writers to whom the manuscript was sent in search of blurbs for the cover responded with glowing comments. Pulitzer Prize-winning columnist Jack Anderson called it "a powerhouse" of a novel. Legendary DEA agent Mike Levine, author of *New York Times* bestseller *Deep Cover*, called it "the first novel since *The Godfather* to take us into the higher echelons of a mob family." Robert Moss, who wrote such novels as *Carnival of Spies*, *Monimbo* and *Moscow Rules* said, "The mafia has inspired numberless yarns, but few that are as exciting or authentic as Nick Vasile's first novel." *Mystery Scene* magazine termed it "One hell of a read!" and Loren D. Estleman, award-winning author of *Kill Zone*, called Nick Vasile "a George V. Higgins for the nineties." There were a dozen other such accolades.

Reviews of the hardcover were uniformly wonderful, the sort of praise you can't buy. *Publisher's Weekly* called *A Member of the Family* ". . . a fast-paced and intricate page-turner . . . The pacing is terrific. Plot, counterplot and subplot swirl cinematically right up to the ironic ending. With its coolly unsentimental look at a particularly unpleasant *dramatis personae*, this novel is a natural for Hollywood."

Can't get better than that, right?

The problem was that the publisher went back on promises—the initial printing was to be 50,000 copies; it ended up being 15,000—and elaborate marketing and publicity plans went by the boards. Nick's book signing appearances were characterized by the books never showing up. (Like virtually every writer, I've suffered the same embarrassment in my career with other publishers). He was guest of honor at a meeting of the International Conference of Private Investigators at the Waldorf in Manhattan, and was to sign books there. No books. When Tedeschi and I tried to buy copies from the publisher for our own use, we were told there weren't any books left in the warehouse. But they never went back to press.

In more than 30 years in the publishing industry, I've seldom complained about a publisher's lack of cooperation and support. I try to understand the business they're in and have been accepting of gaffes and miscues in the publication of my books. But this situation was particularly upsetting, especially for Vasile. As he said bitterly to me one day, "At least with the mob you can believe when they promise you something."

I continue to believe that one day, *A Member of the Family* will become a motion picture, and enjoy republication that will allow a large number of readers to enjoy the story Nick lived, even in its fictional form. Nick Vasile became one of my closest friends, and we planned to treat ourselves to a few days in Las Vegas to shoot craps in celebration of our book being made into a movie. Should that happen, I may go to Vegas myself and throw a string of winning numbers in Nick's memory. Knowing Nick, he might even wrangle a pass from St. Peter and join me.

CHAPTER NINETEEN

"Bury Me in a Catholic Cemetery; the Devil Will Never Look for a Jew There"

Where do book ideas come from?

For a ghostwriter, they usually begin with a publisher that has decided it wants to do a book with a well-known person, or to publish a nonfiction book on a subject it feels will have wide appeal to the reading public. The idea is handed to the ghost, who's expected to create a marketable book based upon it. In order to be successful as a ghost, the writer must be malleable enough to handle diverse subject matter, or write in a variety of other "voices." Dealing with myriad subjects and collaborators has been for me one of the joys of my professional life. I've been forced to learn about many things, and have been exposed to people whose lives and views have been different from mine, and from whom I've learned a great deal. It's hard to go stale as a busy ghostwriter; writer's block seldom strikes.

But for the books that bear my byline, the ideas had to come from me. You never know where or when a good idea will emerge. The genesis for *War in Illinois* occurred early in 1976 while driving on the Long Island Expressway. It led me into months of fascinating research into that insane period of our nation called Prohibition, and ultimately resulted in the book that I consider my best.

It was a sunny morning as I drove into Manhattan from my home on Long Island. I was listening to WCBS, the all-news radio station. CBS film and theater critic, Joel Siegel, came on with a feature about the publication of the *National Lampoon Bicentennial Calendar*, which highlighted infamous days in America's history, as opposed to dates of which to be proud. One he cited occurred on November 12, 1926; the only bombing from an aircraft within the continental United States. (Until 9/11/01.) Siegel reported that the event took place when a bootlegging gang used an aircraft to drop sticks of dynamite on the farmhouse of Charlie Birger, a rival bootlegger.

A few days later, I drove in the opposite direction to Long Island's Stony Brook University where I'd learned that the *Chicago Tribune* was on microfilm going back to the 20s. The gang war between Birger and his archrivals from East St. Louis, the Shelton Brothers, was well documented. The battlefield was southern Illinois, often referred to as "Little Egypt" because of its largest town, Cairo (pronounced Care-O). The more I read, the more I realized I was sitting on a remarkable story that begged to be written.

Charlie Birger was a New York Jew who'd drifted to Williamson County in southern Illinois, at the time a lawless, impoverished coal mining area of the state. Birger, who greeted people with "Howdy-do," and who pronounced his name as one word, CharlieBirger—with the accent on Charlie—idolized Chicago's mob leader Al Capone, and decided to build himself a rum-running empire south of the big city. He put together a ragtag gang that couldn't shoot straight and bumbled his way, fueled by delusions of grandeur, into a dominant position as the area's leading provider of illegal booze.

But the three big, burly Shelton Brothers from East St. Louis coveted Williamson County for their own bootlegging activities and went to war with CharlieBirger. And what a war it was. The Sheltons tried to buy a World War I tank from Henry Ford in Detroit, but abandoned the idea when it was decided it would be too time-consuming to try driving it down to southern Illinois on public roads. So they built a tank, which prompted CharlieBirger to do the same. Things got so out of hand that local government brought in the Ku Klux Klan, led by a crazed gunman named Glenn Young, to restore law and order. That set the Sheltons and Birger against the Klan. When Young was killed, the rival gangs were back at each other's throats, with the Sheltons hiring a couple of itinerant barnstorming pilots and their open cockpit, biwing plane to drop homemade bombs on Birger's treasured Shady Rest, a lodge he had constructed as a fortress against his enemies.

All of this was amply covered in the microfilm archives of the *Chicago Tribune* at Stony Brook. But I needed to go to Williamson County, soak up the atmosphere that was the scrim for the story, and try to find people who'd witnessed the madness that was southern Illinois back in the 1920s. That trip, the first of several, took shape when my 16-year old daughter, Laurie, who never failed to read the obituaries each day, caught an item in *Newsday*. James S. Pritchard, who'd been sheriff in neighboring Franklin County, and who'd been the one who'd eventually ended Birger's crime empire, had died of old age in a veteran's hospital. I called there, got the name of the funeral parlor, called it and reached two of Pritchard's sons. Letters to them resulted in being invited to the home of Charles Pritchard, a highway patrolman. Charles Pritchard, a big, rawboned guy with an easygoing manner, not only provided me with a treasure trove of anecdotal material, he had photos of Birger and his gang, as well as a series of crudely drawn sketches by one Harvey Dungey, a moronic member of the gang who immortalized its madcap adventures with pen and crayon on paper. It was a homerun, a writer and researcher's bonanza.

Because the story was so obviously compelling, Ted Chichak didn't have any trouble selling it to John Kirk, editor in chief of

Prentice-Hall's Trade Book division. Kirk responded positively only three days after receiving a brief proposal I'd written. I signed a contract with them on April 22, 1976, with a delivery date of June of the following year.

Further research and the writing went well. I met people in Little Egypt who knew CharlieBirger, including a member of his gang who'd just gotten out of prison. He agreed to a clandestine meeting at my motel only after we'd gone through a series of cloak-and-dagger moves worthy of an Eric Ambler spy novel. I became so enamored of my trips to southern Illinois that I ended up spending eight weeks there over a four-month span, spending more on my expenses than I'd received as an advance. Researching and writing the book was a labor of love, so remarkable was the tale and its assortment of crazy characters. It was during one of those trips that I came across a facet of the story that I hadn't been aware of before, which added a wonderful new dimension.

There had been a woman, Helen Holbrook, a beautiful young blonde society babe, who lived in a mansion in Shawneetown, a bustling commercial river town. She'd become a mistress to both CharlieBirger and to one of the Shelton Brothers. Her sexual double-dealing eventually led to Birger's downfall, and her own demise. Having a strong female character would round out the story, I knew, and I spent considerable time in Shawneetown delving into Ms. Holbrook's life. There were plenty of people willing to talk about Helen and her scandalous behavior. What fun.

Sheriff Jim Pritchard, with plenty of help from Helen Holbrook, the Shawneetown Dame, eventually tricked Birger into giving himself up for the murder of the mayor of a neighboring town who was aligned with the Shelton Brothers. Charlie was hanged in front of thousands of onlookers who viewed him as a local folk hero, the region's Robin Hood. Birger had two things to say just before the hatch was sprung: "It certainly is a beautiful day." And, "Bury me in a Catholic cemetery. The Devil will never look for a Jew there!" I have photos of Birger's execution on my office wall, along with the Harvey Dungey sketches.

I was fortunate to have a good editor assigned to the project, Don Preston, who'd "edited" Jackie Suzanne's *Valley of the Dolls*. *War in Illinois* was multilayered and populated with a large cast, which necessitated a character list upfront, and maps of the area. Preston worked with me to streamline the story and to provide needed differentiation between minor characters. As I mentioned earlier in this book, a good editor is worth gold; working with a pro like Preston was a treat.

All in all, the experience with Prentice-Hall was positive. They cared about and believed in the book, and were supportive throughout the writing, editing and marketing process. My sole quarrel with them was over the title. I'd proposed *War in Illinois* only as a working title on the proposal. I didn't want it on the finished book, and made my feelings known. But by the time publication neared, everyone at Prentice-Hall liked the working title and insisted it remain. The results were predictable. Although reviews were excellent, and I did an author tour throughout the Midwest, appearing on many TV and radio shows, and giving interviews to print media, sales reflected that the book was considered a "regional book;" sales were brisk in the Midwest, weak everywhere else.

There has been motion picture interest in the book since its publication in the fall of 1978, the most recent from a young producer, Brad Waisbren, who'd read a dog-eared copy while on location for another film. He's been attempting to put together a development deal with a major studio for the past three years. As with *A Member of the Family*, I remain optimistic that this incredible true story, and the saga of CharlieBirger, will one day make it to movie screens.

A screenplay I recently wrote based upon the book has been well received in that strange place called Hollywood. Waisbren waltzed me through a series of meetings in Hollywood—we *took* breakfast, lunch and dinner—and at each meeting the point was made that they would have trouble selling me as the screenwriter "because of your age." The concept of age discrimination evidently hasn't reached L.A. yet. Maybe the story behind *War in Illinois* is too old, too, for Hollywood's designer jeans crowd. We'll see.

I haven't had to live with the title all these years, however. In April 1984, I received a call from one Robert Austin, who heads up a small publisher in southern Illinois, Austin Periodical Services. He told me how much he loved my book, and wondered if it might be possible to publish an edition of his own. By that time I'd gotten back the rights from Prentice-Hall and was free to make my own deals. I told Austin that I'd entertain giving him the rights to publish a trade paperback version (large paperback format as opposed to the smaller mass-market paperback form), but only under certain conditions. I wanted to change the title to *Charlie and the Shawneetown Dame,* and to use my own artist to design a new cover. He agreed. I offered him the rights he sought for the grand sum of one dollar, with provisions for royalties to be paid on each book sold. We signed our agreement in June of 1984, and the book has been published with its new title and cover ever since. My royalty checks arrive twice a year, never big sums, but symbolic to me of the book's worth. Having it remain in print all these years is immensely satisfying. Paul Nathan of *Publishers Weekly* found the deal with Robert Austin sufficiently interesting to write a piece about it for his publication. And I receive to this day letters from people who've read the book, some of whom were witnesses to the gang war between CharlieBirger and the Shelton Brothers. Had I not had the radio on that morning in 1976, I never would have known about the bizarre war between those gangs during Prohibition. Thank you, Joel Siegel.

In 2004, after the rights to *Charlie and the Shawneetown Dame* had reverted back to me, Purdue University Press reissued the book in a trade paperback edition, available in bookstores and online.

CHAPTER TWENTY

"PUT A LITTLE GIN IN THE BABY'S BOTTLE"

The third book on my short list of favorites?

I have a particular fondness for a book I wrote in 1997 with a good friend, Joe Scott, a widely published food, wine and travel writer. It came about when Paul Fargis, another friend and one of the publishing industry's most respected book developers, called to ask if I'd be interested in writing a guide for home bartenders. He felt it was time for a new and better book to replace the popular *Mr. Boston* bar guide.

The notion was intriguing, and I told Paul I'd get back to him.

I called Scott and asked if he'd be interested in collaborating on such a book. He was. We met and started work on a proposal. Because Joe and I shared a background in public relations and marketing (he'd been a PR executive at American, then at Eastern Airlines), we factored our mutual PR experiences into the proposal. What if, we mused, we could do the book in concert with a leading restaurant chain, which would provide useful cross-promotion possibilities?

Sandy Teller, PR practitioner from my Nebel days, who got us through the SADDL episode, has represented the steakhouse chain, Morton's, for many years, and it was through Teller that I'd become friendly with the chain's chairman and CEO, Allen Bernstein. Morton's, an upscale collection of restaurants with locations across America and around the world, seemed a perfect match for an upscale bartending guide. It didn't work. Morton's marketing people, for reasons only they understand, seemed uncomfortable becoming involved with anything not directly related to choosing and cooking filet mignons.

We next tried the Ruth's Chris steakhouse chain, and again came up a cropper, due to some vague internal restructuring going on there.

As it turned out, not nailing down a restaurant partner proved to be a blessing. Again, we played the what-if game. What if we were to arbitrarily choose the world's 50 greatest bars, contact their managers and bartenders, and base the book on solid advice from these professionals? A brainstorming session with our wives resulted in an impressive list of 50 establishments, approximately 35 of which either Joe or I had personally visited over the span of our careers. Because we felt it was necessary to have national and global geographic diversity, we chose additional cities in which neither of us had personal knowledge of their bars, and enlisted friends in those places who conducted their own limited Zagat-like surveys to come up with the most popular watering holes.

Once we had our 50 bars selected, we created a lengthy questionnaire, which, after securing agreements to cooperate by phone, was sent to each of the bartenders at these establishments. The results were gratifying. The bartenders came back with dozens of their personal recipe variations on popular drinks, as well as drinks of their own creation. And they provided plenty of anecdotes about celebrities they'd served, their idiosyncrasies, unusual drink requests, and in some cases their behavior when at the bar. In addition, they answered a long list of questions including identifying the sort of customers that pleased them the most, or drove them nuts.

Armed with this material from the pros behind the bar, we set out to research the origins of the most popular drinks, and the history of alcoholic beverages. Fargis had sold the project to John Duff at Perigee Books, part of the Berkley Publishing Group, a division of Penguin-Putnam, and we were assigned a veteran freelance cookbook editor, Jeanette Egan, who worked with us from her home in Arizona. Everyone had agreed with our suggestion that we not go the route of most bar guides in which every drink known to man is included, three-quarters of which will never be made or tasted, at least not by anyone with standards, or a minimally functional palate. In addition, we wanted to make the book readable, a source of information for home bartenders who wanted to serve up some fascinating tidbits along with the drinks they were serving their guests. Most reviews pointed out that the book was a joy to read, as well as a useful guide to drink recipes. We'd succeeded.

The World's Best Bartenders' Guide was published in 1998. Although neither Joe nor I liked the cover (some people who bought the book on amazon.com and reviewed it there even commented on the bad cover), it didn't seem to negatively impact sales. It sells well to this day, and has become a popular business gift, resulting in substantial bulk sales around the holidays.

Why am I particularly fond of this book? Like working with Tony Tedeschi on *A Member of the Family*, collaborating with a pro like Joe Scott made the hardest aspects of the project seem easy and enjoyable. It provided me with a welcome diversion from the murder mysteries I've been immersed in for years. And, the historical material we collected gave me yet another subject area with which to become familiar.

Oh, about the title of this chapter. When I was born, my mother, God bless her Anglo-Saxon soul, put a little gin into my baby bottle each night to help me sleep. I was a very good baby, and to this day I consider a cold, dry martini to be one of life's supreme pleasures.

*   *   *   *   *

I can't leave the subject of favorite things I've written without mentioning the liner notes I wrote for a jazz album by Oliver Jones. Oliver grew up next door in Montreal to the great jazz pianist, Oscar Peterson; his piano teacher was Oscar's sister, Daisy. After many years traveling in the Caribbean as musical director for a popular calypso singer, Oliver decided to devote his career to playing jazz, and set out to make his mark in that challenging musical genre.

My wife and I met Oliver one afternoon in Montreal. A sign in the window of a downtown hotel said that a jazz duo was performing for the cocktail hour. We went in, took a seat, and sat in appreciative silence as Oliver, and his bassist, Charles Biddle, who also owned a popular jazz club in the city, played stunningly beautiful and complex music. Cocktail pianists seldom provide more than pleasant, non-challenging listening. But here was a world-class piano talent spinning out lush, sophisticated music, supported by a rock-solid bass player.

We spoke with Oliver during an intermission and exchanged cards. I bought two cassettes Oliver's manager had there for sale, and we returned to New York. This was during the period I was working part-time as a DJ at WGSM in Huntington, and I started playing cuts from Oliver's cassettes, sending him air-checks of those portions of my shows. A solid friendship developed over the ensuing years as Oliver fulfilled his dream to become one of the world's most respected jazz pianists.

One day, I received a call from his manager, Carol Clarke, who asked if I'd like to write the liner notes for an album Oliver was cutting with a trio at Greenwich Village's jazz club, Sweet Basil. *Would I like to?* Try and stop me. We caught the trio's sets, accompanied by a number of friends as well as Ruth Ellington, the Duke's sister, whom I'd met through Peckham Production's Tom Detienne. The Duke was dead by this time, and following Oliver's gorgeous rendition of *My Funny Valentine*, Ruth exclaimed, "Oh, how my brother would have loved him." I led off the liner notes with her comment.

I mention this episode because I have never in my career been as thrilled to receive a finished product as I was when Carol sent me the actual album. Receiving a copy of a book you've written is always exciting. Seeing a magazine article with your byline is invariably a kick. But that album, a 12-inch LP, satisfied me as nothing else ever has. It certainly had nothing to do with money; I refused payment for it. Both sides of the framed album hang proudly in my home. It reminds me each day how being a writer has brought me into contact with wonderful, talented, decent people like Oliver Jones.

CHAPTER TWENTY-ONE

HONING THE CRAFT AND REAPING THE REWARDS

"Nothing in the world can take the place of persistence. Talent will not; nothing is more common than unsuccessful men with talent. Genius will not; unrewarded genius is almost a proverb. Education will not; the world is full of educated derelicts. Persistence and determination alone are omnipotent."

I agree with Calvin Coolidge. While I believe I possess some talent, and have put it to optimum use throughout my writing career, attitude, openness to ideas and possibilities, and a commitment to working hard have played a bigger role in whatever success I've achieved.

Too many writers I've known squander their talent because of negative attitudes. They consider themselves artists, and blame everyone else for their lack of success—publishers, agents, the great unwashed reading public, even the world at large. They show up at important editorial meetings after having had too many drinks, or display an arrogant disdain toward the very people with whom they'd be expected to collaborate. They can't bother cleaning up their manuscripts because "that's what editors are for." God forbid anyone should want to change a word of their writing, even when it comes from a skilled, experienced professional whose suggested edits will result in a better book. A few such writers, of course, go on to achieve great success and can afford to posture this way. The majority cannot.

Whatever I'm writing at the moment is the most important thing I'll ever write, and maybe the last.

I agree with what that great British literary moralist, Kingsley Amis, once said about writers. Amis, as respected as he was as a novelist and essayist, also tried his hand at ghostwriting when he ghosted the James Bond novel, *Colonel Sun*. Ian Fleming, the originator of the 007 series, had died in 1964, and the publisher decided to continue with other authors writing under the name Robert Markham. It's suggested that Amis also completed *The Man With the Golden Gun* after Fleming's death, although that's never been validated. Amis said of writers, "Any proper writer ought to be able to write anything from an Easter Day sermon to a sheep-dip handout." I've written plenty of "sheep-dip handouts" but never an Easter Day sermon. But I'd be happy to if the opportunity ever presents itself.

The 1980s continued to be a fruitful time for me as a writer and ghostwriter. I wrote most of my nine J.D. Hardin westerns for Playboy Press during this period, as well as a handsome leather-bound book for *Conquistadores Del Cielo*, an exclusive organization of top commercial aviation executives that meets each year at a ranch owned by one of them. This project came through Jeff Kriendler, for whom I'd written speeches when he was head of public relations for Pan Am.

Bill Adler introduced me to Marjorie Margolies-Mezvinsky, a former award-winning NBC-TV journalist from Philadelphia, who would go on to become a one-term Democratic congresswoman. Her husband, Ed, was also in Congress (they met when she interviewed him for NBC), and they went on to create one of the most remarkable extended families I've ever known. Prior to their marriage, Marjorie was the first single woman in America to have adopted a foreign child, bringing Lee Heh from Korea in 1970, and Holly from Vietnam in 1974. A book she wrote about those experiences with veteran writer Ruth Gruber, *They Came to Stay*, received excellent reviews and was commercially successful. Ed brought children into their life from a previous marriage. They kept adopting, and having their own children, until their household consisted of 11 kids and assorted others benefiting from their generosity.

Adler had suggested to Marjorie that she write a novel about women in the TV news business, and we collaborated on *The 'Girls' in the Newsroom*. That title had accompanied the manuscript right up through final production, but Marjorie decided at the last minute that the term "girls" was sexist and derogatory. Because of the expense involved, the publisher, Charter Publications, refused to change it. The resolution was to place single quote marks around the offending word, and the novel was published in 1983. It was a strong story of three women vying for a top network anchor spot, and contained a fair number of graphic sex scenes, which proved to be problematic when Marjorie ran for Congress in 1992. Her opponent pointed to the book as proof of her "immoral character" as a candidate (shades of Nick Vasile's *Sado Cop* being used in court to destroy his credibility). She prevailed, and as a freshman member of the 103rd Congress went on to cast the deciding vote on President Clinton's first budget, which angered enough of her Philadelphia Mainline constituents to cost her a second term. She's an exemplary woman whose friendship I treasure to this day.

Two other ghosting jobs came to me in the 1980s through Allan Wilson at Lyle Stuart's publishing house. A former NYC cop had drafted a story based upon a case with which he'd been involved while on the force. It was a good story, but he was no writer. I took on the assignment of crafting it into a publishable novel, resulting in *Raven*, successfully published in hardcover in 1987, and softcover in 1988 by Berkley. This former cop then came up with a second story, which Wilson asked me to ghost. I agreed, although I was really too busy to take on another project at that moment. Tony Tedeschi collaborated with me and we wrote *Baby Farm*, a bizarre, twisted novel that wasn't nearly as successful as *Raven* had been. Only readers as perverted as the characters in the book would have enjoyed it.

In the early 80s, Lyle Stuart again entered my life, pairing me with Gerald Stein, president of Iron Gate Products, the fancy food division of the restaurant "21," and an expert on caviar. Stein was a delightful collaborator, and our efforts resulted in *Caviar, Caviar, Caviar*, a $75 coffee-table book that told readers everything they could ever possibly want to know about those wildly expensive little fish eggs. As with so many ghosting assignments, this one allowed me access to a world I'd never thought about—the high stakes world of caviar. Allan Wilson edited the book, and Lyle pulled out all the stops to promote it. Writing and having my name on a pricey, large format book filled with color photographs to accompany the text was ego-satisfying, and a copy is proudly displayed on my coffee table. It was a smooth project, but one aspect of it stands out in my memory.

At the time I was writing the book, the U.S. Government had imposed a ban on the importation of all goods from Iran. Because so much of the best caviar comes from Iran and its advantageous location on the sturgeon-rich Caspian Sea, the ban seriously impacted the pocketbooks of America's leading caviar purveyors. That led to underground smuggling of caviar into this country, much of it coming through Copenhagen where an illegal caviar smuggling center had been established.

Gerry Stein told me in exquisite detail how this illicit movement of caviar into the United States was carried out, and it became a chapter in the book titled "The Ayatollah and Me." It was a fascinating tale; I later used what I'd learned as the basis for a crime novel I went on to ghost for a well-known person.

Years after *Caviar, Caviar, Caviar* was published, I received a call one morning from a U.S. attorney in Miami. After confirming who I was, he informed me that Gerry Stein was being charged with illegally smuggling caviar into the States through Miami, and wanted me to come to Florida to testify at his trial. At first, I thought he was joking. But then he talked about "The Ayatollah and Me," reading paragraphs from the chapter, and making the point that it served as a blueprint for how Stein had carried out his alleged criminal activity.

"Look," I said, "this is all very interesting, but I'm not about to testify against Gerry Stein. Why should I? He's a very nice guy and . . . ."

"You have a fax number?" the U.S. attorney asked.

"Yes," I said, and gave it to him.

A minute later, a subpoena directing me to appear as a witness crept through my fax machine. It also subpoenaed any tapes and notes I had in my possession.

I didn't think it was legal to serve a subpoena by fax, and said so. What I didn't say was that I thought prosecuting someone for bringing in fish eggs, banned or not, was a waste not only of taxpayer money, but of law enforcement's time.

This U.S. attorney had obviously done his homework before calling. He knew the name of every famous person for whom I'd ghosted a book, and the title of every one of those books. His message was veiled but clear; if I didn't prove to be cooperative, his knowledge would become public knowledge.

A few days later, two men arrived at my office bearing an original copy of the faxed subpoena. I dreaded having to testify against Stein. Our relationship had been good, and I liked him. I considered calling him but thought better of it. I was certain he wouldn't want to talk about it. Besides, I was to be a witness. Making contact as a witness with a defendant in a criminal case wouldn't go down very well with the prosecutors. I gathered up my tape-recorded interviews I'd done with Gerry, and pages of notes I'd written, and waited for the next call. I also consulted with an attorney about whether I'd be on shaky legal ground if I refused to turn over my research materials. His advice to wait and see how things played out was good advice. All charges were eventually dropped against Stein, and I was spared the unpleasantness of having to go to Miami and testify.

Gerry Stein now lives in Miami where he's known as the "Mr. Caviar," selling top-grade caviar by mail order across the country. I erased my tapes and shredded my notes, and I buy my New Year's Eve supply from him each year. All I know is that if I intend to honor the tradition of serving caviar on New Year's Eve, my books had better continue to sell. Gold is cheaper than fish eggs.

*　　*　　*　　*　　*

The decade of the 80s also provided me an opportunity to indulge myself in two other professional pursuits I enjoy, performing as a jazz musician, and working in radio.

Clarinetist Charles Nostrand and his swing-era quintet was much in demand, playing the Benny Goodman–Lionel Hampton song book, and I found myself working dozens of weekend jobs with him that were both financially rewarding and musically satisfying. The affairs at which we performed were generally hosted and attended by older men and women who wanted no part of the rock-and-roll or disco scene, with DJs playing music at insanely loud levels that makes conversation impossible with the person sitting next to you at a table. I've reached a point where I dread being invited to weddings or bar mitzvahs, even involving loved family members, because of the noise levels that soon drive me from the room. Why people holding such events allow a DJ, or live band with massive speakers cranked up to their maximum volume, to ruin their parties will always remain a mystery to me.

The help wanted ads in *Broadcasting Magazine* prompted my return to radio. A station in Huntington, Long Island, WGSM, advertised for a disc jockey. What caught my attention was a description of the sort of musical programming the station featured—Sinatra, Basie, Ella, Louis, Goodman, Bennett and other artists I admired and enjoyed. I sent a letter to WGSM's program director, Jim Ferguson, and was invited in for an interview. After cutting a few demo tapes, I was hired. I knew it would be impossible for me to take on a full-time job because of the books I had under contract, but I worked out a deal in which I would be the fill-in DJ when full timers were out sick or on vacation, as well as doing my own regular Sunday show.

I was on the air at WGSM for four happy years. The Sunday show built up a loyal following, and I even got to play vibes with area big bands at station promotional parties attended by hundreds of listeners.

Being on the radio, and performing as a musician, gratified my ego, no question about that. Spending one's professional life working alone as a writer doesn't offer the sort of instant gratification provided by these other pursuits. There's no applause for writers, no phone calls from happy listeners. A writer spends months and years working in solitude on a book, turns the finished manuscript over to a publisher, and waits a year or more until the book is published. Is it selling? Are those people buying it actually reading it, or placing it alongside hundreds of other unread books on their shelves? Did those who read it actually like it? Some will write letters; I've received countless letters over the course of my career, and answered every one of them. Letters from readers are the only direct link a writer has with the public, along with book signings at which the writer can actually meet and shake hands with those buying the book. My many trips across the Atlantic on the QE2, and more recently the Seabourn Sun, have been among the more satisfying experiences of my life. Again, ego comes into play. I get to speak to large audiences about my career as a writer, and then get to meet the audience members individually and sign books they've purchased from the ship's bookstore.

Of course, being invited to speak on these ships has other advantages. I've met some wonderful people who've become close friends, including the British thriller writer Craig Thomas and his wife, Jill. Craig was writing techno-thrillers before Tom Clancy, and as far as I'm concerned does it better.

On one QE2 crossing, my wife, Renée and I were table partners for the entire trip with the wonderful mystery writer, P.D. James (Baroness James; Phyllis is a member of the House of Lords), and her charming editor and friend, Rosemary Goad. Actually, Phyllis is a "crime writer," the preferred British term for authors writing about murder. Here's a portion of how Baroness James described one aspect of that Atlantic crossing in her excellent memoir, *Time to be in Earnest*, published in 1999 in England and in the States.

"We found we were to share our table, always at first a depressing prospect. But the two passengers—Donald and Renée Bain—were delightful, entertaining and companionable Americans. Donald, among his varied literary achievements—he is the author of the Murder, She Wrote *series—writes books for celebrities who want to be published authors without the actual bother of having to write themselves. He was extremely discreet about his clients, but I can see the attraction. The book sells on the celebrity's name and the writer collects 50 per cent of the royalties. But it is not without its disadvantages, particularly when the celebrity draws a languid hand across his or her brow and complains about the emotional stress of creative writing, not to mention the publicity, is becoming too much. Under Don's guidance I threw craps in the casino, the first time I have ever gambled. I limited myself to $100 and left the table with $198. Rosemary played the one-armed bandits until I confiscated all her quarters."*

Renée and I remain friends with Phyllis James and Rosemary Goad, and Craig and Jill Thomas, and treasure those friendships that came out of a chance meeting aboard the QE2.

Without letters from readers to indicate their pleasure or displeasure with a book you've written, or comments at book signing events, a writer has only the reaction of reviewers upon which to gauge whether the book is being well received. Reviewers of any creative act wield tremendous power. They can close a show, diminish the value of a painting, or in the case of books convince bookstores, and by extension book buyers, not to order or buy books. Good, honest, well-meaning book reviewers provide a useful service to the reading public—and to writers. I've learned quite a lot from thoughtful reviews of my books, and have incorporated some of their comments and criticisms into future writing projects. But there are those reviewers who view the space they're given in their publications as a license to show how clever and creative *they* are, which generally results in cute, negative turns-of-phrase that do not fairly reflect the book being reviewed. Too, there are reviewers who believe that if they aren't critical of a book, they aren't doing their job. Because they're predisposed not to like anything written by anyone else, their comments are worthless. Virginia Kirkus, whose review service is one of the industry's most active, seems to fall into this "if you can't say something bad about a book, don't say anything" category. A number of writers, including this one, have learned to shrug off Kirkus reviews of their books and even laugh about them. They're no help to anyone, reader and writer alike.

* * * * *

So many projects, so little time.

In 1985, I formed Hyphenates, Ltd. with my wife-to-be, Renée Paley, a former newspaper editor and experienced business writer. The small corporation was established to provide editorial assistance to business, and we went on to work for dozens of companies, most notably Robert Half International Inc. (RHI), the first specialized staffing firm, founded by Bob Half and his wife, Maxine, as a one-office, mom-and-pop operation. After building it into a successful international franchise business, they sold the company to a corporation headed by Max Messmer, a visionary business leader who has continued to expand the business into an industry leader, with more than 330 offices worldwide, and listing on the New York Stock Exchange. Hyphenates continues to be editorial consultant to RHI, a long and mutually beneficial marriage.

It was also in the 80s that Jim Grau put me together with Abe Hirschfield, New York's Israeli-born, enigmatic, multimillionaire parking lot magnate who ran for every elected office available in New York State, and who, at the time I write this, serves prison time for having been convicted of plotting to murder a business partner. Abe wanted to write his autobiography, and I agreed after a long Saturday lunch at the Friar's Club to write a proposal. I spent considerable time with Hirschfield and his family, and came up with a proposal that ran more than 100 pages. I was paid for it; to my knowledge it never resulted in a published book. Abe went ahead and self-published the proposal as a thin book, in actuality more of a campaign brochure for his latest run for office. The last time I saw him was at Donald Trump's Mar-a-Lago in Palm Beach where he's a member. This was before his conviction. Abe is a strange, often funny man, whose ego knows no bounds, but who provided me with a few months of interesting experiences as he squired me around Manhattan. There's nothing I enjoy more than meeting and spending time with people whose lives deviate from the so-called norm, men and women who've broken some of the rules (but preferably not the law), and who march to their own internal drummer. Abe Hirschfield certainly falls into that category.

Joe Ziehl, the pianist with whom I played early in my career at the Sombrero Club, and I started a business in the 80s, providing short radio shows to public relations interests. Each show offered advice on a variety of subjects, with the client's name woven into the scripts. I wrote them, and Joe and my former wife performed them, recording them in Ziehl's Forest Hills apartment. It was successful for a few years, but Joe decided to strike out on his own and formed a competing company. I didn't have the time to pursue it alone and closed up shop.

But I did find the time to become the American Cancer Society's national radio voice. Through Hyphenates, Renée and I wrote, produced and directed the society's annual radio fund-raising campaign, using a variety of actors and actresses in the vignettes, and with me making the pitch at the end of the show. It was an enjoyable five-year run, although awkward at times for this smoker. Lunches with the cancer society's brass found me making multiple trips to the men's room for a fast cigarette. I assume they thought I had a five-year urinary tract infection, but were too polite to ask.

A dream project was offered me in the 80s, writing jazz great Lionel Hampton's autobiography with him. Working with this master vibraphonist would have been a thrill, and I enthusiastically pursued it. But Lionel had so many people surrounding him, each of whom were to receive a piece of the pie, that it left virtually nothing for the writer. When I complained, one of his entourage said, "You're just the writer."

"You're just the writer."

I walked away from a project with baseball great Yogi Berra because after everyone else took their share of the money, I was left with very little. This was not Yogi's doing, however, who I understand is one of the nicest people in the world. It was the people around him who viewed me as "just the writer."

Well-meaning people have approached me countless times to tell me they have a wonderful story to tell, and want me to collaborate with them. "All you have to do is write it," they say. And I say to them . . . .

* * * * *

The decade of the 80s was a busy one for me. But aside from the projects I've mentioned above, there were two that have defined my writing life ever since.

The first occurred in 1980 when Ted Chichak called and asked if I was interested in ghosting a murder mystery novel for a well-known person. The three of us met for lunch, and I walked away with the commission to write the book. I've been writing novels in this series ever since, a book a year, most of them well reviewed and appearing on many bestseller lists throughout the country.

The second is the subject of the next chapter.

CHAPTER TWENTY-TWO

MURDER, HE WROTE

Another call from Ted Chichak, this one in 1988, resulted in my having lunch with Russ Galen, a young agent at the Scott Meredith Agency, and Anne Sweeney, an editor from McGraw-Hill. MCA-Universal, whose TV show "Murder, She Wrote" starring Angela Lansbury was immensely popular—it's the third longest running TV series of any kind, and the longest running detective mystery series in TV history—had decided to capitalize on the show's popularity by launching a series of original murder mystery novels utilizing the TV characters, with the byline to be shared by the writer and Jessica Fletcher, who existed only as the character played by Ms. Lansbury. It was a pleasant lunch. Galen, a personable, bright guy who would later leave Meredith with Ted Chichak and Jack Scovill to establish their own literary agency, and who's been tearing up the publishing industry ever since, suggested that the books take place in more exotic places than Jessica Fletcher's fictitious hometown of Cabot Cove, Maine. Sweeney agreed. Galen then asked whether I was sufficiently "sophisticated" to make use of foreign locales.

"I don't know," I replied, "but I've been to every county fair in Indiana."

It was one of those rare times when I came up with the right line on the spur of the moment. Usually, such responses come to you hours or days later. Galen sensed my pique, and the subject of my level of my sophistication wasn't raised again. We discussed possible settings for the first book in the series, and I lobbied for London, a city with which I was familiar after having enjoyed many trips there.

I left the luncheon excited about being a part of the proposed series, and went to work on the book, which I titled *Gin & Daggers*. McGraw-Hill published the hardcover, and Avon did the softcover in 1989, with Michael Joseph bringing out a British hardcover in 1990.

Prior to starting the book, I called MCA to see if they had some sort of specs used by the various writers working on the show, character sketches of Jessica Fletcher and other characters, their likes and dislikes, clothing and food preferences, hobbies and other details I could use. No such thing existed, I was told.

I watched every episode of the show I could, and made copious notes. It wasn't until I was satisfied that I knew everything I needed to know that I began the actual writing. I learned after the book's publication that I'd missed something important. Letters poured in from readers chastising me for having Jessica rent a car in London and race to a manor house in the country to head off another murder. The TV character, Jessica Fletcher, doesn't drive, the letters said, some of them downright nasty. She gets around Cabot Cove on her bicycle. Lesson learned; I wouldn't make the same mistake in the next book.

But it seemed that a second book wasn't to be. McGraw-Hill's division that published *Gin & Daggers* was closed down, and the "Murder, She Wrote" series descended into limbo.

But then Signet, one of publishing's leading paperback houses, stepped into the picture and picked up where McGraw-Hill had left off, offering me a four-book contract. Fourteen years later, with 25 books having been written and a contract for four more, "Murder, She Wrote" is alive and well, in reruns of the TV show on cable television, and in the bookstores. Remarkably, every book in the series continues to be in-print and available to book buyers. (A list of books in the series, as well as other books written or ghostwritten by me, appears at the end of the book.)

Aside from the obvious financial rewards of writing the "Murder, She Wrote" series, there have been other less tangible advantages. Because each book takes place in different cities across the nation and around the world (with the exception of a few set in Cabot Cove), I've traveled to these cities to experience them firsthand. The yearly lectures aboard ship came as a direct result of the series. I've been invited to make a number of public appearances to talk about writing the series and writing in general. And there are the letters from readers, hundreds of them, almost all laudatory, with an occasional note pointing out to me something I'd misstated about Jessica or other characters. Fans of the TV show number in the millions, and they are passionate about the series and its characters. I love receiving those letters, and take pleasure in responding personally to each one.

There was one letter in particular that I found especially amusing. The cover of each book features a photo of Angela Lansbury, her attire doctored each time via the magic of computer graphics. This particular reader said in her letter to me that she found it amazing how much Angela Lansbury looked like Jessica Fletcher. I had trouble answering that one with a straight face.

I've been fortunate to have had some wonderful editors with whom to work on the series, including Ellen Edwards, Dan Slater, and more recently Kerry Donovan. Their hands-on, total involvement has benefited the series greatly, and made my life easier.

Because of MCA-Universal's involvement, the administration and decision-making process is somewhat complicated. Cindy Chang, a dynamic young executive who handles MCA's publishing tie-ins, and her equally capable boss, Nancy Cushing Jones, are intimately involved in virtually every aspect of the series. Naturally, MCA has a significant stake in the Jessica Fletcher character, and in preserving her image. Cindy must approve all settings and story lines for future books, and each manuscript receives her thorough vetting.

Being handed a character like Jessica Fletcher is a dual-edged sword. When I first started using her in books, she'd already been shaped by a variety of TV writers, and by the wonderful actress who plays her, Angela Lansbury. I was aware of the restrictions placed upon me by Cindy and MCA, and treaded carefully in how I handled this precious character. But over the course of the series, I've managed to change her to some extent to serve my interests, but only slightly. I have Jessica sipping a glass of wine or from a snifter of cognac now and then. In one book, I had her taking flying lessons; she doesn't drive but now has her private pilot's license. And I injected the possibility of romance in this TV widow's life. Viewers always suspected there might be a romance between Jessica and her friend, Dr. Seth Hazlitt. While that may still be the stuff of conjecture, I preferred to introduce another male into her life, Scotland Yard Inspector George Sutherland, who meets Jessica in the series' first book, *Gin & Daggers*. Theirs is, of necessity, a platonic relationship, but the handsome, dashing Sutherland has made it clear in a number of subsequent books that he'd like to move their relationship to another plateau. And Jessica has indicated that there could be the possibility of that happening somewhere down the road.

I don't know how long the series will continue, although there seems to be no reason at this juncture for it to end. Publishers publish books to make money, and "Murder, She Wrote" has been financially successful from the beginning, with sales increasing with the introduction of each new book. Writing the series has been nothing but a positive experience for me. As far as I'm concerned, it can go on forever, provided, of course, that I go on forever, too.

EPILOGUE

Writing one's memoirs is, of necessity, an exercise in self-indulgence. What you hope is that the life you've lived is sufficiently interesting to justify a recounting of it in book form, with a price tag on it that the reader is willing to pay. That the publisher of *Murder, HE Wrote* has committed editorial talent, as well as production and marketing costs, to publish the book indicates an interest on their part. I thank them for that. But whether you, the reader, shares that interest remains to be seen. I'd love to know because sales don't always correlate with reader satisfaction. Send a letter.

My professional life has changed dramatically since "Count" Hans Ashbourne paid me to write excerpts from books that didn't exist, or Dr. Louis Sunshine sat me in a dentist's chair and screamed "Humah! Humah! Humah!" My days of chasing every potential project—of saying "no" to nothing—are over.

These days, I content myself working on the latest book in the long-running series I write for a well-known person, and books in the "Murder, She Wrote" series. My world is more idyllic than it had been. Hyphenates turns down most projects offered it because time has become more precious, although we continue to provide editorial services to Reesa Staten, Max Messmer and the other good folks at Robert Half International. My wife, Renée, who has her own gig as vice president of communications for the Association of Independent Commercial Producers (AICP), has also turned her considerable writing experience to collaborating with me on the latest "Murder, She Wrote" books. The books are better for it, to say nothing of easing my schedule.

I still play an occasional jazz concert as a vibraphonist, although breaking down, packing up, setting up, and breaking down again that unwieldy instrument tempers my desire to go out and perform. But I still practice almost every day, running through tunes I'd like to learn, and looking for more interesting chord changes to songs I've been playing for years. Walking away from the computer to run through mallet exercises, or to play *How High the Moon* or *Lover Man*, provides a welcome break from the words on the screen.

I'm especially pleased that some of my older books have been published again. Books can have a very long life, and some of mine have been resurrected, including *Charlie and the Shawneetown Dame; The Control of Candy Jones;* and, as mentioned earlier, *Coffee, Tea or Me?*

* * * * *

I often think of my father's love of four-legged animals and his fondness of quoting Lincoln on the subject. I share his feelings and have been blessed with a variety of dogs and cats, all street saves, and each possessing a personality distinctly different from the next. My dog Jumper lived beyond 18 years. My beloved Jessie, named after my famous fictitious collaborator, Jessica Fletcher, made it to fifteen. I miss her. These days, I head downstairs to my office, followed by Wendell, our old cat, and Maggie, a Maine Coon, who thinks she's a dog.

I have my own favorite quote, from Anna Sewell, who wrote *Black Beauty.* "There is no religion without love, and people may talk as much as they like about their religion, but if it does not teach them to be good and kind to other animals as well as humans, it is all a sham."

* * * * *

Writers—veterans or beginners—should write, and I do every day. You learn from writing. There isn't a thing I've written over the past 45 years that didn't teach me something about the craft. That I've managed to make a decent living all these years from, as Vonnegut once said, "putting little black marks on paper," never fails to impress me. It hasn't made me rich, but what is "rich?" TV personality Dave Garroway once said that being rich meant to him being able to take a cab whenever he wanted. It means different things to different people. For me, it means being able to pay the bills, put aside money for that rainy day, to have raised my family in some comfort and educate my children, and to indulge in occasional trips, and meals out at favorite restaurants.

* * * * *

Until recently, my wife, Renée, and I lived in a semi-rural area of Westchester County where there was no Lake Tower Inn or Jolly Fisherman at which to while away my lunches, and beyond. We now live in a large condo on a lovely lake in Connecticut where we both work. I eat lunch at home these days, venturing out only occasionally to meet with Charles Flowers, a wonderful writer and raconteur; Phil Leshin, former bebop bass player with Buddy Rich and more recently Lionel Hampton's manager; Dick Mann, a former top PR executive whose conversational ability has few rivals; Tony Tedeschi, with whom I collaborated on Nick Vasile's *A Member of the Family,* some books ghosted for business leaders, and the cop novel, *Baby Farm;* and a semi-monthly luncheon club, "Men With Time," founded by musician and record exec Mike Millius, which includes Pulitzer Prize-winning theater producer Ken Marsolais, retired marketing genius Tom Molito, award-winning photographer and magazine publisher John Shearer, resident sage John Renwick, bon vivant and quipster Jeff Lasdon, and Leshin and Flowers. I treasure their friendship. It's probably a healthier life; the first martini of the day isn't poured until sunset. The daily three-martini lunches with a wonderful assortment of characters is a fond memory. Whether that's a good thing or not is irrelevant. Aging, and a more stable financial life, have made it inevitable. Do I miss it? Of course I do. No one calls me "kid" anymore.

*   *   *   *   *

Being a writer has been good to me. It's enabled me to meet many interesting, often skewed characters, and to experience situations I never would have encountered if I hadn't been exposed to them because I was a writer.

If you're an aspiring writer, I hope my experiences, and the modicum of advice I've dispensed in this book, will be helpful.

If you've read the book simply because you were interested in how someone makes a living as a writer, I hope my anecdotes have been interesting and enjoyable to read.

In either case—as I used to say on the radio—thanks for listening.

Books Written by Donald Bain

The "Murder, She Wrote" Series

Gin & Daggers—U.S. Hardcover McGraw-Hill (1989)—Jessica Fletcher & Donald Bain, U.S. Softcover Avon (1989), British Hardcover Michael Joseph (1990), British Softcover Michael Joseph (1991)

Manhattans & Murder—Signet (1994)—Jessica Fletcher & Donald Bain

Rum & Razors—Signet (1995)—Jessica Fletcher & Donald Bain

Brandy & Bullets—Signet (1995)—Jessica Fletcher & Donald Bain

Martinis & Mayhem—Signet (1995)—Jessica Fletcher & Donald Bain

A Deadly Judgment—Signet (1996)—Jessica Fletcher & Donald Bain

A Palette for Murder—Signet (1996)—Jessica Fletcher & Donald Bain

The Highland Fling Murders—Signet (1997)—Jessica Fletcher & Donald Bain

Murder on the QE2—Signet (1997)—Jessica Fletcher & Donald Bain

Murder in Moscow—Signet (1998)—Jessica Fletcher & Donald Bain

A Little Yuletide Murder—Signet (1998)—Jessica Fletcher & Donald Bain

Murder at the Powderhorn Ranch—Signet (1999)—Jessica Fletcher & Donald Bain

Knock 'Em Dead—Signet (1999)—Jessica Fletcher & Donald Bain

Gin & Daggers (Reissue)—Signet (2000)—Jessica Fletcher & Donald Bain

---

Trick or Treachery—Signet (2000)—Jessica Fletcher & Donald Bain
Blood on the Vine—Signet (2001)—Jessica Fletcher & Donald Bain
Murder in a Minor Key—Signet (2001)—Jessica Fletcher & Donald Bain
Provence: To Die For—Signet (2002)—Jessica Fletcher & Donald Bain
You Bet Your Life—Signet (2002)—Jessica Fletcher & Donald Bain
Majoring in Murder—Signet (2003)—Jessica Fletcher & Donald Bain
Destination: Murder—Signet (2003)—Jessica Fletcher & Donald Bain
Dying to Retire—Signet (2004)—Jessica Fletcher & Donald Bain
A Vote For Murder—Signet (2004)—Jessica Fletcher & Donald Bain
The Maine Mutiny—Signet (2005)—Jessica Fletcher & Donald Bain
Margaritas and Murder—Signet (2005)—Jessica Fletcher & Donald Bain
A Question of Murder—Signet (2006)—Jessica Fletcher & Donald Bain
Three Strikes and You're Dead—Signet (2006)—Jessica Fletcher & Donald Bain
Coffee, Tea or Murder?—Signet (2007)—Jessica Fletcher & Donald Bain

The "Coffee, Tea or Me?" Series

Coffee, Tea or Me?—Hardcover Bartholomew House (1967)—Trudy Baker
& Rachel Jones
The Coffee, Tea or Me Girls' Round-the-World Diary—Hardcover Grosset
& Dunlap (1970)—Trudy Baker & Rachel Jones
The Coffee, Tea or Me Girls Lay It on the Line—Hardcover Grosset &
Dunlap (1972)—Trudy Baker & Rachel Jones
The Coffee, Tea or Me Girls Get Away From it All—Hardcover Grosset &
Dunlap (1974)—Trudy Baker & Rachel Jones
NOTE: Softcover editions of all four books published by Bantam Books.

Other Comedies

Tender Loving Care—Hardcover Bartholomew House (1969)—Joni
Moura & Jackie Sutherland, Softcover Fawcett (1970)
Girlpower—Softcover Fawcett (1971)—Kathy Cole & Donna Bain
How to Make a Good Airline Stewardess—Fawcett (1972)—Cornelius
Wohl & Bill Wenzel
If It Moves, Kiss It—Fawcett (1973)—Joni Moura & Jackie Sutherland
We Gave at the Office—Fawcett (1974)— Laura Mills & Pauline Burlick
Fly Me—Fawcett (1974)—Cornelius Wohl & Bill Wenzel
Teachers Pet—Fawcett (1975)—Janet McMillan & Mitzi Sims
The Casting Couch and Me—U.S. Hardcover Walker Publishing Co.—
Joan Wood, British Hardcover and softcover—Peter Elk, U.S. soft-
cover Pocket Books (1976)
Wall Street & Broad—Dell (1976)—Teri Palmer

J.D. Hardin Western Series

The following nine softcover titles were published by Playboy Press
between 1980 and 1983 under the byline J.D. Hardin.
Bloody Sands
The Spirit & the Flesh
Death Flotilla
The Lone Star Massacre
Raider's Revenge
Raider's Hell
Apache Gold
Bibles, Bullets & Brides
Death Lode

"Toma" Novels

The Airport Affair—Dell Publishing (1975)—David Toma & Jack Pearl
The Affair of the Unhappy Hooker—Dell Publishing (1976)—David Toma
& Jack Pearl

Historical Romantic Novels

Daughter of the Sand—Playboy Press (1978)—Pamela South
The Eagle & the Serpent—Jove (1982)—Lee Jackson
Texas Lily—Charter Books (1987)—Stephanie Blake

Crime Novels

Sado Cop—Playboy Press (1976)—Nick Vasile
A Member of the Family—Hardcover Tor (1993)—Nick Vasile .
Softcover—Forge (1995)
Raven—Lyle Stuart (1987)—Mike Lundy
Baby Farm—Lyle Stuart (1987)—Mike Lundy

Other Books

The Racing Flag—Pocket Books (1965)—Bloys Britt & Bill France
Veronica—British Hardcover W.H. Allen (1969)—Veronica Lake, U.S.
Hardcover Citadel Press (1969)
The Case Against Private Aviation—Cowles Book Co. (1969)—Donald
Bain
Long John Nebel—Macmillan Publishing Co. (1974)—Donald Bain
The Control of Candy Jones—Playboy Press (1976)—Donald Bain

Club Tropique—Fawcett (1978)—Donald Bain

War in Illinois—Prentice-Hall (1978)—Donald Bain

Charlie & the Shawneetown Dame (Reissue of War in Illinois)—Austin Periodical Services (1984)—Donald Bain

Caviar, Caviar, Caviar—Lyle Stuart (1981)—Gerald M. Stein & Donald Bain

The 'Girls' in the Newsroom—Charter Books (1983)—Marjorie Margolies

The World's Best Bartenders' Guide—HP Books (1998)—Joseph Scott & Donald Bain

*   *   *   *   *

Contractual obligations prohibit Donald Bain from publicly taking credit for an additional 25 novels ghosted by him, as well as four nonfiction books written for business leaders.

INDEX